THE COMPLETE IDIOT'S GUIDE® TO

Guerrilla Marketing

by Susan Drake and Colleen Wells

ALPHA

A member of Penguin Group (USA) Inc.

For Gabriel and Faith, inspiration to us both.

ALPHA BOOKS

Published by the Penguin Group

Penguin Group (USA) Inc., 375 Hudson Street, New York, New York 10014, USA

Penguin Group (Canada), 90 Eglinton Avenue East, Suite 700, Toronto, Ontario M4P 2Y3, Canada (a division of Pearson Penguin Canada Inc.)

Penguin Books Ltd., 80 Strand, London WC2R 0RL, England

Penguin Ireland, 25 St. Stephen's Green, Dublin 2, Ireland (a division of Penguin Books Ltd.)

Penguin Group (Australia), 250 Camberwell Road, Camberwell, Victoria 3124, Australia (a division of Pearson Australia Group Pty. Ltd.)

Penguin Books India Pvt. Ltd., 11 Community Centre, Panchsheel Park, New Delhi—110 017, India

Penguin Group (NZ), 67 Apollo Drive, Rosedale, North Shore, Auckland 1311, New Zealand (a division of Pearson New Zealand Ltd.)

Penguin Books (South Africa) (Pty.) Ltd., 24 Sturdee Avenue, Rosebank, Johannesburg 2196, South Africa

Penguin Books Ltd., Registered Offices: 80 Strand, London WC2R 0RL, England

Publisher: *Marie Butler-Knight*
Editorial Director: *Mike Sanders*
Managing Editor: *Billy Fields*
Senior Acquisitions Editor: *Paul Dinas*
Development Editor: *Nancy D. Lewis*
Production Editor: *Megan Douglass*
Copy Editor: *Ross Patty*

Cartoonist: *Steve Barr*
Cover Designer: *Bill Thomas*
Book Designer: *Trina Wurst*
Indexer: *Johnna Vanhoose Dinse*
Layout: *Ayanna Lacey*
Proofreader: *Aaron Black*

Contents at a Glance

Contents

Introduction

Guerrilla marketing is a phrase coined by Jay Conrad Levinson in his 1984 book, *Guerrilla Marketing*. Levinson describes guerrilla marketing as unconventional and inexpensive marketing methods geared toward small businesses. Since then, guerrilla marketing has been used to describe unconventional marketing methods of all types and sizes. Buzz marketing, word of mouth marketing, grassroots marketing, viral marketing—these are all part of the loosely defined concept of today's guerrilla marketing.

What applications does guerrilla marketing have for your business? *The Complete Idiot's Guide to Guerrilla Marketing* is here to help. We'll explain the basics of marketing, along with a wide variety of the new and innovative methods that we collectively call guerrilla marketing. You'll find lots of real-life examples in each chapter as well as interesting facts and suggestions for you to try.

How to Use This Book

Crack open this book to find endless ideas on guerrilla marketing methods—some may be familiar, others, not so much. It's a whole new world out there so let's get started!

Part 1, "To Market, To Market ..." covers all the basics of traditional marketing. You'll find out why marketing is necessary and how it's changed since the introduction of the Internet.

Part 2, "Modern Marketing Marvels," highlights the power of personal recommendation in marketing. You'll find out how to get people buzzing about you so they can influence others.

Part 3, "To the Internet and Beyond!" gives you in-depth information about the many new tools available online. From viral marketing to mobile marketing, we've got the inside scoop on leveraging the power of the Internet to market yourself.

Part 4, "The Nuts and Bolts of Guerrilla Marketing," takes you into the trenches of guerrilla marketing. Filled with specific tools and methods to get you armed and ready for battle.

Extras

I've developed a few helpers you'll find in little boxes throughout this book:

> **Brainwaves**
>
> These stories will spark ideas and help you learn right and wrong from the experts.

def•i•ni•tion

These will help you talk the talk of a marketing professional.

 Booby Traps

Steer clear of these pitfalls, or you'll have a painful experience with competition.

 Here's the Buzz

Want a hot tip on how to make buzz marketing work for your brand? These quickies will show you how.

Acknowledgments

Our first thank you goes to Sheree Bykofsky and Janet Rosen at Sheree Bykofsky Literary Agency. After almost 10 years, they continue to bring us projects with wonderful publishers. Paul Dinas, with *The Complete Idiot's Guide* series, is an awesome human being, and we thank him for his intelligence, flexibility, and graciousness.

We both owe our undying gratitude to Susan Gross, whose contribution to this book is so tremendous that she is actually the third author. Beyond lending us her Internet research super powers, she also provides the glue that holds our whole operation together. And Kirby Gross has provided immeasurable patience and moral support throughout.

We also appreciate the genius and contributions of Lori Frazier, managing partner, RedRover. Scott Drake did his usual impeccable job of proofreading.

Trademarks

All terms mentioned in this book that are known to be or are suspected of being trademarks or service marks have been appropriately capitalized. Alpha Books and Penguin Group (USA) Inc. cannot attest to the accuracy of this information. Use of a term in this book should not be regarded as affecting the validity of any trademark or service mark.

Part 1

To Market, To Market ...

Marketing isn't all glamorous advertising and slick promotions. It's a science that helps you differentiate your product or service so that potential customers become true-blue fans. And let's face it: unless you own a Fortune 500 company, you probably don't have the marketing and advertising dollars to get in that game. Fortunately, technology has ushered in an entirely new category of marketing that doesn't have to break the bank. But before we jump too far ahead, let's consider the basics.

What Is Marketing?

In This Chapter

◆ The four Ps of marketing

◆ What customers want

◆ Building relationships

◆ Fixing problems

In 1972 Marlon Brando stuck some orange peels in his cheeks, adopted an Italian accent, and uttered the ultimate marketing intention: "I'm going to make him an offer he can't refuse."

Although the Godfather's methods weren't exactly mainstream, his sentiment is the essence of marketing. The reason any business uses marketing is to make its product or service simply irresistible to the consumer. It offers a customer a deal that's so desirable the customer simply can't wait to buy.

Textbooks describe marketing as the ongoing process of pricing, promoting, and distributing a product or providing a service to customers. Many of us think of marketing as merely advertising or sales; however, it should actually be a several-part discipline that is very well thought out.

The Inception of Marketing

Marketing is such a commonplace concept it's hard to imagine that once upon a time no one even thought about it. If you think of the word "marketing," you can imagine that it got its start when people went to a market to buy or sell goods. Consider that even as recently as the mid-1900s there wasn't significant product competition. Soap was soap, and when you ran out, you bought more soap.

In the late 1940s, that began to change. After World War II, products began to proliferate, and whereas soap used to be just soap, now there were "new, improved" brands. Procter & Gamble introduced Tide in 1946, and it became the high performance, reasonable price alternative. The next year Colgate-Palmolive introduced Fab detergent. Although my memory isn't encyclopedic, it seems that I recall back in the '50s laundry detergents were produced under just a handful of brands, including Tide, Fab, and Duz. Real innovators in the market were Wisk and Axion, liquid products rather than powdered. Woo-hoo! Now that's differentiation.

This is about the time when marketing began to be a real science. Suddenly products had competition, which made it incredibly important for companies to wisely conceive, price, advertise, and distribute their wares.

Brainwaves

One of the strangest examples of innovative marketing hit the streets in the 1970s, when an advertising executive named Gary Dahl figured out how to get people to pay $3.95 for gray pebbles. He hooked people by calling it a "pet rock," and selling it with a "Pet Rock Training Manual." The fad made Dahl a millionaire (in 1970s dollars that was a lot) and remains one of the most entertaining examples of marketing we've heard.

Whether it's a face-to-face act of exchanging goods or services, the most important factor to remember in marketing is that it's a two-party system: a seller and a buyer. The actual transaction involves each person giving the other something he or she wants. The seller gives a product or service, and the buyer gives, well, most often, money.

The key elements of marketing are represented by four Ps:

◆ Product: This is what you sell, whether it's a tangible item or a service, such as home cleaning or package delivery.

◆ Pricing: This is what you expect a customer will pay for your product.

◆ Promotion: How will you tell your story to the public?

◆ Placement: Who will buy your product and where can they get it?

We'll talk about each of these in this chapter.

Product: Meeting the Customer's Needs

If you want to sell something, the first thing you should ask yourself is: Do people need or want what I have to offer?

Just because you have a fantastic idea for a refrigerator that has a fish tank display in the door doesn't mean that other people will believe they can't live without it. *Supply and demand* are the foundation of all marketing. If there's no demand, you'll get stuck with a lot of unsold supply! Unless you want a boatload of your product sitting in your garage indefinitely, you'll do well to consider whether you have a sellable product.

def•i•ni•tion

The **law of supply** states that supply is directly proportional to price; the higher the price of the product, the more the producer will supply.

The **law of demand** states that demand is inversely proportional to price; the higher the price of the product, the less the consumer will demand.

The **law of supply and demand** states that the market price of a product or service is the intersection of consumer demand and producer supply. If the price for a product drops, people will demand more of it than producers can supply, which results in a shortage of the product. The shortage of the product then drives consumers' willingness to pay more for the product. On the flip side, if price is very high, producers will make more product than people want to buy, thus creating an abundant supply. When this happens, producers are willing to lower their price until it reaches a point where consumers want to purchase the product again. The goal is to balance supply and demand so that both are equal—meaning, producers are prepared to sell the same quantity that consumers are willing to buy.

Two Types of Customer Desires

Customers buy products for one of two reasons:

◆ They need the product to support their lifestyle. Commodities like bread, milk, or baby diapers fall into this category.

- They want it because it makes them feel good. Stylish handbags, plasma TVs, magazine subscriptions, and mountain bikes line up in this category. These are things you can live without, but don't want to.

To ensure success, you must be selling a product that falls into one of these categories. Sometimes you can actually create a "need or want mentality" among consumers by developing a meaningful new product, but this is an iffy situation with no guarantee of success. And it's a lot harder to create a new demand than to fill an existing need or want.

Identifying a customer need requires inside-out thinking. This is another way of saying that you put yourself in your potential customers' shoes and consider how they feel about what you're selling. While major corporations do massive research to investigate customer need and make sure they're on target, you can do your own form of research in a simple, low-cost way. How? If you're planning to start a business, ask the people you know, or the people you think might be interested in your product. If you're already in business, ask your existing customers. Let's pretend that your business is a delivery service. Here are some questions you could ask:

- Do you ever use a delivery service? If so, how often? If not, why not?

- What types of things do you send by courier?

- What timing is important to you when you need something delivered? Give them a choice of timing such as one hour, two hour, one day, or whatever makes sense.

> **Brainwaves**
>
> You can get a feel for customer interest in your product by informal research done through a simple printed questionnaire, quick interviews in person, phone calls to people you know, or an e-mail survey.

- What factors are most important to you in selecting a courier? Again, give them choices, such as speed, reliability, cost, friendliness, guarantee, 24-hour availability, and so on.

- What courier service are you using now? Is there anything that would make you switch from the courier you're now using?

By asking these questions, you can determine customers' need for your service and also judge what your competition is doing right and wrong.

Price: What Will They Pay?

The second P of marketing is price. Having a great product is one thing; getting people to pay is quite another. The second question you should ask yourself about your product is, what is it worth to the customer?

In pricing your product it's essential that you balance two things: what it costs you to deliver the product, and what people will pay. The difference between those two items is your profit.

In the process of creating your business plan—you do have a business plan, right?—you probably have taken into consideration what your operating costs are and how much money you expect to make. But just in case, let's think about how you can appropriately price your product.

The cost of delivery includes a variety of things: raw goods; labor costs, including wages and benefits; transportation; insurance; advertising; overhead, such as office space or equipment; and taxes. In accounting lingo, this is called *COGS: cost of goods sold.*

When you've computed what it costs you to make and deliver your product, the next step is to project how many units you think you will be likely to sell over a certain period of time. It's best to be conservative in your estimate; lots of businesses fail because they're too optimistic about how much they can sell.

def•i•ni•tion

Cost of goods sold (COGS) is an important number to calculate before pricing your product or service. This is a need-to-know figure before you begin guerrilla marketing.

After you know how many deliveries you think you can make, you can then figure out what you must charge your customer in order to pay for the goods and realize something leftover for you. To figure this out, simply divide the number of items you sell into the cost of delivering them. For example: $100,000 COGS ÷ 5,000 deliveries = $20 per delivery.

This means that the minimum you can charge to break even is $20 per delivery. If you expect to make any money, you'll have to charge more than that. Now, let's assume your competitor has been in business for 20 years, has an established clientele, and only charges $20 per delivery. There is no way you can compete with this company if price is an important factor. So consider these three possibilities.

◆ You might be able to offer something extra, something of value that makes your service worth more to the customer. If you delivered a free cup of coffee with each package, maybe you could charge $1 more. The key to making this work is that you have to find something that the customer believes makes your product a greater *value* than that of your competitor. By charging more without significantly increasing your costs, you can enjoy something left over.

◆ You might find a way to reduce your COGS. Maybe you work a deal with a local auto dealer to lease or purchase the delivery vehicles for a lower price, or you bargain with a service station owner to buy gas cheaper.

◆ If you sell more deliveries than your competitor, you could decrease the cost per delivery. If you're new to the business, this is a very risky proposition. Before you can get up to speed, you could be out of money.

 Booby Traps

In a classic example of marketing gone wrong, Coca Cola misjudged the market when it introduced New Coke. With one of the strongest brands in the world, Coke has created an incredibly loyal following. In fact, some people have such an emotional connection to the brand that you could describe it as an old family friend. Yet in 1985, having watched Coke's market share decline over a number of years, the company decided to change the formula of the original Coke.

Very shortly after the product's introduction in April, a small subset of vocal Coke lovers took to the airwaves and protested vehemently against the new formula. New Coke— and Coca Cola management—became the butt of jokes by talk show hosts, the subject of nationally syndicated columns, and a source of irritation on the part of bottlers. The company received thousands of negative phone calls, and a psychologist who listened in reported to Coke that complainers sounded as if they were describing a death. New Coke was withdrawn from the market just three months later.

Management made a fatal error in not considering what customers wanted.

Promotion: Let's Talk about Your Ingenious Product

The third P is what this book is all about: how to tell the world about your refrigerator/fish tank or your delivery service. You can shout it from the tops of buildings or go door to door like the old-fashioned vacuum cleaner salesmen, but there are many more effective ways to let people know you're here. There are, of course, some very traditional methods of promoting, such as advertising and public relations, but we're here to tell you about some new, improved ways to get your message out. Check out Chapter 3 for more info on the traditional stuff; the rest of the book is about cool, new techniques, many of which are available through the miracle of technology.

Don't underestimate the power of a simple message. Being able to articulate your product's benefits in one statement is critical in any type of promotion, especially guerrilla marketing.

Placement: Getting the Product to the Customer

The fourth element of marketing is distribution, but that's problematic because it doesn't start with a P. So in the interest of alliteration and parallel construction and making the marketing formula easy to remember, someone wisely changed it to placement, creating the fourth P.

Placement describes how you get your product into the hands of your customer. You might decide to put it in a retail store, sell it online, or promote it through a catalog. The trick is to put your product in your customers' hands with as little effort on their part as possible.

Another part of placement has to do with who you're selling to: senior citizens, Baby Boomers, teenagers, young adult males? Placement defines all of these and will come into play in helping you determine how you reach your *target audience*.

And speaking of target audiences, your goal should be to create a relationship with them. Does that mean you have to go on a date or do couples therapy with your customers? No, but it does mean that you should approach them as if they are more than just a one-off sale.

def•i•ni•tion

Your **target audience** is the primary group you are marketing your product to. Even though your business may appeal to many different types of people—and all business is valuable business—when you are promoting a product, you want to focus on the group of people who are most likely to want what you have to offer.

Here's the Buzz

Studies show that it costs about five times more to get a new customer than it does to keep one. If you want to spend your marketing dollars wisely, concentrate on how you can build long-term relationships with your existing customers.

And while you're at it, remember that word of mouth is the best advertising of all. If you make your customers happy they'll tell all their friends, who may then become customers themselves.

Relationship Marketing Ensures Success

Long gone are the days when customers were simply numbers on a tally sheet of sales. Customers have so many product choices that you may be one of a long line of potential companies they can do business with. Consider one product: jeans. A person who wants to purchase a pair of jeans can choose from thousands of stores with a variety of brands and styles. As a jeans manufacturer, you hope that your customers will find something in your jeans they don't find in others, whether it's style, comfort, fit, durability, or price. You don't want them to buy just one pair of jeans from you; you want them to buy jeans from you again and again. And if you sell other products, such as shirts or shoes, you want them to come to you for those as well.

> ### Brainwaves
>
> Levi Strauss has definitely created a fan club with its Levi's jeans. Some customers swear by Levi's and wouldn't buy any other brand. Not only does the company garner accolades for its wonderful product, it also earns respect for being a responsible corporate citizen. Among its high standards are ethical and diversity guidelines. In addition, the company sees the bigger picture.
>
> From the Levi Strauss website:
>
> "In the late 1980s, employees at Levi Strauss & Co. began to raise concerns about the working conditions of people making our products overseas. This led executives to begin to work on a supplier code of conduct that would ensure all individuals making our products were being treated with dignity and respect and working in a safe and healthy environment."
>
> Levi Strauss now operates under its Global Sourcing and Operating Guidelines, which, when instituted in 1991, made the company the first multinational apparel company to do so.

A Guarantee of Performance

You tell your customers you have a great product, right? But can you be certain that it will absolutely always satisfy them? Is there such a thing as no defects, ever? Probably not. So when something goes wrong, what are you going to do about it?

Many companies offer a satisfaction guarantee, assuring customers that if anything goes wrong they'll replace the product free of charge, or give the customer their money back. Well, that's just too risky, you say? Think people might take advantage of you? Might put you in the poorhouse? Not likely.

In fact, the most expensive thing you can do is *not* give someone their money back when they're entitled to it. If you think satisfied customers tell their friends when they like you, let us assure you that dissatisfied customers tell lots of people—at least 15— and those people will tell people, and, well, you get the drift. You might as well flush your marketing dollars down the toilet if you're going to let people go away unhappy, because they'll generate more negative buzz than you can possibly overcome.

Rule number one in ensuring that customers love you is their belief that they can trust you to fix it if something goes wrong. Most people are reasonable and fair, and they won't expect you to give them their money back unless they're entitled to it.

Loyalty as a Goal

In the last 10 years, the word "loyalty" has become increasingly a part of market researchers' discussions, as well as a hot topic in board rooms around the world. While we used to measure our success with customer satisfaction surveys, we've now discovered something pretty important: customer satisfaction doesn't necessarily drive repeat business.

Yes, satisfied customers may come back. And they may tell their friends about your product. But they may also be quite easily swayed to try a different product. Thus, just making people happy wasn't a guarantee of success.

The search for a stronger indicator of success ended in the adoption of loyalty as the new buzz word. But now the question is, what creates loyalty?

Emotional Connections Take Center Stage

Customers become loyal only when they enjoy a series of consistently excellent experiences over time. But there's more to it than that, because loyalty has an emotional facet as well as a rational one.

How do loyal customers act?

- ◆ They repeatedly choose your product.
- ◆ They are patient if you screw up.
- ◆ They tell their friends about you in a positive way.
- ◆ They aren't easily lured away by price considerations or a new fad.

Brainwaves

Loyalty implies action, not just words. And it includes a deep emotional connection. Think about people who use a Mac computer from Apple. Apple is a heartthrob brand with a personality. When Apple announces a new product, people await its launch as if they were expecting a birthday present. Apple computers are far outnumbered by the ubiquitous Windows-based PC, and Mac users have to go to some degree of trouble to function in a PC world. Still customers swear by all things Apple. Try converting a Mac user to a PC and you'll see a look of horror on the person's face. Because of the quality of the product, and *the emotional tie* customers feel, repeat business is all but guaranteed.

Love Conquers All

Patriots are loyal to their country. Fans are loyal to their sports teams. Why, people are known to wait 18 years to get season tickets to the New York Giants games. And in Boston, diehard fans waited out an 86-year drought, sticking by the Red Sox until they experienced the elation of their team winning the 2004 World Series. People are loyal to their family members, pets to their owners.

It's rather unusual, however, to see "undying loyalty" among customers. Yet it is possible. Take for example the Volkswagen Beetle. By 1974, 21 million of the somewhat daffy looking but reliable and affordable "Bugs" had been sold. Despite customer protests, Volkswagen took the Beetle off the U. S. market in 1974. And then, in 1998, the Beetle returned. Still small, reliable and predictably round, the Beetle was greeted with enthusiasm by Baby Boomers who had owned one the first time around, and by new users who were equally intrigued by the funny little car. The car maker now includes a flower in each new car, perhaps a nod to the "flower power" of the generation that originally made it a success. The Beetle represented an emotional experience for owners that lasted through the 22 years the car was off the market. Ten years after its reintroduction, it's going strong.

For those who question the relationship between loyalty and profit, consider that the Beetle now stands as the best-selling automobile in history.

The lesson is clear: the best marketing plan is one that incorporates avenues for building loving relationships among customers.

Here's the Buzz

You might think that having a customer experience a problem is the worst thing that could happen. Not really. Research has shown that when a customer has an issue, if you fix it in a way that meets or exceeds their expectations, they become more loyal than before they ever had a problem! Think about the last time you were dissatisfied and reported the problem to management. Did they respond in a genuinely concerned way and do everything they could to make it up to you? If so, we'll bet you like them more than ever.

It Worked For Them

Hampton Inn Hotels instituted a 100% Satisfaction Guarantee in the 1980s, becoming the first hospitality company to create a true service guarantee. The guarantee said that if you weren't satisfied with your stay, you didn't pay. Period. Most important about the guarantee is that it didn't include any bargaining, like a half-price discount or anything less than a full refund of the night's stay. And, believe it or not, every employee was empowered to refund the guest's stay. Sure, there were skeptics at first, but the positive press coverage, awesome word of mouth, and tremendous guest loyalty it generated proved them wrong. The company discovered that for every dollar it paid out in refunds, it collected about seven in repeat business. The brand still has the only unconditional guarantee in the hotel industry.

Missing the Big Picture

In late 2006, Cingular announced that they would begin charging an additional $5 a month to more than four million subscribers who are using old analog and TDMA (Time Division Multiple Access) cell phones, in essence forcing those who haven't converted to new GSM (Global System for Mobile) technology to either upgrade or cough up what can only be described as a nuisance fee. Why would they do this? They need to convert their network to one type of signal so they can provide a larger portion of their network to their larger GMS audience. And while Federal Communications Commission legislation requires that all cell phone carriers in the United States must continue to provide analog service until 2008, if all their customers are converted, they could convert sooner. (They would not have to provide the older technology if they didn't have customers using it.)

Through this $5 a month fee, Cingular is charging some of their most long-standing customers, most likely their most loyal customers. The extra revenue created by this fee is estimated to be $23.5 million per month.

For its part, Cingular issued a statement to Associated Press explaining that as the number of analog and TDMA customers decreases, "the per-customer cost of using that network is increasing considerably. That's why we made a decision to impose this charge."

The statement also points out that, "Customers can avoid the charge by switching to our GSM network and equipment. The combination of coverage, service quality, devices, and advanced features on GSM is superior to TDMA."

As you can imagine, this decision was met by a firestorm of criticism from angry bloggers and tech writers. How different would this have played out if Cingular had simply rewarded people for switching instead of punishing those that didn't? Yes, they did offer discounts to people who purchased new phones, but the overall effect was negative. Just look on the Internet for evidence.

The Least You Need to Know

- Marketing is a complex process of offering the right product to the right customer at the right price.
- The four Ps of marketing are product, pricing, promotion, and placement.
- Building strong relationships with customers is the only way to succeed in the long run.
- Loyalty, rather than customer satisfaction, is the most effective marketing tool.
- Fixing problems in an outstanding way can create loyal customers.

Chapter 2

Why Is Marketing Necessary?

In This Chapter

- ◆ Creating awareness
- ◆ Delivering your brand promise
- ◆ Targeting the right audience
- ◆ Understanding consumer behavior

Kevin Costner's character in the movie *Field of Dreams* heard a voice telling him, "If you build it, [they] will come." It's a nice thought, but not many of us have the fortitude to mentally generate bleachers full of fans. In reality, people won't flock to buy your product unless they know about it. That's where marketing comes in. It's a disciplined way of telling people what you have to sell, what your *brand promise* is, and why they should buy.

def•i•ni•tion

Brand promise is what you tell customers they can expect from your brand. Your promise may be outstanding service, high quality, low price, reliability, high style, or whatever you are prepared to deliver to the customer on a consistent basis. A brand promise doesn't usually change. Customers who buy Dove soap have always expected something gentle and pure, and they still do. And remember how FedEx revolutionized the package delivery business when it suggested you choose FedEx "when it absolutely, positively has to be there overnight?" They were guaranteeing on-time delivery.

It All Begins with Brand Awareness

Before anyone can buy what you're selling, they have to know about you. Sounds simple, right? Not quite. People have to be told time after time after time about a new product before they really catch on to what it is. Suppose you've just opened a new muffler shop. You put up a big banner on your store and have a week-long grand opening celebration. You get a local radio station to come out and broadcast their drive time talk show from your location. You've put flyers in people's mail boxes and on windshields. You even mortgaged the house to put a big ad in the newspaper. Great. A week after the big celebration, who remembers that new muffler place? Not many people. In your situation, people only think about muffler shops when they need a muffler. By the time Joe's muffler falls off, it may have been six months since your launch. So Joe goes to Midas because he can remember their name. Midas has high brand awareness and you don't.

Things might be different if you had a different kind of product. A few years ago, we noticed a building going up on a parking lot near our house. A big building. Hmm, we wondered, what's going up there? Soon a sign appeared: "Coming soon: Malco Paradiso Theater." (Malco operates the majority of movie theaters in Memphis.) Hooray! We were excited because we'd been wishing we had a theater this convenient to us. We waited and anticipated and were some of the first customers to pass through the doors. Why? Because they had something we want and use several times a month. They were filling a need. And while the Malco name helped, it was our desire for a movie theater that made us remember Paradiso.

Do you have a product that people are anxiously awaiting? Or are you selling something that they will think of only when they need it, like a muffler?

Here's another consideration: are people in the habit of using a different supplier? For instance, suppose you open a dry cleaner. Most people are already using a dry cleaner, and they're probably in the habit of going to one that's either convenient or that does a good job, or both. So how are you going to get them to think of you when they're headed to work and drop off their cleaning on the way? You will have to do something to make people change their habit. If you've ever tried to change a habit, you know how hard that is. What kind of incentive will you give people that will make them think of you first?

To be successful, you have to stay at the top of your customers' minds. That takes ongoing effort.

Consistency Is Key

I'll bet that you could recall at least 10 memorable advertising slogans off the top of your head, couldn't you? I certainly can: McDonald's "You Deserve a Break Today," Coke's "The Real Thing," Alka-Seltzer's "Plop, Plop, Fizz, Fizz, Oh What a Relief It Is."

I can even remember slogans from my childhood! What a great job these ad agencies do in creating memorable moments. And more important, when agencies create ads, they reinforce the same simple message incessantly. The statement of the brand promise replays in every single ad. Eventually, the consumer comes to associate the brand, or product, with an idea or benefit that they can expect to receive from using the product.

In fact, even as a company or product's ads evolve, they tend to reinforce the same product benefit. An award-winning Alka-Seltzer ad from the 1970s has a man saying, "I can't believe I ate the whole thing." The company reintroduced the ad in 2006 with actor Peter Boyle and Doris Roberts, his TV wife from *Everybody Loves Raymond*. The product benefit—relief from stomach ills—is still viable.

Short Attention Span

You don't have long to catch a person's attention, whether they're watching TV, reading a magazine, or driving down the street looking at a billboard. If you don't capture their interest in about the first five seconds, you will lose them forever. And you're competing with a world full of images and sounds that range from cell phones ringing to stories in People magazine to electronic billboards and high definition TV. Stop the insanity!

That's why it's so important to think of your product in a very simple, straightforward way. Most ads center around one idea or product benefit.

Focus on Benefits

What's in it for the customer? That's what your message should contain. Some companies talk about their product's features, when what they should be talking about is the outcome of the features. For example, what if Delta Airlines did ads about their airplanes that described their speed, sleek design, or reliability? Who cares? What we care about is that we arrive safely and comfortably. So an ad should talk about the outcome of their speed, design, and reliability: passenger comfort and timely arrival. The details of how it happens are irrelevant.

Frequency Counts

Have you ever noticed that TV ads seem to play over and over? That's because people have to see a message about 20 times before it sinks in. By now you'd think that Crest toothpaste would be drilled into people's heads. Still, those ads for gleaming white teeth keep on coming. Even a brand as famous as Crest has to stay in front of the public.

I've always thought that as the advertiser, just when you're sick to death of the same old message, the customer is just beginning to remember it.

Products, Products Everywhere: How Can They Decide?

Assume you want to buy a roll of toilet paper. Should you buy Charmin, Scott, Kleenex Cottonelle, Quilted Northern, Angel Soft, Sunrise, or one of the numerous house brands? Decisions, decisions. How can a poor consumer decide?

Fact is, there are so many brands it's hard for anyone to know what makes one a better choice than another. That's where marketing comes in. Good marketing clearly differentiates your product from the competition in a brief, easy to remember way. Back to toilet paper. A legendary TV advertising campaign created a name for Charmin by introducing a character named Mr. Whipple. His job at the supermarket was to protect the super soft toilet paper from customers who just loved to squeeze it. His tagline, "Please don't squeeze the Charmin," clearly stated to the customer that it was soft toilet tissue. The differentiation was important to consumers who were tired of using rough toilet paper on their tender derrieres.

What Makes Your Product Better Than Another?

Naturally you think your product is better than others. But you need an objective assessment of your product's features and a comparison with the competition to know exactly what makes it better or different. Remember, it doesn't matter what you think about it; what customers think is what matters.

Perhaps your product is made with all-natural ingredients, does something another product doesn't (like make your hair shine or clean mildew faster), or costs less than another. There are two requirements before you define this as your brand promise:

◆ You must be sure that you can deliver it consistently, time after time.

◆ You should make sure they are factors your customer is interested in.

I, for example, love my Jeep Grand Cherokee. I don't care if it costs more or less than other SUVs. I bought it because it has the features I want. A car salesman who tries to sell me a different brand on the basis of price might as well be spitting in the wind. I am unimpressed by price arguments. My Jeep has been reliable for six years. True, I don't drive it much, but still, I haven't had a problem with it in six years. Could you sell me another brand of automobile? Maybe. But you'd better be prepared to prove to me how it will be more dependable than my Jeep has been, and that it has the same or more features … for a comparable price.

What Does the Customer Want?

There may be many things about your product that make it wonderful. But which ones are important to your customer?

When you're determining what factors constitute your brand promise, make sure you're highlighting the things that are truly important to the customer. And the way you find that out is to ask them.

How Do You Stack Up?

Make a checklist of all the features you feel are admirable about your product. Now take the list to a sampling of the people who will potentially buy it. Ask them to rate the things that are important to them. You may be surprised to discover that what you think is important is only secondary to them—and vice versa. Here are some factors that tend to influence a buyer to buy: price, track record, dependability, quality, ease of use, availability of a guarantee, ease of getting service for the product, convenience of getting the product, high quality, uniqueness, and reputation.

Here's the Buzz _____

Customers may be aware of your product or brand in very conscious ways or in more subtle ways. To understand just how familiar they are with you and to gauge whether you're top of mind, you can check on their aided awareness and unaided awareness. Aided awareness is what customers think when they're asked specifically about your brand or product. Unaided awareness is when you ask generic questions that don't mention your product or service. For example, an aided question might be, "Of Rite Aid, Walgreens, or Super D, which pharmacy would you say provides the best service?" In that case, you have suggested that you're interested in one of those brands.

An unaided awareness question would say, "When you need a pharmacy, which one do you think of first?" You haven't given the person any clue about pharmacies at all. Whichever brand they mention would have the highest unaided awareness.

Here's another way to find out what they think. Ask them to describe your product's pluses and minuses without listing any that you think are important. This will give you a more accurate read on what people genuinely think is important.

Now remember, you're armed with information about what's important to people who buy what you sell. Promote the outcomes of those features to demonstrate the benefit to the customer.

Appealing to Your Target Audience

Here's the thing about consumers: not all of them will want what you're selling. That's why we talk about target audiences. You see, it's a waste of money to direct your marketing efforts to people who will never have any intention of buying your product or service. For example, it doesn't make much sense to try to sell senior citizens skateboards, right? That's an exaggerated example, of course, but when you're on a limited budget, you certainly don't want to waste your dollars trying to appeal to people who aren't suited to your product.

You can't afford to market to everyone on the planet, or even in your city. The best way to invest is by identifying the people the product is intended for and aiming your messages at them.

Consumers and How They Behave

There is a whole science around consumer behavior that describes why and how people purchase products. Is it even possible to quantify all the factors that affect us in the marketplace? A host of factors go into the decision-making process. The three biggies are:

◆ Social, including family influences, friends, opinion leaders, social class, and so on.

◆ Demographics, such as age and gender.

◆ Psychological, including attitudes, personalities, lifestyles, and motives.

Your Momma Told You ...

Probably the influencer we think of first is our family and our upbringing. I'll bet you can look in your refrigerator and see some things that you saw in your mother's refrigerator. Is that Hellman's mayonnaise? French's mustard? And what about those Oscar Meyer wieners? If you're like many people, you probably continue to use some of the products that you grew up with. Family influences are pretty strong, and they may show up in choices like the automobile you drive, the type of house you live in, and yes, what brand of toilet tissue you buy (and which way you position it on the toilet paper holder!).

What did your parents teach you about values? If one of your values is to be frugal, you'll probably select products that represent a bargain. (Unless, of course, you're rebellious and have gone in the exact opposite direction.) On the other hand, if looking successful is important to you, you may even spend beyond your means to appear to have made it.

Other societal issues come into play, too. Anyone who lives in California can attest to how cultural influences can affect marketing. For instance, we're guessing that people who live in this "green" state are more likely to buy hybrid cars than those who live in Texas, where the oil industry is *big*.

Issues such as political leanings, ethnic origin, and family income—they all affect how you buy.

The Age of Aquarius

Demographics is a science that analyzes population according to density, distribution, and personal characteristics such as sex, marital status, age, and other defining qualities. Knowing, for example, where a large population of unmarried males live could help you understand where to sell sports cars, frozen food, or sports bars.

Or think about how McDonald's might determine where to build a restaurant with a playground. Surely they wouldn't put one in an area where there were mostly senior citizens, but they would locate one where there are lots of families with young children.

def•i•ni•tion

Demographics is the science of looking at population and defining it statistically according to people's age, gender, marital status, number of children, household income, and other characteristics that describe them. These numbers are important to marketers and others who want to influence certain groups. The recent divisive political climate, for example, groups people in "red" and "blue" states according to whether the state is more inclined to vote Republican or Democrat.

Psychological Factors

We're all driven by things we may not even be aware of, such as motives to be seen as sexy or successful or to be loved. We may be influenced by our lifestyle choices, like whether we're athletic or inactive, prefer artistic endeavors or sports, like to get involved in community activities, and so on. We talked earlier of family influences and whether we rebel against our parents or our upbringing. These and other psychological factors go into our decision-making when it comes to buying a product.

Social Factors

Peer pressure is a real, true thing that drives people to buy. We're influenced by people we go to church with, play sports with, and live next door to. If we live in an affluent neighborhood, we may want to purchase things that our neighbors have, such as upscale playground equipment for our kids or a trendy car. If we're environmentally conscious, it will affect what we purchase. And if we're married with children versus single with a pet, we'll make different decisions, too.

Financial Considerations

Economic status is certainly a driving force in buying decisions. In many cases, price tolerance is directly affected by how much money the person has to spend. That, of course, assumes that people are living within their means. But with the almighty credit god shining on people in every economic bracket, even those at the low end of the income scale can sometimes buy, buy, buy, no matter what the price.

Did you have any idea marketing was this complicated? It's true, there's a lot to think about. Rather than teach you every aspect of marketing, we simply want you to be aware of the many elements that play a role in selling to the customer. The more you understand, the better you can see how important it is to choose the right approach, whether it's buzz marketing or TV ads.

What Makes People Buy?

The first thing to consider is what kind of product are you selling?

◆ Higher priced items—when people are considering an expensive item such as a washer/dryer or a car, they put more thought into it. Because they're making a bigger investment, they may shop more carefully for a good price and for features such as reliability.

◆ Necessities—when people are shopping for necessities, they fall into two categories: bargain hunters who will choose the product that best fits their definition of price/value; brand shoppers who will stick with a brand that they trust.

◆ Impulse items—some things just call your name, like that adorable sweater in a to-die-for green or the dark chocolate candy bar at the grocery store checkout counter. When you're in the throes of an impulse, you may consider the price, argue with yourself that you don't need it, but often go right ahead and buy it anyway. You're the victim of an impulse purchase.

People's approach to buying the kind of product or service you're offering will depend on what type of product or service it is.

Because people have so many choices of products that offer the same features, considerations have changed a bit. Whereas consumers used to buy a soap that had some differentiating factor, like aloe or Shea butter, today every brand offers soaps with those elements. So when people buy, they tend to base their decision more on loyalty and their emotional connection to your product or the service you deliver than they will the actual product itself or the price.

The Decision-Making Process

Decision-making at its best is a five-step process.

1. The consumer recognizes that he or she has a need. At this point, they may or may not have a product or service in mind to fill the need. They may simply know that they have itchy skin and would prefer not to have itchy skin.

2. They conduct an information search about the product or service that will meet their need. They may simply cull through their memory banks for products they already know about that cure itchy skin, they may ask friends for recommendations, or they may do a more formal search online or through a pharmacist.

3. They look at all the options of products that may alleviate their itch. They might take into account the price, availability, reports of effectiveness, and other factors that tell them which product is the best value.

4. They buy the product and use it.

5. They decide whether the product is satisfactory or not. Did it cure the itch? Did it have an obnoxious smell? Did it wear off too soon? At this point, they determine whether they would buy the product again and perhaps whether they would recommend it to others.

This process can be a long one or a short one, depending on how urgent the need is—how bad it itches—and how much the person already knows about the options. In some cases, the steps may be short-circuited. If the person already has experience with an acceptable product, they might jump straight from step two to step four, skipping the options segment completely.

And if the person is caught up in an impulse situation, they might go straight from one to four without any thought whatsoever!

Maslow's Hierarchy

No marketing book is complete without a description of Maslow's Hierarchy of Needs. Abraham Maslow, born in 1908, was a psychologist who theorized that human beings exhibit needs on a prioritized basis. He created a pyramid of five levels of these needs, which are, starting at the most basic:

◆ Physiological Needs: These are the things we need to survive, the most basic needs such as air, water, food, and sleep. Until these needs are met, nothing else matters.

◆ Safety and Security Needs: People need physical safety, job security, and sufficient money.

◆ Love and Belonging Needs: Once people get beyond worrying about whether they can survive, they desire to belong to a group and to have loving relationships.

◆ Esteem Needs: Esteem needs show up in a desire for recognition and appreciation, along with self respect.

◆ Self-Actualization Needs: The highest needs on Maslow's pyramid are those that lead us to seek fulfillment. This is where people begin to develop ethics and humility, creativity, and solutions to the world's problems.

From the marketing standpoint, it's important to know what level of needs you are seeking to fulfill with your product. You would never try to market self-actualizing products to people who are just trying to survive. By recognizing what level your audience is on, you can appeal to their particular needs.

Two Types of Buyers: Consumers and Businesses

The majority of our discussion has been about consumers and their behavior. But there is another type of buyer: a business. In marketing jargon, this is called B2B, or business-to-business selling.

Let's think about an office supply company that provides copy machine paper to businesses. The factors that affect a company's buying are different than those that affect an individual. Here are some factors that weigh more heavily in a B2B situation:

◆ Price: A business has to live within a budget and must make wise, cost-conscious decisions about any purchases.

◆ Logistics: Do you deliver? How quickly can you respond to an order? What are your hours? What kind of shipping do you offer? Can you expedite shipment?

◆ Payment terms: How do you expect to be paid? How long does the company have to pay its bill? Will you set up an account or do they have to pay on delivery?

◆ Quality: Are your products always high quality? Perhaps the company doesn't need the highest quality, so they weigh the quality against the price. Do you offer a variety of quality levels to choose from?

◆ Customer service: Is your service responsive, reliable, and hassle-free?

Businesses are always looking for the price/value equation, that is, they want the best value for the price.

Keep in mind, though, that even when you're marketing to a business, the quality of the experience that the company's people have with your people will make or break the long-term relationship.

Booby Traps

In our business, we find that people often want things fast, high quality, and cheap. We always joke among ourselves that they can choose any two of the three, but not all three. They can get it fast and cheap, but the quality will suffer. They can get it fast and high quality, but they'll have to pay a high price. They might even get it high quality and cheap, but it will take a long, long time! We don't recommend that you necessarily tell the client this but for your own benefit, be careful not to promise all three or you probably won't be able to deliver.

Targeted Marketing vs. a Shotgun Approach

Before we had sophisticated systems of identifying consumer segments and communicating with people on a more individual basis, companies had to use a *shotgun marketing* approach. This means they put out messages to huge numbers of people hoping to capture some buyers among a hodgepodge of consumers. For example, a high-end ladies shoe store would advertise in the newspaper or on television and the ad would be seen by men, women, children, teenagers, senior citizens, rich people, poor people, factory workers, and a variety of others. Most of them would never be in the market to buy shoes from that store. In essence, the store had to shout its message to everyone in earshot, even though only 10 percent of the people might be interested.

def•i•ni•tion

Shotgun marketing sends messages to a broad audience that includes a large percentage of people who are not potential customers.

During these shotgun days, every type of business under the sun would advertise in these same types of media: automobile dealers, farm tractor sales, toy stores, and pizza parlors would all line up side by side, sending messages to the same large group of consumers. Then they crossed their fingers and hoped that the people who read the ads would buy something from them.

As our marketing knowledge has evolved and our understanding of consumers has grown, we have developed a more effective approach that we call segmented marketing. We take a gigantic audience (in our city, state, country, ethnic group, and so on) and we divide it into smaller groups that are likely to buy our products. An example of a market segment would be females aged 10 to 12 in the South. Instead of trying to sell a preteen product to everyone in the country, you would narrow your field of concentration to these girls. By narrowing your target, you get a greater return on your investment, that is, a higher likelihood that a greater percentage of your audience will purchase.

Targeted marketing allows you to spend your dollars where they count, rather than throwing them away talking to people who aren't potential customers.

The Least You Need to Know

◆ You're competing for people's attention, so keep your message simple and memorable.

◆ Market the benefits of your product, appealing to your audience's needs.

◆ Understand what motivates people to buy so that you can develop marketing tools that they can relate to.

◆ Targeted marketing is more cost-effective than spending your money to inform people who don't even want or need your product.

Chapter 3

Traditional Marketing Techniques

In This Chapter

- ◆ Using traditional marketing methods
- ◆ PR and media relations
- ◆ Face-to-face marketing opportunities

Ever since Eve "sold" Adam the apple, people have been using various techniques to get others to buy what they sell. From billboards to TV ads to cola taste tests, most companies adopt a combination of standard methods to create awareness of their products, provide incentives for people to try them, and convince consumers that their products are a must-have.

Traditional marketing techniques do still work; however, they can be expensive and sometimes not as effective as newer guerrilla marketing tactics. So that you may choose wisely, read on to learn about the most common traditional forms of marketing.

Advertising Sends Your Message Far and Wide

When we think of marketing, most of us think first about advertising. Advertising is the art of telling your potential customers about your product via paid messages through vehicles like television and radio ads, newspaper and magazine ads, on billboards, and other media.

But listen up: years ago advertising guru Fairfax Cone said that advertising is what we do when we can't go see someone. So, if you're a consultant or other business person with a small group of clients, you could conceivably sell to them without ever once using any form of advertising. In fact, that face-to-face relationship would be more powerful than any ad could ever be. You'd do well to save your marketing dollars and invest in a few lunch dates to show your appreciation.

Few of us, however, are able to reach all of our customers, or potential customers, by buying them a Caesar salad. We may turn to advertising.

Reach and Frequency

When you start thinking about where and how to advertise, there are two terms you should know: reach and frequency.

The term reach refers to just how broad the extent of the medium's impact will be. For example, a daily newspaper ad has a very wide reach, because newspapers have lots of readers. Conversely, an ad in a local specialty publication for knitters has a much narrower reach, being seen by a small audience of like-minded individuals.

Frequency defines how often your message will be seen. A one-time daily newspaper ad has limited frequency if it appears only once. A radio ad repeated 12 times a day has much greater frequency.

If you are advertising knitting supplies, you don't really need widespread reach. You will effectively communicate your message through the specialty knitting publication. And because knitters are likely to hang onto a publication with patterns in it, they're likely to see your ad repeatedly as they refer back to the publication.

On the other hand, if you're advertising a furniture store, you'll want to achieve higher frequency so that you create awareness and are top of mind when people want to buy furniture.

Although it is generally thought that you want broad reach and frequency, you're better off with highly targeted advertising unless you're promoting a service that's used by a wide variety of consumers.

Select Your Medium Carefully

Advertising can be an effective tool as long as you use it properly. As with any marketing approach, you need to consider who your target audience is and where they go for information about products like yours. For instance, if your product is one that people need to see and fall in love with, you will definitely not want to advertise it on the radio. On the other hand, if you're advertising burgers, car radios are a good place to reach hungry people.

We once worked with a client who sold insurance management services to local corporations. He was enthralled with the idea of advertising online and wanted to put a banner ad on other people's websites. So, we asked him, who buys what you sell? Turns out his audience was limited to about 200 key people in mid-size corporations in the city. Here's one huge reason why putting a banner ad on a website wouldn't work for him: there was no guarantee that his audience would even go to the website at all, and even if they did, there was little likelihood they would buy his type of product from that one small mention. And furthermore, why spend money with no guarantees? He would have been much better served by creating a marketing plan that would reach the audience in their businesses in a very personal, one-on-one way.

Our client had the ability to follow Cone's advice and "go see" his potential clients, which made it silly and a total waste of his money to advertise.

When it comes to advertising, you can pick locations as traditional as newspapers, magazines, and radio ads, and as unusual as bathroom stall doors or traveling billboards. The trick is to catch people where it counts.

Television Advertising

Television advertising can be effective if you need to reach a broad number of people from all walks of life. For example, if you sell retail products such as furniture, you can attract customers from a wide area in your city. After all, people will shop for furniture outside their neighborhood. On the other hand, if you run a lawn service, you don't want customers all over town; it's more cost-effective for you to serve people in neighborhoods that are close to each other. TV advertising would be a waste because you would be selling to lots of customers you don't want.

When you're deciding if television advertising will work for you, you should rely upon an advertising expert to recommend the best way to approach it. Think about these questions:

- ◆ What benefit do people get from using my product and service?

- ◆ What one thing do I want people to know about my business?

- ◆ When are people likely to buy my product? In other words, is it seasonal, such as swimming pools, or do they buy year-round?

- ◆ Is it important that I show the product?

Have you seen those annoying commercials where people shout their message repeatedly? If you think those ads are bad, think again. Sometimes the most effective commercials are the ones that drill themselves into your brain with their inane messages or totally obnoxious characters. We're not recommending annoying your potential customers, but we do suggest that you make sure your ad is very, very memorable.

Radio Advertising

Think about all the time you spend in your car. Most of us have at least a 15-minute drive to and from work, plus errands and road trips. And consider this: unless you have Sirius or XM radio, you probably hear all the ads on your favorite station over and over. Because there's no fast-forward button on the radio and most of us tend to listen to one station without switching, radio ads for the right kind of product can be much more engaging than television.

> **Brainwaves**
>
> During the early part of the twentieth century, the best way to reach a mass audience was via radio. Almost every household had one, and listening to radio shows was a beloved family event. Did you know that the term soap opera refers to radio dramas that were sponsored by soap manufacturers?

Something to remember about radio ads, though, is that people won't write down phone numbers or addresses while they drive (at least we hope they won't). If you need to give them directions to your place of business, tell them a landmark to look for, like "at the intersection of Poplar and Highland" or "next door to the Paradiso movie theater."

Naturally, "drive time," when the majority of people are going to and from work, is a very popular time to advertise because you reach more people.

Promotions and Special Offers

Part of the challenge of selling is getting customers to try your product for the first time. This is called trial usage. Habits are hard to change, and if you want people to switch from a product they're already using to your product, you first have to overcome their habit. There's a saying that we all prefer "the devil we know to the devil we don't know." In the business world, it means that we're inclined to keep using a product that's not perfect just because it's easier than changing the way we've been doing things.

If your product is absolutely new and innovative, you have to overcome people's skepticism about paying for something that may or may not live up to its promises. Again, you may have to give them an incentive to try it.

You can generate trial usage by offering something for free or at a discount, giving away a gift with purchase, or otherwise enticing people to check it out.

Booby Traps

One particular store that I shop at frequently offers me 5 percent off coupons from time to time. If I spend $100 on a dress, I get only $5 off. I shirk those off because it's not worth my time to go there for such a small savings, especially if it's for an unplanned purchase. I can stay home and save myself $95. In fact, I'm a little insulted that I could spend so much money there and they offer me a paltry 5 percent discount. At the same time, when they send me a coupon on my birthday for $25 off, I always go. That seems like a sizable savings. Whatever you're offering must be significant enough to matter.

One of the oldest tricks in the book is the buy one, get one free offer. This does two things for you: first, it gets the new customer in the door. Second, it ensures they buy something. Restaurants get a third bonus—the additional customer who comes along as a date or companion!

Public Relations: No Free Ride

Public relations—also known as PR—is the art of gaining the support of the different groups whose opinion of your company is important. To do that, you manage your image in the public by trying to influence how the media portrays your company.

def•i•ni•tion

A **third-party endorsement** is when someone not associated with your company says good things about your product or service or about your company's way of doing business. This can come from a customer, the media, or someone in the community who has an opinion about you.

How many times have we heard people say, "Public relations is free advertising?" Not true. Good public relations is hard to come by and requires savvy action on your part. The difficult part of PR is that you really have no control over how others perceive you, so you have to work hard to influence them to speak nicely about you. The object of PR is to get a *third-party endorsement*, which means someone objective sings your praises. What makes a third-party endorsement so valuable is that it carries more weight than if you or someone who works with you talks about your good qualities. It's more believable because the person doesn't have anything to gain by saying good things.

How to Get PR

PR arises from the things you do that are noteworthy and newsworthy. For example, if you have a grand opening at your new store, receive an award, get elected an officer of an association, lay off a lot of employees, or do something scandalous or illegal, you're likely to generate interest from the media—whether you want it or not.

Whenever you invite the media into your world, keep in mind that you can't control what they say about you. If you have any skeletons, you can bet the reporter will ask you about them. Be prepared with a well-thought-out answer.

Brainwaves

When Sara Blakey came up with the idea of Spanx (footless pantyhose), she decided to act as her own PR agent. She sent a gift basket containing Spanx to Oprah Winfrey with a note thanking her for being her inspiration. Presto! Her product took off like wildfire.

Developing Relationships with the Media

While you can't control the media, you can develop good relationships with them and hope for the best. Here are some guidelines to follow when you're working with reporters.

The best thing you can do is be prepared. You should have handy in your file a few one-liners that are good sound bites, highly quotable, and provide information other people don't know. Reporters love a good quote with pithy statements. Think about your company and write down three solid sentences about what you do and how you do it. Use active verbs and unusual descriptions, not corporate baloney. Here's an example for a company that coaches speakers: "We teach our clients how to mesmerize audiences." "When our clients get on stage, they create earthquakes in the audience."

◆ Be honest and upfront.

◆ Don't try to get coverage of a nonevent. Wait till you truly have something meaty to talk about.

◆ Try to make the reporter's job easy by having all the facts at hand, along with some interesting personal interest information or other colorful background that the reporter may use for a sidebar.

◆ Always remember that reporters are working on deadline and they need quick responses. Respect their need for speed and be available to talk to them. Otherwise, without information from you, they may just move on to a story about a source who is available in a timely fashion.

Issuing News Releases

Usually, when companies do something noteworthy, they send out a press release to the local media providing the facts and background of the situation. The media might simply write a story using the information you've submitted or they might contact you to get more detail.

If you want to create good relationships with the media, you will send out a release only when something truly interesting happens. And it has to be interesting to other people, not just to you! People who inundate the media with mundane or inane information quickly alienate reporters. Once they've identified you as a nuisance, they will write you off and not pay any attention to your news releases, even if the information is valid. It's like the boy who cried wolf.

> **Brainwaves**
>
> Use quotes to make your press releases more interesting. There are many websites that offer lists of quotes on every imaginable subject. Some examples are www.quoteland.com, www.famousquotes.com, and www.thinkexist.com. Or you can just drop by the bookstore and get your own copy of *Bartlett's Familiar Quotations*.

Responding to Media Inquiries

There are times when news about your company reaches the media without your sending out information. If something favorable has happened to you, be ready to comment about it, giving short, positive comments. If something unfavorable has just come to light, you may want to respond defensively but be careful.

Face-to-Face Marketing Opportunities

We talked earlier about the best sales opportunity being the one where you're right in front of your prospect. If you have a product you can carry around with you, you're armed to sell wherever you go. Another face-to-face strategy is to use the technique that has worked so well for companies like Avon cosmetics, Amway, or Mary Kay Cosmetics, all of which take the product to the people's homes. Being able to demonstrate a product up close and let the prospective buyer use it with friends is a tried-and-true technique.

Brainwaves

The Direct Marketing Association (DMA) is the leading global trade association of business and nonprofit organizations, using and supporting direct marketing tools and techniques. DMA advocates industry standards for responsible marketing and conducts research and education. Founded in 1917, the DMA today has more than 3,600 members from the United States and 46 other nations, including the majority of companies on the Fortune 100 list. Check out the website at www.the-dma.org.

Direct Mail

All that stuff that ends up in your mailbox? You may call it junk but marketers call it direct mail. Direct mail is usually sent via snail mail either to your office or your home. It can include special offers, announcements of sales, coupons for dollars off, free dinners, credit card offers, catalogues, or other wonderful information about how you can give someone your money. Direct mail is good for information that a person needs to have a little time to review, may want to hang onto (like a coupon), or could file away in their financial files. The trick is, you must give people a way to react to what you've sent them like a date and time for a sale, a subscription form to fill out and return, or another *call to action*. Don't let them off the hook by letting your item end up in the trash.

def•i•ni•tion

Call to action is the part of the sales pitch where you ask someone to do something to purchase. Call a number, sign a coupon, or send in a form, just anything that gets them one step closer to a commitment to buy.

Community Relations Builds Friends

What company doesn't want to have a good relationship with the community in which it operates? Certainly if you are perceived as a good corporate citizen, you'll find it easier to do business and enjoy more support from the citizens in your community. Don't you feel positive about a company that you see helping others or doing something to make your city a better place to live? Everyone does.

Being a good citizen doesn't have to cost a lot of money. You don't have to underwrite the construction of a Cancer Survivors Park or build a house for someone to make an impact. Simple volunteerism can create a great name for your company. Here are some ideas:

- Gather a group of friends and employees, wear T-shirts that say what company you represent, and walk together in a fund-raiser.

- Participate in a corporate spelling bee to raise money for literacy programs.

- Set aside a half day on Friday once a month to clean up a certain part of the neighborhood where your business operates.

- Serve as a safe haven for kids.

- Mentor underprivileged students or judge essay contests.

When you're active in the community, you will automatically meet others who share your interests and concerns. When you've created relationships with like-minded individuals in other companies, you may want to co-sponsor an event that will bring visibility to you both. By parlaying your resources, you can increase the size of your community contribution and also the size of your reputation. Everyone benefits.

The Least You Need to Know

◆ Radio ads should never include information people need to write down.

◆ Promotions and special offers work when you want people to try your product for the first time.

◆ When you invite the media to an event, understand that you cannot control what they say about you.

◆ Making ads memorable is the key to success.

Chapter 4

A Whole New World

In This Chapter

- ◆ Why traditional marketing methods have been diluted
- ◆ How Internet usage has shifted the business landscape
- ◆ The Internet makes guerrilla marketing easier
- ◆ Why guerrilla marketing tactics work

Most companies can't afford to hire magician David Blaine to hang suspended over Times Square to drive Thanksgiving Day sales. But if you consider how over-stimulated most consumers are, it takes an ingenious gimmick such as this just to get their attention. And beyond that, most consumers are tired and jaded when it comes to traditional marketing and advertising anyway. Why? People are simply less trustful of messages spoon-fed to them by companies who have a vested interest in convincing them to buy their stuff.

Today news of real customer experiences spreads like wildfire thanks to the Internet. Fortunately for consumers, companies that fail to live up to customers' expectations can't hide any more. If your product isn't up to par or your service is substandard, it's going to be part of the public and permanent record faster than you can say "blog."

But as long as you're on the up and up, the proliferation of electronic tools is tremendously good news. You have at your fingertips a brand new, cost-effective way of reaching customers. This new high-tech world we live in offers dozens of ways to create free (or nearly free) buzz. By mastering *guerrilla marketing* techniques, you can take advantage of inventive, but inexpensive methods that create buzz about your product, with and without the help of technology.

def•i•ni•tion

Guerrilla war is conducted in an irregular manner by independent troops. In the marketing world, **guerrilla marketing** has come to mean unconventional marketing techniques intended to get maximum results from minimum resources invested. The term was coined by Jay Conrad Levinson in his book, *Guerrilla Marketing*. Certainly, in the battle that goes on for customers, a war analogy could be an accurate description of techniques that we can use.

What Is Guerrilla Marketing?

Guerrilla marketing means getting people's attention in an unconventional way. It's about maximizing your creativity instead of draining your bank account. The Internet is guerrilla marketing's ultimate best friend because it provides the opportunity to reach communities of people who formerly were only accessible to companies with deep pockets.

By far, the most common guerrilla marketing tactic is buzz marketing. In buzz marketing, the goal is to generate excitement and encourage people to talk about you so that they spread your message either through personal word of mouth recommendations or virally on the Internet.

Brainwaves

New methods of marketing are evolving even as you read this book. Don't be surprised if you see some of the terms we use being used in slightly different ways in other information resources. The precise definition of ambient marketing, for example, might vary slightly based on your source. And guerrilla marketing, in some circles, is synonymous with stealth marketing. We don't see it that way because we envision guerrilla marketing as a thoroughly wholesome methodology, whereas stealth marketing is just plain underhanded. Bottom line, don't get caught up in the terminology. Just concentrate on understanding the concepts and figuring out how you can use them in your own business; you'll be a guerrilla master in no time!

Why Guerrilla Marketing Methods Work

Guerrilla marketing techniques rely on a lot of elbow grease on your part, along with the so-called "kindness of strangers." That is, it typically requires grassroots involvement from customers—or potential customers—who get excited about what your product or service does.

For a small company without a lot of money to spend, it gives you ways to make a small investment go a long way. And you can do that by being very hands on and letting information about your company grow *organically*, or naturally, from one person to another. For a larger, more established company, it allows for broader reach.

Although guerrilla marketing doesn't include slick advertising, it does require exceptional creativity. And that's easier said than done, because just about anybody can clog up the airwaves, cables, and networks with their messages. Average citizens are creating videos and uploading them to *YouTube*. People from every demographic are communicating using methods previously reserved for top secret government agencies. Why, even the average 12-year-old child can become a vocal and highly visible participant in dialogues taking place in cyberspace. Let's face it: it takes something pretty unusual and clever to catch people's attention these days.

def•i•ni•tion

In marketing, **organic** refers to promotion that happens naturally simply because customers become passionate about your product.

YouTube is an online video community founded in February 2005. YouTube allows absolutely anyone to upload videos from just about any source, including their personal video cameras. You'll find everything from cute animal footage to embarrassing hidden-camera videos: humorous, informative, embarrassing, cute, clever, or obnoxious. It is free to watch and upload videos on YouTube.

People Want Interactivity and Connections

Even though you have lots of competition for a customer's "mind space," there's never been a better time for guerrilla marketing. Now, more and more established companies are jumping on the bandwagon for one good reason: guerrilla marketing works! In the old days, when the computer was in its infancy, and technology hadn't become our friend, we used to talk about "high tech vs. high touch." That meant we couldn't let technology substitute for human interaction. And while things have changed a lot since then, the "high touch" element has remained an essential part of effective marketing.

As technology has become a more integral part of our lives—one we're increasingly comfortable with—consumers still long for more authentic communication. They're leery of mass marketing methods. Sure, direct mail pieces come "personalized" with the intended customer's name printed on them, but most people are savvy enough to know that there's no genuine connection behind that. As a result, they've developed a taste for communication that intrigues and involves them, as opposed to communication in which they're being communicated "at." Enter guerrilla marketing: it's both inexpensive *and* effective, so it's fast becoming the first choice of companies both large and small. Now is the time for guerrilla marketing. Here's why.

Internet Broadens Your Reach

Water cooler conversations aren't a new phenomenon. Consumers have always discussed with their friends the products they use, the services they prefer, the shows they watch, and the companies they think are cool. But now, rather than talking with a select few in their immediate social or business circles, your targeted audience members can use the many and varied digital communication methods available and widespread online access to spread a message to an infinite number of potential customers! People from every demographic are now engaging in conversation on message boards, through blogs, by podcast, and by uploading video messages to YouTube. They rate products online and provide feedback about product sellers to the general public. Never before has information had the capacity to be disseminated so quickly. And at a time when television viewers are able to fast forward through commercials using their DVR box, reaching users in nontraditional ways has never been so important.

One of the simplest forms of spreading information quickly lies in the "forward" button on your e-mail program. We've all received one of those alarming urban myth e-mails. You know the type: "Beware of people who are drugging victims who wake up in a bathtub filled with ice and discover that someone has stolen their kidney. Pass this on to all your friends!"

Or surely you've received forwarded pictures of spectacular Grand Canyon sunsets or pictures of Earth from space, or a kitty or puppy photo album. In one day, information can go from one person's inbox to the computers of hundreds of thousands of receivers—or more.

New Ideas Easily Implemented Through Technology

Just 15 years ago, it would have been hard for your average professional marketer to envision a time when you could reach millions of people instantly, by simply pressing a button. (Of course there's a bit more to sending an e-mail than just one click of a button, but you get the idea: it's much easier than ever before.) But that was before mass e-mail distribution became a common practice. The idea was novel in the beginning, but without restraint many marketers bombarded us with "too much of a good thing" turning a viable medium into a dirty word—*spam*. But we digress.

The digital age has ushered in an era where you can spread a potent message without spending thousands of dollars on printing and mailing. No more production schedules that include print time and fulfillment. Messages that in the past cost thousands of dollars to distribute can now be disseminated for a fraction of the cost. And it's not just about instant advertising. Companies can now get customer feedback easily and inexpensively via online opinion polls. Through blogs and message boards, company representatives can engage in a conversation with their audiences and give customers what they really want: a genuine interaction instead of a targeted marketing message. And the best part of getting instant feedback—companies can make adjustments quickly when necessary.

Brainwaves

In 1937, Jay Hormel invented a food product called SPAM. The recipe for SPAM Classic, as it's called today, included ham, pork, salt, water, sugar, sodium nitrite, and potato starch. Hormel Foods held a contest to name the new product, offering a $100 prize to the winner. A man named Ken won. Since then, Hormel Foods has sold six billion cans of SPAM. The low-cost, canned food was used in World War II to provide nutrition to soldiers. Talk about marketing ingenuity: Hormel Foods now actually has a SPAM museum in Minnesota, a SPAM fan club, and SPAM gift items such as caps, silver charms, antenna bobbers, and coffee cups. There's more info on the www.hormel.com website.

In modern usage, the term spam has come to mean a bunch of unwanted junk mail sent in bulk to lots of people. In some cases, juvenile computer delinquents, criminals, and jerks with truly evil intentions create spam with the deliberate purpose of clogging up your e-mail box.

An Internet Presence Is an Absolute Must

What's the first thing you do when you want to know more about a company? If you're like most people, you probably jump online and check out its website. It's the fastest, easiest way to get comprehensive information about everything from how much money it makes to who its executives are to how to buy its products. Want some history on SPAM or spam? The Internet's got it. Need to know where you can find a Pottery Barn Outlet store? Check. In fact, the biggest surprise you can get is when you *don't* find a company on the Internet. Absence will just about destroy a company's credibility these days.

Companies that sell to the public certainly need digital connectivity. In fact, it's virtually the cost of entry.

So many transactions are happening on the Internet these days; not only purchases, but also conversations—conversations that make business happen. Corporate bigwigs have to come out from behind the closed doors of a boardroom to interact with consumers. We all want to be heard. As a result, the Internet has moved from being a virtual playground for teenagers and tech geeks to being a virtual cocktail party.

Many respected and successful companies have a presence of some sort on the Internet, and they are exchanging meaningful dialogue with their customers. This is extremely powerful because it increases the authenticity of their relationships with the public. What an amazing shift; it's truly launched an entire culture change.

A Two-Way Exchange

Internet usage has also increased the amount of data businesses can collect during a single transaction. Every time someone fills out a sign-up page or completes a short survey, the company can collect information about who the person is, what they like and don't like, where they shop, how old they are, and so on. Businesses now know more about their consumers' wants and desires than ever before. With such intelligence, management can truly understand customers, develop products and services to suit them, create incentives, and, when necessary, shift their perspective to develop a fresh relationship with their customer base.

def•i•ni•tion

Facebook is an online network founded in 2004. It was originally exclusively available to college and university students. Facebook is now open to anyone with an e-mail address. Various social networks exist within Facebook, including communities centered around places of employment, high schools, universities, colleges, and even regions. Facebook is still largely a college-centered community (www.facebook.com).

To understand just how much the Internet and the proliferation of digital communication methods have changed the way business is conducted, consider that even the CIA has a *Facebook* page. Yes, you read it correctly—the real Central Intelligence Agency has a Facebook page to recruit students to join its National Clandestine Service (NCS), the organization that oversees human espionage operations by the 15 U.S. Intelligence agencies including the FBI and Defense Intelligence Agency. Welcome to the new millennium.

Digital Marketing Is "Green"

The fact that *An Inconvenient Truth* won an Oscar at the 79th Academy Awards is evidence of our increasing awareness and concern about global warming. At a time when our desire to make a difference is at an all-time high, digital marketing is more appealing than ever.

E-mail and websites save thousands of reams of paper on a daily basis. Just look at Apple and the introduction of the *iPod*. Sure, immediate delivery and individual song purchasing are the primary drivers of this industry revolution, but do a search online for "iTunes, positive environmental impact" and you'll find blogger after blogger touting the environmental savings of iTunes. With Apple selling five million songs each day, just imagine how much our landfills are spared in jewel cases, inserts, and CDs, not to mention the chemicals used for printing and pressing and the gas used to deliver all those elements to their desired locations.

Digital media gives our "I need it now" society two highly valuable commodities: instant gratification and the opportunity to "do the right thing" for our planet. And you can leverage this marketing advantage, too.

Brainwaves

Instead of using the trite "click here to join our mailing list," why not showcase your green thumb? Instead use "Click here to join our eco-friendly mailing list. Our company is proud to encourage others to use less paper to protect our environment."

A great example of this in action is SavATree, a tree, shrub, and lawn care company that serves Connecticut, Washington D.C., Maryland, Massachusetts, New Jersey, New York, Pennsylvania, and Virginia. On their site, they offer users the option to sign up for electronic-only communications. Here's how they phrase it:

"Help us save trees! Submit your email address. Please submit your email address so that we may begin communicating with you electronically. We pledge to use your email address only as means to enhance the quality of customer service we are able to provide. You can review our complete Email Promise below."

There's An Everything-Technical Craze

Two years ago YouTube didn't even exist. Today, more than 100 million videos are viewed on the site every day, and the site now boasts roughly 20 million unique visitors each month. Need evidence that hits closer to home? How about that forwarded e-mail from Grandma or Grandpa in your inbox? While there are those few hold-outs who are hoping for the return of the Pony Express (such as our friend, Timothy), the role technology plays in our everyday lives is only going to increase in the coming years.

Already, the line between the online community and reality has become increasingly blurry and there's no sign this will slow down. You might see the latest viral video featured on the national news. (EepyBird's Diet Coke and Mentos stunt was featured in a segment on *The Today Show,* for example.) Television shows have blogs and message boards. If you're not already on, you'd better jump on board and make the most of the ride.

> **Brainwaves**
>
> The Internet and its widespread use have so drastically changed the way we do business that every business is impacted, no matter how far removed it is from technology. If you've resisted getting online, it's not too late. Check out *The Complete Idiot's Guide to the Internet* for some basics on getting started.

Distrust of Traditional Marketing Techniques

In this case, a few bad apples really have spoiled the barrel. Because some advertisers are shamelessly guilty of deceiving the public, people do not trust companies to tell the truth and nothing but the truth especially when it comes to marketing. Like it or not, consumers are savvy. They value recommendations from interpersonal relationships more than targeted messages created by slick ad agencies. But they can still be fooled.

Enter stealth marketing, which is a term used to describe undercover marketing efforts meant to appear as though they occurred naturally. Although stealth marketing is often associated with guerrilla marketing because it's an inexpensive and attention-grabbing strategy, it is not something we recommend. It is almost certain to backfire when your deception becomes public knowledge. And even if you aren't discovered, being successful in business is about building solid relationships. Solid relationships are never built on deception. Guerrilla marketing, as we see it, should be innovative and upfront. To read more about stealth marketing, see Chapter 10.

Booby Traps _____

Always represent your company and your offerings in the most accurate way possible. Don't over-promise and under-deliver because the truth will always prevail. Bloggers all over the world are poised and ready to expose the disingenuous. Keep in mind, too, that the Federal Trade Commission (FTC) works to uncover deceptive marketing. Their mission is to protect consumers from fraudulent, deceptive, and unfair business practices.

The Public Suffers Information Overload

Television, e-mail, billboard ads, magazines, cell phones, Blackberries, news feeds, and instant messages … all of us are subjected to hundreds of messages each day. The glut of information makes it increasingly hard to communicate effectively with your target audience. Buzz marketing, a form of guerrilla marketing, can help you stand out in today's overstimulated environment.

> ### Brainwaves
>
> *The Complete Idiot's Guides* (CIGs) started in 1993 as a line of easy-to-understand computer books for people who were intimidated by software and related technology. Because of their immediate success, the line of books was expanded to include a variety of other topics. Why were they so successful? Because they are a direct assault on information overload!
>
> In 2005, scientists in the UK found that a relentless influx of information can lead to "info-mania," a condition that was shown to lower people's IQs by up to 10 points. So the truth is: you, dear reader, are incredibly smart. People who read *The Complete Idiot's Guides* are anything but idiots—they are very smart individuals who simply know better than to put themselves through information overload just to determine the need-to-know facts about a subject. Why lower your IQ when you could just read a *Complete Idiot's Guide?*

Proliferation of Product Choices Creates Confusion

The Internet has given us nearly limitless purchasing options. Now, instead of being confined to buying items in your neighborhood, you can order products from almost any place on Earth. But with so many options, buying decisions can become more complicated. How do you differentiate yourself from your competition? Using guerrilla marketing to create a buzz is an effective way to get your product or service in front of your customer at the point of purchase.

We Value Coolness and Connoisseurship

Forget the idea that being a nerd is undesirable. Having the latest technological gadget, like the hot new cell phone, is cool and trendy. Being in the know about our ever-evolving methods of communicating is hip. The list of must-have gadgets and gizmos grows by the day.

Full disclosure: even with knowledge you aren't immune. We've added Apple's new iPhone to our wish lists, although we did not camp out overnight for it. And no, Apple did not solicit our endorsement. They've just successfully created product advocates in us.

Technology Makes Guerrilla Marketing More Effective

Throughout history, the advent of new technology has wielded the power to shift big businesses. Airplanes changed the face of transportation. Refrigeration drastically impacted food industries. And so, technology has impacted the marketing community. And while technology-based solutions are not yet typically stand-alone marketing strategies, using digitally based marketing tools is quickly becoming a viable way of promoting yourself.

> **Brainwaves**
>
> IDC, International Data Corporation, provides data, analysis, and advisory services on information technology (IT) markets, trends, products, vendors, and geographies. According to their research, "On a typical day, 19 million people go online to research a product, and for 2006, online retail purchases exceeded $100 billion." That's billion, with a "b."

Guerrilla marketing efforts that before only reached hundreds of people can now reach thousands, even millions. Although guerrilla marketing is typically associated with low-cost options, more and more dollars are being spent on nontraditional methods. Traditional marketing is getting a smaller share of the budget as nontraditional methods gain in popularity and in use. Current trends suggest that we should expect even further transitioning toward digital marketing in the future.

Technological Marketing Methods

We'll go into more detail later in the book, but here's a quick description of some methods that have resulted from the availability of technological tools:

◆ Blogs—user-generated online diaries that allow users to respond

◆ Social networks—online communities where people network and share information

- Tagging—way of labeling web content such as blog entries to enable users to easily find your stuff

- RSS—messages are delivered directly to users' desktops, bypassing e-mail filters

- Podcast—a recorded audio session that can be shared and played as MP3s

- Bluetooth—wireless technology that allows you to send messages to people's personal devices (like mobile phones) using short-range radio frequency

The Least You Need to Know

- Even if you think you're immune, the Internet has changed the business playing field.

- Creating a buzz using guerrilla marketing methods can help your product stand out to information-saturated consumers.

- If you aren't reaching your customers online, your competition probably is.

- Internet-driven guerrilla marketing methods aren't the only ones available, but they're fast becoming the first line of defense in marketing.

Part 2

Modern Marketing Marvels

Reaching people has never been easier or more affordable. From buzz marketing projects like "Free Hug" campaigns to grassroots efforts like "Spread Firefox," it is now possible to reach millions of people for a fraction of the cost of your old-school ad campaign.

People Who Know People: Influencers

In This Chapter

◆ Why influencers can reach your customers when you can't

◆ Where to find influencers to promote your company's product or services

◆ Preparing influencers to communicate your message

◆ Celebrity marketing, product placement, and product seeding

Having the right person endorse your product at the right time to the right audience can move mountains in the way of sales. Just look at UGG boots. Even though the boots have been around for nearly 200 years, they weren't "hot" until *Baywatch* babe Pamela Anderson started wearing them. It'll be interesting to see how their sales fare now that Pamela has decided to ditch the footware after discovering that the boots are made of sheepskin. And while hiring a celebrity may not be an option, you can still find ways to influence people in your target audience.

What Is Influencer Marketing?

Influencer marketing starts with finding someone who has credibility in a certain area, and getting them to visibly use or endorse your product. The concept behind influencer marketing is that when someone cool, smart, successful, or otherwise admirable uses a product, the potential customer will trust that person to have made a right choice. Also implicit in the concept is that if the customer buys the product, he or she will become more like the influencer—that is, girls who wear UGG boots will look more like Pamela Anderson, right? Perhaps not. But when Tiger Woods endorses a golf club, you can bet that millions of golfers buy it because they believe, deep down, that they'll play a better round of golf.

With consumers more skeptical than ever, credibility in marketing is everything. When you're using an indirect selling technique like having an influencer, the effectiveness of your message is dependent upon who is delivering it. For example, would you be more likely to take fashion advice from a columnist at *Vogue* magazine, or from Bob, the paint expert at Home Depot? If you're shopping around for a new MP3 player, you're more likely to heed the advice of your college-age son than your aging aunt. But influencer marketing is about more than expert opinions. It's about appeal, too. People tend to listen to people they admire, even if those people aren't experts. So really, the fundamental questions you must answer to partake in influencer marketing are:

◆ Whose opinion matters to the people I want to reach?

◆ How do I appeal to those people, the influencers of my target audience?

def•i•ni•tion

Influencers are people whose opinion is highly valued by others. Influencers' recommendations are powerful because people heed their advice. These are the people who start cultural trends. A **product advocate** is someone who is willing to talk about your products to other people. Also known as buzz marketers, product evangelists, or word of mouth marketers.

Remember, don't focus directly on your end-user, but rather train your eye on the people your end-users are receptive to. If you can convert them to be true blue fans, *they'll* convert your target audience for you. *Influencers* are especially useful when your target audience has become immune to direct messaging from you (or from marketers in general); marketing through influencers allows you to benefit from association with a person your customer *does* trust. *Product advocates* are powerful; product advocates who are also influencers are explosive!

Why Is It Effective?

Two words: peer pressure. People are easily influenced by people they like or want to emulate. And we're such a part of a "herd" mentality, most of us want to fit in. Look no further than the falling-off-your-behind baggy pants trend. Rumor has it that this trend began in prison. Inmates who were issued ill-fitting clothing (and who were also not allowed to have belts) found themselves walking around with their pants falling off. Little did they know they were at the forefront of a fashion tidal wave. Those first guys may have found wearing their pants this way very annoying, but people wear this style on purpose just to fit in. Go figure.

Here's the Buzz

Movie star Clark Gable, who made hearts throb in movies like *Gone with the Wind*, is credited with a sort of reverse marketing that supposedly occurred as a result of his role in *It Happened One Night*. Directed by Frank Capra, the movie came out in 1934. The story was that a spoiled heiress is running away from her family and meets up with a reporter. They have to spend the night in the same motel room—very racy for the time! Gable takes off his shirt to reveal his bare chest. Ladies swooned and, so the story goes, undershirt sales plummeted. There's no way to prove the sales slump, but it's certainly within the realm of possibility.

Could you apply this to your business?

Finding Your Influencers

It's time to enlist your army of influencers—people who can effectively create a buzz about you. Take a look around and start assembling your forces. Where to start?

No matter what you have to offer, there's someone who can influence your target audience—you just have to find them. They could be analysts, experts, journalists, leaders, researchers, bloggers, authors, enthusiasts, teachers, or professionals— someone is interested in what you're selling. One of the best ways to figure out who your influencers might be is to ask yourself who you would go to for advice if you wanted to purchase what you have to offer.

Turning Advocates into Influencers

By far, the best place to begin looking for influencers is right in your own backyard. Some of the customers you've already impressed are probably highly influential in their social circles—social circles that consist of people *just like them*! Many of them may also be bloggers, analysts, teachers, enthusiasts, and the like. What's great about finding influencers among your existing customers is that you don't have to educate them on your benefits.

Spotting an Influencer

Of course all the people who are buzzing about you are valuable; influencers just have the most impact. Here's how to spot an influencer.

- They're usually well respected.
- They're well connected and they have large social circles.

> **Brainwaves**
>
> Have you ever asked a customer to speak on your behalf? Influencers who are already your customers only need to know you'd like them to talk about you. They may love you to death but may not realize that you're looking for new business. Ask!

- They're great communicators and are usually outgoing and talkative.
- They consider themselves experts in one or more areas.
- They ask a lot of questions because they don't give recommendations without research.
- They're usually early adopters and trendsetters. They're aware of what's hot before it becomes mainstream.
- They like to have the inside scoop.

 Booby Traps

News reporters are supposed to be objective, and if you offer them a free sample of your product they may view it as an attempt to bribe them or otherwise influence them to tell a story that's in your favor. In fact, ethical news organizations have a policy against reporters accepting anything that could be considered a gift. Steer clear of trying to get an endorsement from news people. It could backfire!

Influencers Online

Look for bloggers who are already talking about you. If nobody is talking about you specifically, look for people who are talking about your industry or products or services similar to yours. Begin monitoring buzz that's circulating about your area of expertise. You can do this by subscribing to various blogs via Technorati (www. technorati.com) and reading message boards related to your field. Spend time listening before even *considering* jumping in.

Everyday Influencers Within Your Target Audience

Maybe your potential influencers aren't already customers and they aren't bloggers. How do you find them? Well, think of who you are selling to and find a place to connect with them. Offer a free service, trial membership, open house, sample product—anything to make contact.

Industry Expert Influencers

Who's the go-to person for your industry? Who's blogging about other companies in your industry? Give the experts a chance to sample what it's like to do business with you. Experts are often influencers, so if they enjoy the experience, they're likely to talk about it.

Tap Your Friends and Relations

Employees, family, friends, former sorority sisters or fraternity brothers, co-workers from previous jobs, classmates, suppliers/vendors, other business owners in the community, and local government officials can all be potential advocates for your product. This is the concept behind the business network, LinkedIn— it's all about leveraging your existing resources.

How Influential Are Your Influencers?

Once you've narrowed down your prospects, consider who your best options are. Keep two things in mind: how far is their reach and how powerful is their recommendation? An endorsement from Oprah Winfrey, for example, is both powerful and far-reaching. In fact, when an author is scheduled to appear on her show, the publisher almost automatically puts the wheels in motion to print perhaps hundreds of thousands of copies of his or her book. The publishers know that visibility on Oprah guarantees a best seller.

Even though you might not be able to secure Oprah, you do need to consider the factors that make influencers effective. Think about how many people your potential influencer will come in contact with on a regular basis. Does he or she write a well-respected blog with a wide distribution? Do they reach enough members of your target audience to really make an impact for you? Just how much pull do they have with your audience? How meaningful is a recommendation from them?

P&G (Procter & Gamble Co.) is a great example of influencer marketing at work. When they introduced bubble gum-flavored Pepto-Bismol, a children's-strength version of their tummy-soothing liquid, they didn't go straight to moms; they went to moms' trusted source—pediatricians. Sure, it might have been faster to drench the airways in TV commercials, but their message would probably have been lost in the glut of advertising. By selling specifically to *pediatricians*, P&G, in essence, gets to introduce Children's Pepto one-on-one to countless moms via one of their most trusted resources.

Real Life Example

But what if you don't have the advertising budget of P&G? How could you do this guerrilla-style? A pediatrician's office might also be a good place for you to sell your product if you're a photographer. Offer free services to two of the doctor's patients, with the stipulation that you be allowed to hang samples in the doctor's office. Parents love it because they get free professional photos, the doctors love it because they get to show how much they care about the kids they treat. For you it's a perfectly placed ad that's open to your target audience all day. Make sure your info is displayed alongside the photos.

I inadvertently benefited from this type of situation recently. In a former life I co-authored a book called *Simple Works*, a book of ideas for making life easier and more pleasant. It's a philosophical work with very short chapters. I left a copy of it in the dentist's office. A while later, my sister-in-law, who didn't know about the book, went to that dentist. While sitting in the waiting room she picked up the book. Impressed with the thoughts, she mentioned it to the receptionist, who related that one of the authors had been in the day before. My sister-in-law was thrilled that one of the authors lived in Memphis. At that point, she looked more closely at the cover, and the flap, and realized that I co-authored the book. Perhaps I need to do a better job of simply telling my friends and family about my work!

Arming Your Influencers with Information

Once you've identified your influencers, you need to give them the tools to showcase your wares to other people. Make it easy for your influencers (and any advocates, for that matter) to tell other people why they should choose you over the competition. Keep it simple—something that's easy to repeat. (See Chapter 6 for suggestions on tools to give influencers.)

Brainwaves

Tremor, a marketing service created by the P&G Company, truly understands the power of influencers. They have an entire business devoted to getting new products into the hands of teen influencers. Teens who want to volunteer their opinions on a variety of products related to fashion, music, food, beauty products, and more can sign up to be part of the Tremor Crew. More than one million teens are part of this word-of-mouth advocacy group. Companies interested in working with Tremor can get more information at www.tremor.com.

Motivating Influencers to Promote Your Product

You've identified your influencers and advocates; you've armed them with the tools they need, but don't forget the clincher—what's in it for them. This could be inside information such as a sneak peek at a new product, or it could be as simple as providing a special prize, discount, or free service. You know your audience—give them something that means something to them. It doesn't even have to be anything tangible. You could simply ask people to participate in a focus group. People love to feel like their opinion matters. In fact, in some cases, giving your audience a say in your product development is as powerful as giving them the product itself.

In the 1930s a group of researchers from the Harvard Business School conducted employee research for Western Electric. They wanted to get employees' opinions on various working conditions before deciding what to implement to the entire workforce. In a fascinating turn, the researchers discovered that no matter what condition they put in place, employee productivity increased. They experimented with bright light, dim light, and finally near-candlelight working conditions. Every time, productivity increased. The team concluded that it was the satisfaction that the employees received as a result of being asked to participate in the

---

Brainwaves

The Law of the Few outlined by Malcolm Gladwell in *The Tipping Point*, shows that the opinions of 10 percent of your target market will drive the buying behavior of the other 90 percent. Gladwell describes how a handful of kids from Manhattan's East Village began wearing Hush Puppies shoes and started a fashion trend that resulted in the resurgence of a faltering brand.

decision-making process that drove productivity much more than the lighting conditions. They called this phenomenon "The Hawthorne Effect" to describe the positive effects and advocacy that are generated among people who've participated in research trials.

Finally, never underestimate the power of a simple thank you. Most advocates are selling you because they believe in you. Appreciation is one of the most valuable things you can give them.

Celebrity Influencers/Celebrity Endorsements

If your target audience is highly influenced by pop culture, your influencers might be celebrities. Celebrity *product placement* puts products in the hands of highly influential people in the hopes that they will opt to use those products, become fans, and endorse them. This is different than paid celebrity endorsements and makes celebrity product placements much more powerful. When consumers believe their idol honestly prefers your product to that of to the competition, they are more likely to adopt the same belief. Even better, it costs almost nothing, versus a paid endorsement that could cost millions.

So how does this apply to guerrilla marketing? Celebrity product placement can't be inexpensive, right? Two points:

- ◆ It depends on the celebrity. Most of you probably aren't selling the latest Hermes handbag. That means the target audience for most small- to medium-size businesses is more likely influenced by experts in their areas of interest. In those cases, influencer marketing is accomplished by convincing these experts how valuable you and your product are. Hopefully, once the experts discover your benefits, they'll share the news with your target audience.

- ◆ Celebrity product placement can be affordable if they truly fall in love with your product.

def•i•ni•tion

Product placement is a method of advertising whereby a company pays for their product or logo to be used in a movie, TV show, video game, or other form of media.

Celebrity Gifting

Every celebrity event has an accompanying gift bag. Through this form of celebrity product placement, you donate items that fill up the gift bags. Although you do get high profile attention at star-studded events, you have little control over whether or not you reach your target audience. And of course not just any product will make it into the gift bag. Very interesting for sure, but what if you don't have an item that would merit gift bag placement? What then? You can do the same type of thing, but instead of gifting the Grammy Awards, gift a corporate conference or business meeting. Meeting planners are always looking for cool amenity items to give conference attendees. In fact, trade show organizers love to fill up goody bags with all kinds of junk … er, products, to give attendees.

Finding The Celebrities In Your Midst

Can't afford Jessica Simpson? Consider these sources of celebrities:

◆ Industry celebrities—Every industry has its own celebrities—you know, people who are idolized within that world, but are relatively unknown to the world at large. In the world of musical synthesists, for example, Bob Moog is a total star even though your average Joe has probably never heard of him. (Moog was a electronic music and synthesizer pioneer and has since passed away.) Some bloggers these days are achieving near celebrity status. Another type of celebrity known for an industry might be a cookbook author, or a restaurateur. These types of "celebrities" are much more accessible than the Hollywood elite and their ability to influence people is probably more long-lasting anyway.

◆ Homegrown celebrities—These are high profile influencers—the movers and shakers in your community. In your city, a homegrown celebrity might be a CEO of a company based in your city, the mayor, police chief, morning disc jockey, or local news anchor. In Memphis, for example, Fred Smith, founder and chairman of FedEx, is a high profile and respected guy. Pat Kerr Tigrett, wedding gown designer, is another super celeb. If you have a product that's a fit, do some *product seeding* and see what happens.

def•i•ni•tion

Product seeding is providing your products, free of charge, to people you think are a natural match for your product, and who also are likely to become brand loyalists. Rapper 50 Cent, for example, became a brand advocate for Glaceau Vitaminwater after being provided with a supply of the product by Energy Brands. Consequently, Energy Brands created a new "Formula 50" in his honor.

Product Seeding In Action

Imagine you're a local jeweler and you make handmade jewelry from semi-precious stones. Why not offer your product as an item to the Teacher of the Year at several area schools? Or you could give away a set—necklace, earrings, and matching bracelet—to PTA presidents in your general area.

Booby Traps

Whatever method you use, your influencers must buy in authentically. Never attempt to purchase an endorsement and pawn it off as organic because when somebody figures it out (as they inevitably will), people will see you as manipulative and dishonest, even if your motives are pure. It's fine to solicit comments. Not cool to inflate or invent them.

Offer some coupons and a message encouraging them to tell their friends if they like your wares. Most people want to reciprocate a kindness, and chances are they'll be more than willing to make a recommendation to their friends. And of course, once they've sampled your stuff, they're likely to be itching to get more themselves.

This form of product placement, called product seeding, offers the greatest degree of accuracy in reaching your target audience. With product seeding, you give your product to celebrities (whether Hollywood, industry-specific, or homegrown) that fit your preferred demographic.

Dangers of Celebrity Endorsements

Celebrity behavior can be unpredictable. America's darling of the moment can, in the blink of an eye, find herself splashed all over the covers of the gossip magazines because she was pulled over for driving drunk or worse. And it can certainly be worse. Think Hertz rental cars and football star O. J. Simpson. When Simpson's image went down the tubes as a result of his sensational murder trial, Hertz was identified with a not-so-desirable spokesperson. Fortunately, by acting quickly, brands can usually divorce themselves from the celebrity's bad behavior.

Product Placement in Media

When you see an identifiable, real-life product shown in a movie, television show, video game, or other form of media, it's probably there due to product placement. Seen a movie star drinking a Coke in a movie? Or driving a certain brand of car? Even though it may seem as if this stuff is paraded unintentionally, companies pay for these product placements. Why would you opt for such an undercover appearance? Because getting your product in front of an audience without making an overt sales pitch reaches consumers on a more subconscious level. It's less in-your-face (and less annoying) than typical advertising.

Booby Traps

Be aware—not everyone finds product placement unintrusive. In 2005, the Writers Guild of America, West, along with a group of TV show writers, created a website called Product Invasion to voice their displeasure about being forced to write around blatant product placements. They created spoofs of popular TV shows such as one in which Subservient Donald (a spoof on *The Apprentice*) hypes products such as Bounty paper towels. Another spoof of *Survivor* shows a contestant being forced to say she loves Scope mouthwash.

These writers were fed up with having to write in numerous product appearances throughout various TV shows. From the website … "A cheap and evil force persuaded them to sell their souls … for a can of Pringles? Ok, maybe what we're talking about here does not rank with global terrorism. But we're getting a little tired of advertisers taking over any reality show with a ratings pulse so they can insinuate their miserable products a little bit more deeply into our consciousness. They're getting lazier and less creative." The Product Invasion website also allowed users to "click here for your chance to tell advertisers to keep their paws off your favorite reality shows."

One of the best things about product placement in media is subliminal "ads" are often viewed for years and years to come. Just think about Steven Spielberg's movie, *E.T. the Extra-Terrestrial—every* time somebody watches that DVD they are reminded of Reese's Pieces candy. Many filmmakers and TV producers are proponents of product placement because it means money in their pocket.

Some say that product placement adds to the realism of the work. The film *Minority Report* starring Tom Cruise made heavy use of product placement featuring many major brands including The Gap, American Express, Guinness, Nokia, Pepsi, Reebok, Lexus, Aquafina, and *USA Today*. There are even companies that will secure product placements for you. Creative Entertainment Services (acreativegroup.com) can locate and negotiate product placement for your product, name, or service.

Gameshowplacements.com offers to get your product featured on top game shows and cable network television shows. And these are just two of the many companies that offer these types of services. Keep in mind, too, that with the proliferation of cable network shows and independent filmmakers, there are now more opportunities than ever to strike up your own deal. Product placement in media doesn't have to break the bank. Put on your thinking cap and you'll probably be able to come up with a placement idea that will get your stuff in front of people you want to reach for little or no money.

It Worked For Them

How much impact can influencer marketing have on a product's success? It can literally make or break a product. Just read these examples.

Post-It Notes

If not for the Hawthorne effect, Post-it Notes might have gone the way of New Coke. The glue on the back of today's popular office note was actually created by accident. In 1968, 3M asked one of its researchers to create a new adhesive. Unfortunately, the resulting product was not very sticky at all. The slightly sticky glue was discarded and considered a failure. Six years later a new product development researcher came on board and discovered the abandoned product. He had the bright idea that the weak glue could be used to make bookmarks. The product idea was tested in research to unimpressive results. But before ditching the idea altogether, 3M decided to do some product seeding, placing the sticky notes in the hands of secretaries of high profile CEOs throughout the United States and asking them to find ways to use the product. The secretaries were so pleased to have been consulted on a new product that they were transformed into a legion of influential product advocates. Next thing you know, raves for Post-it Notes were spreading like wildfire around offices large and small.

Gmail

In 2004, Google began offering a free e-mail with 1 Gigabyte of space, then unheard of in free e-mail offerings. The catch? The Gmail accounts were only sent to a select few people—elite Internet users, such as active bloggers from blogger.com, as well as journalists who were invited to review the free Gmail accounts.

A few months after the launch, active Gmail members were afforded the opportunity to send invitations to their friends, but only on a limited basis. Believe it or not, people were actually purchasing the free accounts on eBay because of the buzz-worthy status. Gmail was able to generate buzz using absolutely no traditional marketing and no money spent on advertising. They created the illusion of scarcity, and, because few Gmail accounts were available, everyone wanted one.

Hasbro's "Alpha Pups"

Who better to sell video games to kids than other kids? Hasbro obviously realized this truth in 2001 when they launched POX, a wireless electronic game in which kids would battle aliens who are trying to take over the world. Hasbro identified 1,600 boys who were influential in their schools and they deemed these boys "alpha pups," giving them each a free POX as well as 10 more to hand out to friends. How did they find the boys? Hasbro reps went to Chicago playgrounds and asked kids in the demographic, "Who's the coolest kid you know?" Once they found these "cool kids" they asked the question again. When they found a kid who answered the question by saying "me," they'd found an "alpha pup."

By product seeding with these cool kids, Hasbro started a POX trend. Within just a couple of months Hasbro had moved more than one million units and more than half of Chicago-area schools had a POX rampage in full swing. Unfortunately, we'll never know how far this product could have gone. The terrorist attacks on September 11, 2001, made the idea of alien infectors taking over the world suddenly much less appealing and sales decreased.

> **Brainwaves**
>
> The perception of scarcity enhances influencer marketing. When people think something is available for a limited time only or there are only a few items available, they are moved to the purchase point faster. Think about the craze McDonald's created over Beanie Babies that were only offered for a limited time.

Belly Maternity Clothing

5W Public Relations firm, on behalf of Belly Maternity, sent a supply of the company's baby wear to Brad Pitt and Angelina Jolie in Africa hoping that Shiloh Jolie-Pitt would be photographed in the designer duds. Surprise, surprise—Shiloh was pictured wearing the clothing. The average consumer probably couldn't identify the brand of clothing in the photograph, but you'd better believe 5W Public Relations could and they put out a press release announcing their product placement success.

Organic Celebrity Endorsements—Lifeway Foods

If you think celebrity endorsements are only effective for products that lie within their area of expertise, think again. Celebrities can be effective influencers for products beyond Cristal champagne and trendy handbags—not because we think they're experts in every subject, but because the public at large thinks that because they have money, whatever they use must be the best. An example of a very unglamorous product that's using celebrity endorsement, as well as other types of influencer marketing, is Lifeway Foods, Inc.

Lifeway Foods makes specialty functional dairy foods including Kefir, "a probiotic dairy beverage similar to but distinct from yogurt." In 2006, Lifeway Foods hired a PR agency to pursue celebrity endorsements. The agency sent free samples of ProBugs, an organic whole milk drink designed for kids age two to nine, to Hollywood celebs who have young children. At the company's annual meeting, Lifeway President and CEO Julie Smolyansky said, "I would love to see Tom Cruise's baby drinking ProBugs in a few months." By taking advantage of the Hollywood baby boom, Lifeway hopes to influence its target audience of health-conscious moms, otherwise known as "yoga moms."

Visit their website www.lifeway.net today and you'll find a section labeled "kefir connoisseur." "Hollywood celebrates Kefir with the rest of America! We proudly feature the famous and future famous faces of the growing Lifeway Kefir drinking community. Read why Lifeway Kefir is everyone's kefir of choice," the page intro reads. Click on current celebrities and you'll find various featured celebrities and pro athletes chugging or mugging with the cultured dairy drink. Alongside Tina Fey's picture is the quote "I really like it and my daughter would like ProBugs." On Mary J. Blige's page, the statement reads: "I really like it. I would give ProBugs to my kids." The celebrity comments don't appear to be agency-crafted or paid endorsements.

But Lifeway doesn't rely solely on celebrity endorsement. After all, some people don't share the same values as celebrities. Although celebrities have the money to buy the very best, the public may believe their definitions of "best" are different than most celebrities. For this group of people, Lifeway has more concrete evidence. They have research conducted by scientists, traditional and naturopathic doctors, bacteriologists, and a Nobel prize-winning researcher. They even have information from best-selling author and respected physician Dr. Perricone. The combination of endorsement and scientific evidence makes Lifeway's pitch compelling to a wide audience.

The Least You Need to Know

- ◆ Influencers should truly love you. Never try to buy their affection.

- ◆ If you can't identify influencers among your existing customers, there are plenty of places to find them.

- ◆ Influencers come in all shapes and sizes—they aren't just celebrities.

- ◆ Local celebrities can make impressions that are even more long-lasting than Hollywood celebrities.

Chapter 6

The Power of Buzz Marketing

In This Chapter

- Why buzz marketing is more effective than traditional marketing
- What gets people buzzing
- Ways to get people to buzz
- How to handle negative buzz

Reaching people using guerrilla marketing techniques has never been easier or more affordable. From buzz marketing projects like "Free Hug" campaigns to grassroots efforts like "Spread Firefox," it is now possible to reach millions of people for a fraction of the cost of your old high school ad campaign.

In the 1971 musical *Jesus Christ, Superstar* the apostles sang, "What's the buzz? Tell me what's happening." Buzz refers to an aspect of guerrilla marketing that takes advantage of our tendency to tell others about things we enjoy. Buzz marketing, or word of mouth marketing, sometimes happens naturally when products just catch on. In the '70s, the pet rock craze spread like wildfire—not because of high-powered marketing—but simply because people liked the kooky idea and told their friends about it. Of course now that the power of word of mouth is well-documented, some companies give their buzz a little push start.

What Is Buzz Marketing?

Buzz marketing is also called word of mouth marketing, and it is absolutely the most effective marketing method available. Simply put: buzz marketing happens when people get so excited about what you've got to offer that they tell other people. In effect, they volunteer to become your spokesperson, telling the world how great you are.

Of course having just one person excited about you is not enough to generate buzz. It takes a whole lot of people talking about your product to influence your bottom line. If people aren't catching on and getting excited to spread the word, you don't achieve buzz.

Booby Traps

Be careful not to place so much focus on buzz marketing that you shift emphasis away from the quality of your product and/or service. Buzz won't keep you in the black if the quality of your goods or services is lacking. Even if you get people talking, if their experience with your product is less than expected, your buzz will quickly die.

How Buzz Marketing Happens

Perhaps you own a dry cleaning business and a friend tells a friend about your attention to detail, or how you went the extra mile to meet their needs. That's buzz marketing. And this buzzworthy action can inspire your customer's friend to talk to another potential customer, and that person might talk to two others and those two talk to two others … you get the picture. That's buzz marketing on a small scale. Often buzz is more far-reaching: perhaps you own a restaurant and your unique wait staff uniforms are real attention grabbers. Next thing you know, someone's posted a video of one of your team members on YouTube and you've got customers lined up around the block—all because people are talking about you and your product. It's like a little bee that goes from flower to flower pollinating—and buzzing all the way. The more people you buzz in the beginning, the farther the spread. Not every person who hears something

Booby Traps

Buzz or any type of word of mouth-driven notoriety will eventually die out when the next cool thing comes along. Don't count on it for the long term. Use it simply to get people's attention so that you can show them what you have to offer. Your product must provide value on its own, and be supported by other marketing efforts, to keep your customers coming back.

will pass it on, but some will tell more than one person. If you get an influencer buzzing about you, there's a good chance the buzzing will result in actual sales.

Types of Buzz

Organic buzz is what happens naturally when people discover your product on their own and like it so much that they can't resist telling others about it. You're buzzworthy because you've hit the mark either through customer satisfaction, product quality, or innovation. Interestingly, when buzz happens organically, usually the company's primary focus wasn't on marketing. More often than not, these companies were focused on creating an outstanding product or service, and their actions inspired their customers to talk. This is buzz at its finest!

Amplified buzz is what happens when you set out to make yourself buzzworthy in the hopes of attracting attention. Not to be confused with deceptive marketing techniques (otherwise known as stealth marketing), amplified buzz is simply a campaign or method used to pump up word of mouth and get people fired up about you. Amplified buzz often happens via *consumer-generated media* like blogs or message board posts.

def•i•ni•tion

Consumer-generated media (CGM) is word of mouth on the Internet. It comes in a variety of forms including blogs, message board posts, commentary in forums, and so on. Anytime a person shares his or her opinion, advice, or commentary online it's part of a permanent digital record.

Unethical Amplified Buzz

There's no shortcut to becoming buzzworthy. Real buzz, whether organic or amplified, begins with real people who are genuinely excited about you. No good can come from generating word of mouth about products or services in unethical ways such as paying someone to hype products (as if they were organically inspired), or posing as excited customers online. How do you know when you've crossed the line? When you are deceiving your audience in any way.

Word of Mouth Marketing Association—WOMMA

Word of mouth is such a hot topic that an association has been created to promote and traffic its marketing and applications. Everything you ever wanted to know about word of mouth marketing can be found at the Word of Mouth Marketing Association's website: www.womma.org. WOMMA is an official trade association. Organizations and individuals can join to receive members-only benefits such as access to exclusive research, unprecedented networking opportunities, special event discounts, and unique promotional vehicles. But even if you opt not to become a member, you can still find lots of valuable information on their site. Dedicated to the highest level of integrity, WOMMA published an ethics code for the word of mouth marketing industry on February 9, 2005. From womma.org:

The essence of the WOMMA Ethics Code comes down to the Honesty ROI:

- Honesty of *Relationship:* You say who you're speaking for.

- Honesty of *Opinion:* You say what you believe.

- Honesty of *Identity:* You never obscure your identity.

If you choose to market your product via amplified word of mouth, you would be wise to follow WOMMA's guidelines.

Why Buzz Marketing Works

Buzz marketing works because people trust other people more than they trust company-generated messages. It's simple really: customers know that the company has a vested interest in getting them to buy its products. They also know their neighbor gets nothing out of promoting your product. Of course the neighbor's opinion has more value. Buzz marketing is, for the most part, natural and is accomplished by people who are truly excited about you and your product. Who better to sell you than someone who is willing to promote you for free just because they love you so much?

Generating a Buzz

To be buzzworthy, you have to be unique in a way that is easy to grasp and communicate. Offer your audience something that nobody else in your industry offers. We recently heard of a dentist's office that offers manicures and pedicures while dental treatments are being performed. That is totally buzzworthy! Not only is there a time management benefit (now that's what I call multitasking), but you've turned a necessary evil into a pampering session. What a fabulous brainstorm! So put your thinking cap on and figure out what you can do to make your customers' experience radically different than what they'd expect. That's the first step to creating a buzz.

Begin Building Buzz Before You Take Off

Generating some anticipation for your product before it's actually launched can be highly effective. Be mysterious. Offer only a small amount of information about your upcoming product or development, just enough to create a stir. People are curious by nature. We all want the inside scoop. Movie studios do this all the time through trailers that create interest in upcoming releases. For some really big movies such as *Star Wars* or *Harry Potter* films, the buzz begins a year or more in advance.

Here are some ways to create pre-launch buzz:

- Subscribe to a blog related to your industry and talk about your upcoming launch there.

- Call the newspaper and radio station and see if they are interested in interviewing you about your upcoming launch. Be informative, but still keep a little to yourself.

- Don't spread yourself too thin early on. Remember, you're going to need the lion's share of your marketing push for post-release efforts.

> **Brainwaves**
>
> Begin generating buzz using free online methods before you launch a product. If you can get people interested before something is available, it can really rev up the excitement and anticipation of your product. Think Apple and its cell phone. Just don't start buzzing too soon or people will lose interest.

Avoiding Negative Buzz

The best way to avoid negative word of mouth marketing is by solving any customer issues as quickly as possible. Achieving perfection isn't possible, but most people will not repeat a negative experience to their friends if it was resolved to their satisfaction. In fact, if properly handled, a negative can be turned into a positive success story that can generate its own little buzz.

A friend of ours who's spent many years traveling almost weekly all over the country has service recovery stories galore. On one of her recent trips, she was dining at a well-known upscale restaurant when a runner dumped an entire plate of food in her lap. To make matters worse, her Louis Vuitton bag was sitting unzipped in the seat next to her. Not only did she have food *all* over her clothes, it was inside her purse, too! Not grasping the severity of the situation, the runner offered a wet wipe (as if that was going to help at this point).

Fortunately, the server discovered what had happened, and she got a manager involved. The manager apologized profusely and insisted that he be given the repair and cleaning bills. When the meal was over, my friend was surprised to discover that she had not been charged for her dinner. It didn't erase the unpleasantness of the situation, but it certainly helped.

What could have been a horrifying experience (well, it still was a little horrifying), turned into a story of how dedicated the restaurant was to resolving the issue to our friend's satisfaction. What the management staff at this well-known restaurant chain didn't know is that our friend is exactly the kind of person who should be targeted with buzz marketing. She's a true brand advocate when she finds a company worthy of promoting. She's unswervingly loyal to brands that consistently please her and takes every opportunity to promote those brands.

Buzzers Are Everywhere

Another example from our world-traveling friend relates to her BOSE noise-reducing headphones that she uses when she travels. When her two-year-old headphones malfunctioned, she took them to the nearest BOSE store for repair. Even though they were expensive headphones, they were two years old. Our friend fully expected that they would need to be sent back to the manufacturer, leaving her to manage without them for who knows how long. Imagine how surprised and delighted she was to be waited on by a self-empowered young man who immediately exchanged them for a new pair at absolutely no charge.

From that day forth, anytime she has the opportunity, she shares this positive experience with other potential customers, telling them what a quality product BOSE is and how responsive they are to customer concerns. Beyond that, anytime she needs something BOSE might sell, she looks to them first. Two lessons to be learned from these service stories:

1. You never know who among your customers is likely to promote or condemn your product via word of mouth. You must treat every customer as if they're going to alert the media to share their experience dealing with your company.

2. Never discount the power of saying "I'm sorry," to your customers. Setting a wrong right can speak volumes about how much you care and how dedicated you are to product quality.

Here's the Buzz _____

If you're having a hard time building buzz, do some detective work. Ask your existing customers what you could be doing better. Ask your *new* customers what improvements would be meaningful to them. There may be a product or service issue you've totally overlooked and the act of fixing it could be buzzworthy in itself!

Who Will Do The Buzzing?

So you're focused on product quality and customer service. You've identified your buzz army of product advocates. What's next? Do you just sit back with your fingers crossed hoping your clientele "passes on" the fact that you're fabulous? Of course not. To create an effective buzz, your *product advocates* and *influencers* need two things:

◆ Something to talk about. This can either be a short phrase that summarizes what's buzzworthy about you (a dentist that offers pedicures), a new service you're offering, or a product you've added. You need a topic to start a buzz.

◆ An easy way to share the information. Arm your influencers and product advocates with tools—anything they can use to support their word of mouth. Make it easy so they don't feel like they're salesmen. The easier it is, the more likely they'll buzz.

Tools to give influencers:

◆ Brochures

◆ Product samples

◆ *Elevator speech*

◆ Coupons

◆ An e-mail or web link they can forward

◆ An easy-to-remember phrase about your benefits

◆ Business cards

◆ PowerPoint presentations

◆ CDs/DVDs

◆ Business cards

After you've armed your product advocates and influencers, you need to get involved in the buzzing. If people are talking about you on a message board, get in there and reply. Get out there among the people and connect so that the conversation isn't just *about* you, but includes you as well.

Make sure all your employees know what makes you buzzworthy. They're communicating with your customers and you want to be sure you aren't sending mixed messages. And don't forget: they're buzz marketers, too!

It's A Small World After All

Buzz works because we are all connected. Because we are all intertwined, buzz is able to bridge the gap between demographics. One of our friends, Robin, is a nurse practitioner. What we share with her will likely travel to her office, where there are at least 40 people in the medical community whom we would have never reached through traditional methods.

To get a mental picture of just how connected we all are, let's explore the origin of the social networking concept, a topic that has fascinated humans for decades.

Density of Social Networks

In 1929, Hungarian author Frigyes Karinthy hypothesized that each person on the planet is connected to any other person by no more than five intermediaries. According to her theory, even though the world was growing in population, and the geographical distances were widening, advances in communication were "shrinking" the modern world by increasing the density of social networks. In 1967, Stanley Milgram, a social psychology researcher at Harvard University, set out to verify the "small world" theory by conducting scientific experiments. Milgram found that people in the United States were associated to other people by an average of six acquaintances. Since then, the concept of "six degrees of separation" has been tested through several other experiments and the idea gained notoriety in 1993 when a play by John Guare called *Six Degrees of Separation* was made into a movie starring Will Smith.

Six Degrees of Kevin Bacon

In 1994, three college students took it a step further, creating a game called "Six Degrees of Kevin Bacon." The game requires players to link actors to Kevin Bacon by way of various film roles. The number of connections is the person's Bacon number. The span of people's connections is often surprising. The way people with seemingly no connection can be linked is illustrative of the "small world" theory. For example, Clark Gable has a Bacon Number of 2 because Kevin Bacon was in *Hero at Large* in 1980 with Kevin McCarthy (I); Kevin McCarthy was in *The Misfits* in 1961 with Clark Gable (II).

The "Six Degrees of Kevin Bacon" game was intriguing to mathematicians and computer scientists, including two doctoral candidates from the University of Virginia's Computer Science department. Brett Tjaden and Glenn Wasson created The Oracle of Bacon (http://oracleofbacon.com) that automatically calculates an actor's Bacon number. On the website, you can also find the connection between other actors via three connection methods: movies, TV, or TV and movies. Matt Damon is connected to Marilyn Monroe by only two steps. Matt Damon was in *Legend of Bagger Vance* with Jack Lemmon and Jack Lemmon was in *Some Like It Hot* with Marilyn Monroe. It's actually more difficult than you would imagine to find two actors who have connection numbers higher than seven.

Spinning the Buzz

In an interesting twist, in January 2007 Kevin Bacon harnessed the power of social networking and the popularity of the game by launching SixDegrees.org, a network designed to inspire charitable giving. Visitors to the site can watch a YouTube video featuring Kevin Bacon, in which he discusses the game and the resulting organization. He begins by saying that he was at first horrified at the "Six Degrees of Kevin Bacon" game, thinking it was a joke at his expense. He assumed (and hoped) it would soon fall out of favor with the public. But he goes on to say he's glad the concept stuck around because, he says, "If you take me out of the equation, it's really a beautiful notion. The notion that we are all connected in some kind of way."

Bacon goes on to explain that he loves the idea that each of us is affected by what happens to our "friends and neighbors and brothers and sisters on the other side of the planet" and that we all have a responsibility to take care of one another and help our fellow man. Helping people do that was his motive for creating SixDegrees.org.

On the site, users can find causes that are important to various celebrities and they can donate directly to those organizations. Or users can "become a celebrity" for their own cause by creating their own charity badge that can then be attached to blogs and websites so users can generate donations from others. Bacon will match the donations raised by the top six charity badges up to $10,000.

SixDegrees.org was created in partnership with AOL, Network for Good, and Entertainment Weekly. Just three months after launch, SixDegrees.org had raised nearly $300,000 for a variety of charitable causes. Bacon's partner, Network for Good, allows users to donate to more than one million charities online.

It Worked For Them

Take a look at these ingenious ways that individuals and high profile companies created success stories for their products by using assorted buzz techniques.

The Secret

One of the best examples of the power of buzz is a DVD called *The Secret* by Rhonda Byrne. *The Secret*, an innovative film about the law of attraction, was released in late 2006 on DVD and via streaming Internet feed. A year before *The Secret* was released, an extremely intriguing trailer was circulated around the Internet. (The fact that it is titled *The Secret* probably played at least some part in creating curiosity, as well.) The trailer had millions of people wondering, eagerly waiting to find out what the secret was. Before the release of the DVD and Internet feed, 600,000 copies were already sold. *The Secret* created a feeding frenzy primarily because of its buzz.

New Beetle Colors

In 2000, two new colors for the New VW Beetle (Vapor Blue and Reflex Yellow) were introduced in limited quantities. They were tied to a unique marketing campaign that made the new colors only available by initiating an order online. Only 2,000 of each color were manufactured and the cars were not actually purchased online—a local VW representative would contact users after they entered their information—but nevertheless, the promotion drove people to the Volkswagen website. On the first day, they sold 376 of the special edition Beetles and leads were generated for 1,444 more. The website's traffic increased threefold, with the average time spent on the site doubling from 8 minutes to 16 minutes.

Doubletree Hotels Christmas Eve Milk & Cookies for Santa

Via ads in *USA Today*, *The Wall Street Journal*, and *Time Magazine*, Doubletree Hotels invited parents to bring in their kids on Christmas Eve to receive a holiday pack for Santa. Holiday packs included two Doubletree Chocolate Chip Cookies, a pint of milk, and a card for Santa. The promotion was fitting for the brand because the chocolate chip cookie is a part of the signature warm welcome guests get when they check into a Doubletree Hotel.

Real World Example

Maybe you're a local printing company, and you're currently serving just one person in a building of 600 potential customers. Why not ask that customer for a recommendation? Tell your customer, "If you're happy with our service, please tell your friends and co-workers. We pride ourselves on our low printing costs and word of mouth is one of the ways we keep our advertising costs to a minimum." Mention some of the benefits of your product and service and then give your happy customer some promotional material that outlines these benefits—something that can be shared with his or her officemates. You're on your way to creating an influencer.

Here's the Buzz

Where would you mine for diamonds? In a diamond mine, of course. The sales concept of mining for diamonds means that you look for new customers wherever you found your current customers. For example, if you sell an airport limo service to people in the marketing department of a corporation, why not try to find others in that same corporation who might need the same service? By asking your existing customers for referrals of others who might need the service, you not only get a new list of potential customers, you also get an implied recommendation from the person who gave you the names.

Prepare for Take Off

Before you start buzzing, be sure you're ready to handle a sudden increase in sales. These days, when buzz takes off, it can really drive demand. Be prepared. If your buzz creates its desired effect and customers stop by to check out your product, you want to be able to accommodate them.

The Least You Need To Know

- Find out who's buzzing about you or what's buzzing in your industry.

- "Wow" your existing customers because buzz won't spread without a happy customer base.

- Be sure your influencers and product advocates have an easy-to-share message and the tools they need to pass on your message.

- Motivate people to talk about you by offering incentives and rewarding referrals.

- We are all connected so there's no telling how far your buzz will travel!

"Look At Me!": Stunt Marketing

In This Chapter

- ◆ Why stunt marketing works better than ever before
- ◆ Who should use stunt marketing?
- ◆ Should you do it yourself or ask for help?
- ◆ Matching the stunt with your message

Did you know that the Miss America Pageant began as an effort to draw people to Atlantic City? (It's true, contrary to popular belief, it's not all about the talent.) Any three-year-old knows that making a scene to get attention is downright intuitive. That's why savvy marketers have taken their marketing efforts to the next level: stunt marketing. And it's no wonder that this method has such broad appeal: after all, you can find people on network TV eating disgusting insects and performing feats previously reserved for stuntmen—the more outrageous, the better.

Is It Real, Or Is It Make Believe?

When actors Ashton Kutcher and Demi Moore first started dating, the tabloids thought they were creating a "publicity stunt." Matches made in Hollywood are legendary, with agents creating "couples" for the sake of helping an ailing image, overcoming celebrity invisibility, and even covering up situations that could be perceived to be unfavorable. Even in recent times gay stars have attempted to disguise their sexual preferences in order to be able to be seen as heterosexual romantic leads and such.

In Demi and Ashton's case, Demi was making a comeback in *Charlie's Angels 2: Full Throttle* and Ashton was well known for pranking people on his show *Punk'd*. Of course it turns out they were truly in love, and it was anything but a dramatic ploy to get attention. Still, it's not unheard of for people to do crazy things to create a buzz. When they do, it's called stunt marketing.

Stunt Marketing History

Stunt marketing is at least as old as the 1916 magic act during which Harry Houdini hung suspended upside down in a straightjacket from the top of a building. To this day people talk about his daring escape. And, of course, there's the famous publicity legend from the 1940s: during a Boston heat wave, a chef fried an egg on the sidewalk outside his restaurant. The restaurant successfully captured the attention of the media, not to mention potential customers who were walking by.

Celebrities and musicians have crafted the publicity stunt into a fine art. Their finesse of the media—or lack thereof—means the difference between a career that's made or broken based on how much public attention is centered on them.

Isn't every company's product or service made or broken based on people paying attention—in a positive way? Just because celebrities have fine-tuned stunt marketing doesn't mean others can't jump on the bandwagon. And as "connected" as the world is today—we truly are a global marketplace—there's never been a better time to step into the limelight. E-mail, YouTube, and other online devices mean that if you do create a buzzworthy scene, lots and lots of people can find out about it very quickly.

Why Is It Effective?

First, the obvious: shock sells. Companies and individuals who have something to promote use stunt marketing for two primary reasons: standing out is increasingly difficult and stunt marketing can be accomplished on a tight budget.

Standing Out Is Tough

Consumers today are bombarded with information: billboards, instant messages, e-mails, cell phone calls, text messages, pop-up ads on the Internet, magazine ads, television commercials, promos at the movies, banners at sports games—the list goes on and on. We are inundated with messages from people who want us to use their products or services. So how can a company distinguish itself? Unless you have substantial funds to saturate the very big market with your very creative ads, you might want to consider making a spectacle of yourself.

For the last couple of years, Starbucks Coffee has been performing a brilliant stunt. They hire an actor to drive around with a Starbucks Coffee cup glued to the top of his car, as if he'd forgotten about it. Everywhere he goes people frantically try to alert him to his overlooked java (and, Starbucks Coffee hopes, they might just start thinking they need a cup of their own). Of course, with all the marketing dollars Starbucks Coffee spends, it's impossible to isolate the effect of this particular marketing stunt. But consider this: if you search for "Starbucks stunt" on Google, you get 267,000 pages in return. Blogs have been written about it. Pictures have been snapped and shared. And, of course, here we are writing about it in this book. That's a pretty big return on investment if you ask us.

Stunt Marketing Can Be Cost-Effective

So how much could it possibly cost to hire an actor to glue a cup to the top of his car and drive around? (Think nonpermanent glue.) After all, you aren't hiring Al Pacino. Heck, your brother might even agree to do this for gas money. You could potentially do it yourself if you don't have to mind the store or tend to your customers for the day. The egg-on-the-sidewalk trick cost even less. The restuarant was only out the price of eggs and the olive oil used to fry 'em up. With a little creativity, it is absolutely possible to generate an effective stunt buzz without spending *mucho dinero*.

Not all marketing stunts cost major bucks, but a modest investment sometimes pays off. In 1996, Taco Bell took out an ad in *The New York Times* announcing that it had purchased the Liberty Bell and was renaming it the Taco Liberty Bell. The ad explained that it would still be among the nation's historic landmarks, and Taco Bell would not restrict the public's access to the monument. Taco Bell was simply doing its part to reduce the national debt, and likened its purchase to "adopting" highways, as companies have done for years.

Not surprisingly, people were outraged. Before the close of the business day, the story had reached approximately 70 million Americans. Taco Bell then announced that it was all one big practical joke. It was April Fool's Day, after all. You might think this is an example of bad publicity. Think again. Taco Bell's revenue increased by more than one million dollars over the previous week's sales in just two days. Their investment: one ad in *The New York Times*.

Brainwaves

Some stunts involve grand displays, but when you think about it, many could have been affordable if modified to fit a smaller business. Here's one: Bank of America's Dig for Change promotion.

To get people to open new accounts, they started a program called Keep the Change, which rounds up every debit card purchase to the next dollar and transfers the difference to your savings account. They even match the rounded up funds up to $250 year.

To promote this new offering, they rolled out a stunt promotion called Dig for Change. They plopped a 20-foot couch stuffed with coins in the middle of New York's Grand Central Terminal and invited people to Dig for Change. The concept expanded to malls in other cities, with sports heroes showing up to get in on the dig in some places. Yes, the custom-made sofa probably cost some big dough and the celebrity promoters added to the cost as well. But this could have been done on a small scale with any old sofa. A sofa (or any item) placed in a setting where it typically doesn't belong can't help but grab attention. And when you can capture consumers' attention, you're on your way to capturing their business!

Dangers of Stunt Marketing

Drawing big attention to yourself is inherently risky. There's no way to guarantee that things will go as planned and so there are two very real truths.

If You Fail, It's Very Public

When you stand up and clink your flatware against the wine glass at your cousin's wedding, you better have something good to say because all eyes are on you. History is filled with examples of stunt marketing gone wrong. There's Snapple's "world's largest popsicle" erected on the first day of summer in New York City. Soon after the 25-foot-tall tasty treat was pulled upright by a crane, it was perfectly clear for all to see (what you would imagine Snapple execs would have realized before): 17.5 tons of frozen Snapple doesn't stay frozen for very long in the summer. Chaos ensued as kiwi-strawberry flavored sugary liquid flooded Union Square.

Firemen were called to hose down the streets, and wash away the remnants of the gigantic popsicle. How embarrassing. Surely this is not what the masterminds of this plan had in mind when they engineered the stunt. We'd also be willing to bet there's more than one Jimmy Choo-shoed woman who eschews Snapple to this very day after the infamous popsicle flood inundated NYC streets.

It Can Backfire

Worse than embarrassing yourself, you could actually turn consumers against you. Another example of stunt marketing gone wrong (although their marketers might beg to differ) is U.S. Cellular's Chicago train stunt. They hired a guy to talk on one of their cell phones on the train. His face was painted blue and the back of his hoodie said "Talk Until You're Blue in the Face with U.S. Cellular." All right, sounds interesting. But let's follow it through. How on Earth did they get people to notice he was talking, you ask? There's the rub. He had to be loud and obnoxious and every so often he would tell the person on the other end of the phone not to worry about the minutes, he had free incoming calls on his U.S. Cellular phone.

People who were in the immediate vicinity of the annoying gabber were definitely turned off. Many vowed never to give U.S. Cellular a dime of their money.

But in both of these examples, we must consider that the stories are being retold. And perhaps those who weren't trying to catch some Z's or read the latest bestseller during their commute weren't as repelled. And we have to admit, we're almost sorry we missed seeing the river of Snapple.

> **Booby Traps**
>
> What's worse than embarrassing yourself or creating a backlash? Someone could get hurt. In one of the most extreme examples of stunt marketing gone wrong, an unnamed Norwegian clothing line attempted stunt marketing to particularly horrifying results. A parachuter hired by the company leapt from the Eiffel Tower and fell to his death when the parachute failed to open.

It Can Cost a Lot of Money if It Goes Wrong

Turner Broadcasting apologized—and agreed to paying $2 million—for its stunt gone wrong to promote Cartoon Network's Adult Swim television program, *Aqua Teen*

Hunger Force. The company installed 40 battery-powered, lighted electronic boards around the city of Boston that were intended to simply project images to promote the show. Instead, police and bomb squad units were deployed to investigate the blinking devices that were placed near bridges and overpasses. Authorities, unaware of the stunt marketing campaign, had to shut down highways and subways, disrupting the Boston residents in a major way.

An even more long-lasting effect resulted from the stunt—Jim Samples, Cartoon Network's executive vice president and general manager, resigned after the stunt gone wrong. In another stunt aftershock, Boston City Council filed an order to appeal for a hearing on guerrilla marketing regulations. They've also called on the state to get the FCC involved in investigating marketing practices.

Is A Stunt Right For You?

After reading these cautionary tales, you may think stunt marketing is just too risky. That's understandable and stunt marketing is truly not for everyone. But don't rule it out without giving it some serious consideration. It can be extremely effective if done properly. You just need to figure out a few things before you start.

Just like with any marketing approach, you need to plan. Here are a few ideas:

◆ Gather a group of the most creative people you know to brainstorm with you. Choose people who look at things in a different way. They don't necessarily have to be professionals, just interesting, creative thinkers.

◆ Consider the cost versus potential benefit of your stunt.

◆ Get people to play devil's advocate and try to punch holes in your idea. Try to imagine all the things that could possibly go wrong. If it's a particularly risky venture, legal counsel could be helpful.

Approach stunt marketing in the same way as you would more traditional marketing, identifying your target audience, assessing the impact, potential gain, timing, and so on. And be prepared to determine what the return on your investment was—the actual return, versus what you hoped to achieve.

Awareness or Messaging?

If you are a celebrity, magician, artist, or musician, simply getting people to notice you is the goal. It's really the *only* goal for people who are in the business of entertaining in some form or fashion. But maybe it's your primary goal, too. Maybe you don't have a new program or offering—you just need to let people know you exist. Here's a great example of an awareness stunt pulled off by Barry Potekin of Gold Coast Dogs, a hot dog restaurant in Chicago. For an entire year, Potekin would hail a taxi out in front of his restaurant. He'd then ride around the city telling the driver about Gold Coast Dogs. At the end of the ride, he'd tip the driver and invite him in for lunch. By year's end, Potekin had a huge following of hungry cab drivers, who were willing to spout the virtues of a Gold Coast hotdog to their captive fares and even drop them off for a taste test.

The bottom line: do you need to simply increase awareness or do you have specific messaging you need to communicate?

> **Here's the Buzz**
>
> It's much easier to create an effective stunt if awareness is your only goal. When you have to communicate messaging, more skill and creativity are required.

Is Your Audience Susceptible to Stunt Marketing?

Nothing illustrates this point better than ForeheADS. ForeheADS pays people (primarily students) to display ads—you guessed it—right across their foreheads. Students are required to display the ad for a minimum of three hours in a highly visible venue like a bar, sports event, or the like as required by founder, Cunning (www. cunningwork.com). In return they receive twice the hourly minimum wage. LeaseYourBody.com is another similar program. Participants are paid anywhere from $100–$5,000 depending upon the ad location: neck, forehead, upper arm, forearm, hand, stomach, or lower back. (No, you can't keep the ad hidden. We looked it up.)

If you've ever watched an NFL football game and seen what fans do to their bodies, you know there *are* plenty of people who would agree to put an ad or even more outrageous thing on their bodies. The novelty of this type of stunt is sure to wear off as more people sign on to do it. It will likely become just one of the many messages with which we are bombarded. So the point of this example is: consider renting out somebody's forehead for your logo if your target audience is likely to hang out with people who would do such a thing or admire it in someone else. If you are trying to reach aging Baby Boomers striving for the good life, ForeheADS is probably not a great fit.

A great example of a stunt geared toward the wrong audience happened at the beginning of Monday Night Football in 2004. It was a sexually suggestive spot featuring *Desperate Housewives* star Nicolette Sheridan and Philadelphia Eagles wide receiver

Terrell Owens. It caused a stir and ABC ended up having to apologize. And for what? To entice teenage boys, frat brothers, and manly men across the land to watch *Desperate Housewives*? Is that really the show's target audience? Even if they were planning to catch the women in the room, one has to wonder if a sexy exchange between Nicolette and Terrell would really be the best way to "catch" them.

 Booby Traps _____

When trying to fit your message and your audience, steer clear of reinforcing stereotypes. In 2005, Sony paid graffiti artists to spray paint depictions of their product, the PlayStation Portable, on legally licensed walls in New York, Chicago, Philadelphia, Los Angeles, and San Francisco in an effort to target "urban nomads." Although some ad pros thought this was a very clever idea, others found the ads disrespectful and offensive. If you're not sure where to draw the line, your best bet is to err on the side of caution.

Got a Message? Get Creative!

Even if you know your audience and you have a simple message, creativity is key to pulling off a great stunt. But before you start rolling up your sleeves, complete an honest inventory of your skill set and resources with this handy guide. Answer yes or no to the following:

YES / NO   I am a creative type; I work in a creative industry.

YES / NO   I'm not a creative type, but I know someone who is and he or she is willing to help me.

YES / NO   I know people who are creative types and they are willing to give me no-holds-barred feedback on my stunt marketing ideas.

YES / NO   I'm willing to hire someone to come up with a great stunt marketing idea for me.

You absolutely must be able to answer yes to one of the above questions otherwise stunt marketing is too risky. Don't feel bad: not everyone has the same skills and that's a great thing! You just need to know your limitations.

The nature of stunt marketing means big mistakes are very visible, and the last thing you want to do is come off looking foolish.

Booby Traps

Unless you are a magician or stuntman (or your product is by definition extreme), there's just no reason to put yourself in harm's way. Hanging for 44 days in a glass box from the Tower Bridge in London is just not going to drive revenue for the average business. Even if your company logo is plastered all over the box, it is not likely to generate more than gawking, simply because the medium and the message are not connected. Leave death-defying stunts where they should be: in the movies or in Vegas.

Creating the Stunt

Okay, you've decided on going for awareness or messaging. You've figured out that your audience is susceptible to stunt marketing. You've determined that you have the resources to create a really buzzworthy stunt, and you've resolved not to risk your life (or anyone else's) in the pursuit of publicity. What's next?

Finding the Right Time and Place

If you're staging a stunt, do it in a place where you are likely to find members of your target audience at the time they are likely to be there. It's great to be noticed, but you're not in this for the fame—you're trying to get people to buy your product. If you're a personal trainer and you hope to get some stay-at-home soccer moms signed on, then catch them during school hours at the grocery or a shopping center. Stage a yoga class in the parking lot and give away free sessions. Be sure to avoid school pick up and drop off times.

Connecting the Dots

If awareness of your product isn't your only goal—if you have a message you need to communicate—be sure that the stunt you're attempting is directly connected to your message. In short: don't create the world's largest chocolate chip cookie unless you are a bakery. Don't try to gain entry into the Guinness Book of World Records for washing the most shirts in one day unless you are a dry cleaner or laundromat. Don't do a firewalk downtown unless you're promoting a self-help seminar that includes such an element. Otherwise, onlookers will be left to wonder: What's the point? Keep your product in focus at all times.

Booby Traps _____

If you're an Oprah fan (or even if you aren't) you may have heard that during one of her shows she gave every member of her audience a car. Remember what kind of cars they were? Neither did we. The cars were Pontiacs, and this grand gesture was supposed to draw attention to their new sport sedan. (In addition to being a really charitable thing to do, of course.) Pontiac donated the cars, but chances are most people are under the impression it was Oprah who footed the bill for the cars. No fault of Oprah's: she spent a great deal of time on her show highlighting Pontiac's contribution and product, but somehow Pontiac's contribution got obscured. We're sure the giveaway drove lots of business for Pontiac, but we'll never know how much bang they could have gotten for their 7 million bucks if they hadn't been overshadowed by Oprah's legendary philanthropic reputation. If you team up, be sure not to partner with anyone who can possibly steal your thunder.

Real Life Examples

Of course it's hard to describe how to do this for every type of business imaginable, but here's one. Let's say you are a landscaping company and you want to build your business in a particular neighborhood. Scout the neighborhood for a lawn in need of care (but with great potential) in a high profile location. Maybe it's a corner lot in an area where lots of kids are playing, a spot where people are likely to be driving by slowly. Approach the homeowner and offer him or her a free "fixing up" service in return for allowing you to pull a stunt in his or her yard. After you've performed your magic ask if you can park your truck and landscaping trailer (or whatever you have that displays your company info), in a visible spot while you and your team cut the grass with scissors. Have business cards handy (and give some to the lucky recipient) so interested neighbors can contact you. You could perform this once, or repeatedly until you've built the level of business you want.

Brainwaves
Free services offered in a highly visible way are a sure fire way to attract attention. They're often less risky, too!

Bald People Eat for Free!

If you are bald and you're in Lodi, California, on a Wednesday, it's your lucky day. Go eat at Gary's Uptown Restaurant and Bar and your meal is on the house. If you have half your hair, you get a 50 percent discount. This "just for fun" stunt grabbed the attention of the media, landing Gary and his unique discount in a variety of national publications. Now bald people from across the country are going out of their way to eat at his restaurant. It just goes to show that stunt marketing doesn't have to include a tightrope walker or fire-eater. You just have to be unique.

Stunt Marketing At Its Finest

Talk about making an impression. Competition for quality talent in the online entertainment industry is seriously fierce. That's why the founders of Red 5 Studios went about recruiting in the most unusual way. Here's how they did it and created a 100 percent response rate.

Red 5 Studios created a top 100 list of people whose work they admired. They researched the people on their wish list and then set about to get their attention. How could they lure the best of the best away from their already successful jobs? Red 5 looked to Pool, a San Francisco-based design firm, for help. Together, Pool and Red 5 created an amazingly clever campaign.

Say you're among the top 100. Here's how your day would have gone. You're at your desk when the mail guy brings over a FedEx package for you. You open it up to find a box. A very attractive box with some words written on it—"Not the end, a beginning, a new beginning." You open that box and find another with still more words. As it turns out, the boxes are beautifully-adorned nested boxes and the words make up a message. Each box is more intriguing than the last and then the final box offers up its prize: an iPod engraved with the receiver's name on it. The iPod's one audio file is a personalized message from Red 5 President Mark Kern, telling you why you're the right person for the job. You're given a key to access a private website where you can learn more details about the company who sent the boxes and the iPod and exactly what job they've hand-selected you for. Wow. Who wouldn't love for something like this to happen? Kudos to Red 5.

Stunt or Mishap? You Be the Judge

Every now and then something happens to cause a commotion and we are all left to wonder: was that a clever stunt or an unintentional mishap? The world may never know.

Letter *from* the Editor?

George, a magazine co-founded by John F. Kennedy, Jr., once ran a letter *from* the editor that was perceived by some as a publicity stunt. In the letter, J. F. K., Jr. described his cousins Joe and Michael as "poster boys for bad behavior." Of course John-John's comment may have been totally genuine and it may have been Joe Kennedy's retort—"Ask not what you can do for your cousin, but what you can do for his magazine"—that fueled the "publicity stunt" perception.

Super Bowl XXXVIII

When it comes to stunts, Super Bowl XXXVIII in Houston had it all. First, there was the wardrobe malfunction. Both Justin Timberlake and Janet Jackson eventually admitted that they intended one aspect of their halftime show to be a stunt, but neither cops to the "full exposure" that actually took place. During the portion of their medley performance that featured his song "Rock Your Body," Justin sang the line, "Gonna have you naked by the end of this song," at which point he reached over and ripped the front of Janet's clothing off to reveal her bare right breast, nipple shield and all. Immediately afterward, CBS received a record-breaking 200,000 calls from people who were offended by the stunt. Jackson and Timberlake said that while they had planned the clothing ripping ahead of time, they had not intended to take it all off.

Jackson, Timberlake, and everyone else involved apologized, but it was too late for damage control. America Online, a halftime show sponsor, was given a $10 million refund by the NFL. The NFL promised never again to let MTV produce their halftime show.

But wait, there's more! Cue streaker Mark Roberts sporting only a g-string and a tattoo promoting the Internet casino GoldenPalace.com. The stunt never made it on the air.

Here's the Buzz

If you're hoping to attract the attention of television cameras, keep the visual aspect of your stunt in mind. The more visually stimulating your stunt is, the more attention you'll get from image-driven media.

Mark Roberts is a famous Brit who makes a habit of running naked (or nearly naked) through various international events. To date, he's performed nearly 400 streaks with a heavy emphasis on sports games. Mark has also contracted with GoldenPalace.com to streak on their behalf. On his website, Mark accepts PayPal donations that he gives to a different charitable organization for each streak he performs. You can't say it's not an attention-grabber.

The Least You Need to Know

◆ Stunt marketing can be very effective and inexpensive if done properly.

◆ Stunt marketing is easiest if you simply want to increase your product/service awareness.

◆ Stunt marketing can be disastrous if done improperly—don't attempt it unless you have a well-thought-out plan and you're sure you've got a good idea.

◆ If you're not a creative type, get someone who is to give the thumbs-up to your stunt idea. Better yet, get them in on the brainstorming session!

Chapter 8

"Try It, You'll Like It": Experiential Marketing

In This Chapter

◆ Purpose of experiential marketing

◆ Places to conduct experiential marketing

◆ Using free services and product samples to build business

◆ Is experiential marketing right for you?

Who would ever believe that thin, silk long johns could keep you as warm as thermal underwear? You probably wouldn't unless you tried them. *Experiential marketing* brings us back once again to the days of vacuum cleaner salesmen going door to door so customers could actually try the product on their carpet. (It seems like everything goes back to those vacuum cleaners, doesn't it?)

The reason experiential marketing is important and effective is that people long to have one-on-one interactions. Again, high touch is important to people who have grown tired of being just one of the masses.

def•i•ni•tion

Experiential marketing consists of marketing experiences designed to immerse the potential customer in the brand. Ideally, experiential marketing engages as many of the five senses as possible.

What Is Experiential Marketing?

Perhaps one of the most famous experiential marketing examples is the classic taste test conducted to determine whether people prefer Pepsi or Coke. Another form has been around for quite a while, too: the "you've won a trip to Orlando" phone call that invites you to take a free trip if you'll agree to listen to a sales pitch about some real estate opportunity in the Sunshine State. The idea is that if you actually do something, you're much more likely to buy into it.

There are two ways to approach experiential marketing.

Sampling Your Product

Every marketer has this goal: to get someone to try the product. This is called driving *trial usage*. Marketers go to any lengths to get people to just give them a shot. One of our clients, a hotel company, uses promotions such as weekend specials and other special offers to get customers to stay with them that first time. It's the surest way to let people understand and learn to love the features that you want them to be aware of.

This type of experiential marketing allows people to give your product or services a test drive, just like auto dealers have been doing for years! Beyond giving the customer a chance to experience what you have to offer and see how great your stuff is, it also builds relationships and establishes trust. Offering the "experience" of your product face to face builds the relationship; letting someone try the product tells them you believe in its quality and are happy to take the risk of letting them see it up close and personal. This is especially effective when you have a product that is so superior to the competition's offering that people will not be able to fully appreciate it without experiencing it for themselves.

def•i•ni•tion

Trial usage seeks to get a customer to try your product for the first time in hopes they will like it and continue to choose it. Sometimes companies offer discounts; free coupons; buy one, get one free; and other methods of getting people to walk through the door.

Think about how you've gotten a CD of AOL in the mail, or a sample of detergent left hanging on your front door knob, or a perfume in a magazine. Marketers know that the cost of offering samples is small compared with the success they get from giving customers a test ride.

Entertaining to Build Loyalty

The other type of experiential marketing doesn't necessarily offer a direct product experience, but rather builds familiarity and fondness for the brand itself. This type of experiential marketing offers the audience something that they enjoy while subtly infusing the message of product superiority. In many cases, the mere exposure to your brand in an enjoyable setting is enough to turn the tide in your favor when it comes to point of purchase.

The ultimate goal in both types of experiential marketing is to create an entertaining, interactive experience that communicates the essence of your brand. If you've got a unique product, experiential marketing can be one of the best tools in your arsenal.

Hampton Inn hotels several years ago introduced a new, more comfortable bed, along with other guest room enhancements, in all of its hotels. They hired teams of "bed heads," actors who had mussed up hair and Hampton T-shirts, to appear in highly visible locations such as Times Square in New York. The areas where they appeared also happen to be feeder markets for their hotels. Feeder markets are cities that lots of their customers hail from. In addition, the areas were cities where influential media operated.

In another experiential effort, Hampton displayed its bed at a hotel industry trade show and had a judge try out its product as well as that of the competition. A risky strategy, but one that paid off; in fact, the Hampton bed won.

Why Is It Effective?

Although countless market research studies have proven the effectiveness of experiential marketing, you don't have to be a statistician to know that people are more likely to consider purchasing something they've tried first-hand or something they've associated with an enjoyable experience. Just think back to the old Life cereal commercial—"Try it, you'll like it." It captured a universal truth: seeing is believing.

> **Brainwaves**
>
> Experiential marketing is often known to trigger impulse buys. The offer of instant interaction can help get your audience to fall *for you* (and then hopefully fall *in love with your stuff*). Because the fun of participating moves people into a buying frame of mind, be sure to have the ability to sell whatever it is you offer. Whether it's a product they can walk away with or a service they can order, be sure customers can purchase it on the

Places to Conduct Experiential Marketing

Fortunately, there are dozens of ways to conduct experiential marketing. Deciding where to connect with your target audience and what "experience" you want to offer is key. The trick is to give people a real taste of what you do so they will want to follow you anywhere.

Trade Shows

If your product is new to the marketplace, trade shows are a great way to make a splash. But it's not the most inexpensive venture in the world. The price of a basic 10'×10' booth varies based on the size and importance of the trade show. For your entry fee you get a spot on the floor, and perhaps a table, chairs, and section of carpet. If you want electricity, an Internet connection, or other special item you'll pay extra. Plus, you will have to create your own signage and display materials.

There is quite an art to creating an effective trade show booth. Here are some things to consider:

- ◆ Make it inviting enough to draw people in.

- ◆ Offer a free giveaway, a door prize, or other reason for them to stop by. It helps to do an entertaining or funny item that other people will want. For example, people love silly items like neon necklaces. If they see someone wearing one, they'll ask where the person got it. A perfect chance for the wearer to direct people to your booth. Be sure to put your logo and contact info on the giveaway.

- ◆ Give them a reason to give you their business card or contact information. Some trade shows provide a scanner that will enable you to load the information directly into a computer.

- ◆ Man your booth at all times. No telling how many sales you might lose if someone wants to stop by and you're not there.

◆ Have handouts that are simple and will fit into a pocket. The information you want people to have should be sufficient to get them interested and direct them to your website or toll-free number.

If you envision going to a lot of trade shows, hire a professional trade show designer to create a portable display that you can reuse. Certainly, you can use a do-it-yourself kit to customize your exhibit, but in the long run it's probably better to get direction from people who do this for a living. Depending on what your product is, you could pay for the exhibit with just a few good sales. And when a professional creates a display for you, you have assurance that the material is durable, packable, and shippable.

When you're budgeting for trade shows, remember to consider costs for your travel and hotel, as well as shipping costs, signage, and, of course, meals.

Just remember that the more entertaining and enjoyable you make your booth, the more impact you'll make.

To locate a trade show related to your industry, take a look at TSNN.com, where you can search 15,000 trade shows, exhibitions, public events, and conferences. Be on the look out for events that match your area of expertise. The trade shows your competition may already attend are the ones you should consider.

> **Brainwaves**
>
> Many trade shows will allow you to go as an attendee instead of a sponsor. The primary benefit of a trade show is networking and you don't have to have a booth to network! Send out your friendliest team member (or two) and let them start connecting even if you can't yet afford a booth.

Mall Carts or Kiosks

If you have a seasonal business or you need a jumpstart for your product, this could be the way to go. You will need some money to get started. Costs vary, but startup costs typically range between $1,500–$10,000 depending upon whether you lease or purchase the cart/kiosk. In addition, you'll have a monthly rental fee for the mall space that could run $500–$1,000 or more, depending upon the mall and the season. Some malls charge a percent of your sales, as well. The best way to start is to rent a cart for a limited time and then see how it goes. It's not unheard of to get in for $1,500 and pay $600 rent a month. Market trends show that mall sales are on the rise. If you only stayed for two months, just think how much exposure you could get for your product. Just don't forget that the whole idea is offering a sensory experience. Make sure people get a true feel for your product or service when they stop by, and be sure they know where to find you when (or if) you are no longer at the mall.

> **Brainwaves**
>
> One of the secondary benefits of experiential marketing is that it allows you to receive customer feedback on the spot. When you get out there one to one with your target audience, you're opening up the lines of communication. You'll be surprised what you can find out just by being available. Existing customers will tell you what they like or don't like and potential customers will tell you what they're looking for in a product. Be sure to take notes so you can tweak your offerings if necessary.

Whether you're considering a trade show booth or a mall cart or kiosk, be sure to inquire about security and insurance. You certainly don't want someone walking away with your laptop, a trunk full of your product, or other essential items. And believe us, at conferences and trade shows, lots of things turn up missing.

Free Services

Nothing gets people more excited than the word "free." (The word "sale" is a close runner-up.) If you're a massage therapist, offer free chair massages at the health food store during lunch hour. Hand people your card and you may get customers to come to your store.

Do you fix people's computers? How about a "tech support station" offering free advice outside of Office Depot? You'll have to get permission from the store owners, of course, but most welcome the extra attention because it benefits them, as well.

Open Houses and Launch Parties

Launching a new product or service? Throw a party or have an open house and invite your best prospects. Give away or demonstrate your wares. Even if you've been in business awhile, who says you can't reintroduce yourself? Besides, people are always looking for an excuse to party.

If your office isn't an ideal location for an open house, do it at a restaurant. Have a theme and make it truly enjoyable. Be sure not to apply to much pressure to buy during the event. Remember, you are trying to give people an experience of your product—even if they don't buy at the party, you've planted a seed. Make sure they remember the fun they had and how much they enjoyed your product, not the fact that you were making a sales pitch.

Make sure you set reasonable expectations for any experiential marketing event. Walking away with a few solid contacts is truly a success. If you get goldfish bowls full of business cards, that's fantastic! If not, don't be quick to underestimate your success. Building a business of integrity takes time, and there's no shortcut to experience. Just keep doing the right thing, and you'll come out on top!

Seminars or Consultations

Offering free expert advice or lessons in your field is a great way to show people what it's like to work with you. If you're a law office, offer a free bankruptcy seminar. You're an interior designer? Offer a free class on window treatment options. If you're a writer, offer a resumé writing seminar. One critical element to the free seminar: you absolutely must deliver valuable information at the seminar. Don't attempt to "bait and switch" (only giving something of real value to paying customers) because it will damage your reputation. Yes, you may be giving away services to people you will never see again, but you may also gain customers who need much more than the limited service you've provided. Another important note: save the sales pitch until the very end.

And here's a bonus: if you offer valuable information, the people who attend your seminar will pass it along and recommend you to their friends. Remember, word of mouth is the best sales tool ever.

Here's the Buzz _____

Build trust with your potential customers by offering for free something they would typically have to buy. Your natural instinct might tell you not to give away your offerings for free, but in reality, the goodwill you create could actually drive business your way. When you offer something of value to people who want to go the "do-it-yourself" route, you're also speaking to the many people who don't want to do it themselves. Those who opted to take your do-it-yourself advice on their small projects will certainly keep you in mind when they have bigger projects.

Product Samples

Food manufacturers have had a handle on this for a long time. Grab people at the point of purchase, engage them in the experience of tasting your product, offer them a discount, and count up the sales. Experts say sales from a demo can boost one-day sales up to 400 percent. And that doesn't even include the sales generated from people who regularly purchase the product afterward. Visit Costco on a busy day and you could leave with a full stomach. So the bottom line is: if you have a product that people need to try in order to buy, give it away!

Sponsor an Event

Another way to gain access to your audience and get your product in their hands is by sponsoring an event. Possibilities include:

- Local fairs or festivals
- Art exhibits
- Fitness/health screenings
- 5K runs
- Blood drives
- Craft fairs
- Outreach efforts/food drives
- Charity galas

Look for events that are likely to draw people in your *market segment*. Sponsorship levels will vary and you can either donate samples to be provided in goodie bags or you can man a booth at the event to provide services or product samples. (If you are a massage therapist, a foot massage station at a 5K run would be very popular. You could walk away with a handful of new clients.)

def•i•ni•tion

Marketers often divide people into distinct groups that they believe are driven by similar motives and similar needs, known as **market segments**. In other words, people who come from the same demographic grouping. People within a market segment are thought to respond in the same way to various marketing tactics, thus improving the efficacy of these marketing strategies.

It Worked For Them

Some companies have created an experience that is as compelling as the actual product. Check out these memorable examples of experiential marketing.

Wells Fargo Stagecoach Island

To target clients of the future, Wells Fargo Bank launched an online, multi-player, role-playing video game inside a virtual world. The video game targets young adults and through entertainment teaches them about financial responsibility.

Players choose a character and are allotted money to use on their "island adventure," which includes exploring parks, dance clubs, chic shops, amusement parks, and more. Players can earn more money by answering trivia questions at the Virtual Learning Lounge, which is based on Wells Fargo's Hands on Banking financial literacy program.

The game teaches the basics of money management in a medium that is extremely popular: online gaming. By integrating an educational aspect into an entertaining environment, Wells Fargo has made the most of experiential marketing. Best of all, it has an entire audience of future customers—educated consumers who understand how to manage money—who have developed a bond with the Wells Fargo brand name. Genius!

Trader Joe's

Trader Joe's is a really cool privately owned grocery store chain with over 250 stores in 20 states. The company is steadily growing. They offer the basics like bread, butter, and milk, along with exotic foods, but you won't find a lot of branded items in their stores.

Unlike conventional grocery stores, Trader Joe's stores are always on the lookout for new products and they add 10–15 new products every week. (They also discontinue products as they go out of season or if the item is not a big hit with customers.)

Trader Joe's puts their mouth where their money is: they taste every product before they decide to sell it, promising: "We tried it! We liked it! If you don't, bring it back for a full refund, no questions asked."

All the foods they offer are made with nongenetically modified ingredients. And while it's true that the great food, great prices, and their friendly, upbeat culture are all huge factors in their success, they also make heavy use of product sampling. All day long, from 9 A.M. to 9 P.M. Trader Joe's employees conduct demonstrations, cooking food and offering taste tests. Customers can smell coffee brewing and taste the unique items so they can experience the benefits. So far it seems to be working. Trader Joe's has a cult-like following and is steadily expanding.

General Mills' Cereal Adventure at the Mall of America

In the Mall of America, you'll find an eye-popping example of experiential marketing created by Chicago Scenic for General Mills. The General Mills' Cereal Adventure is an interactive experience that takes visitors from "Farm to Factory," showing how the manufacturing process of cereal works. The experience is as much educational as it is fun, which makes it appealing to both kids and parents.

Children begin the adventure at the "Farm and Mill" section where they witness the grain growing on the farm. In the "Control Room" they can touch and press various controls before moving to the "Cooking Room," where they'll perform tasks to mix the grain and water and plunge it into the oven. The "Dough Extruder," gives kids the chance to make the dough into Cheerios before they send it into the "Puffing Area" where Cheerios erupt out of a giant Cheerios Volcano. The next to the last stop is the "Toasting Room," where the cereal gets a blast of hot air before its final destination— the "Finishing Area," where the all-important packaging takes place.

Kids who visit the General Mills' Cereal Adventure at the Mall of America can also create their own cereal blend, choosing which cereals will go into their mix. They name the cereal and decorate the box. Their customized cereal creation is sent to the cereal adventure retail area where it can be purchased. Happy kids take home their own unique cereal and can share it with their friends.

Of course, the poor parents may then have to buy multiple varieties of cereals if the kids want to continue to mix their own hand-made recipe.

The Least You Need to Know

- ◆ Experiential marketing can be used to build brand awareness or get hands-on exposure for your product.

- ◆ Experiential marketing is great for products that are unique or new to the marketplace.

- ◆ Experiential marketing should offer something of value to the target, even if it's only entertainment.

- ◆ Offering free services or seminars is a great experiential marketing method.

Chapter 9

Location, Location, Location: Ambient Marketing

In This Chapter

- ◆ Ambient marketing methods
- ◆ Sponsorships and partnerships
- ◆ Unusual ambient marketing locations

Ambient marketing is all about being in the right place at the right time. Buy Dry Idea deodorant and you may get a coupon for the competition's product printed on the back of your receipt. Ambient marketing directs advertising at a customer at a time when they are most likely to be receptive to the message. The key is choosing the right vehicle and the right outlet.

What Is Ambient Marketing?

Planes flying over spring break beaches with banners trailing behind announcing happy hour at a local bar, banners that hang at sports arenas, and ads on grocery shopping carts are all types of ambient marketing.

Because it aims to reach customers as they go about their daily activities, ambient marketing is also called place-based marketing. The goal is to get the message to the consumer wherever they are, ideally when they are in the right frame of mind to purchase your product. Because ambient marketing can be done literally anywhere, it's definitely worth consideration.

The idea that it might be profitable to get consumers thinking about your product by plastering its image on things consumers see during the course of a day is not a new marketing concept. It's been around for years. We've become very accustomed to seeing messages on park benches, coffee cups, grocery carts, both inside and outside buses and other public transportation, and the list goes on. But there's more to ambient marketing than just smacking your logo on a bunch of random stuff. With ambient marketing, the idea is to put your logo or message on things or in situations that catch your target audience's attention at the point of purchase or at the very least, when they are open to considering what you have to offer. Here are just a few examples of ambient marketing:

- Billboards on bus stop benches

- Ads on shopping cart returns

- Company name on dry cleaning bags or hangers

- Sports team sponsorships

- Signs on exterior or interior of public transportation

- Logo items, such as backpacks

- Advertising messages on product packaging

- Fly-by airplane banners

- Skywriters

- Racks of brochures on area attractions or services

- Posters in restrooms

- Brochures in strategic locations such as doctors' offices

- Yellow pages ads

- Search engine ads

Here's the Buzz

Out of house advertising reaches your customers when they are out of the house. Billboards are a traditional example of this type of advertising. Television commercials and direct mail, on the other hand, typically reach customers in their homes.

- Banner ads on web pages and retail sites
- Coupons on grocery store aisles
- Advertising on movie screens
- Tradeshow booths

Is Ambient Marketing Subliminal?

Don't confuse ambient marketing with subliminal messages. Subliminal advertising happens when advertisers attempt to tap into our subconscious minds without us even being aware that we've received a message. We've all heard the stories: drive-in movie theaters flashing the words "Drink Coca-Cola" and "Eat Popcorn" on the screen very quickly, thus increasing concession sales; ice cubes in liquor ads containing pictures of naked women in an attempt to appeal to our subconscious desires; and rock 'n' roll songs that spout satanic propaganda when played backward. Despite the lack of definitive proof that these techniques work, in the 1970s the FCC made it illegal for "broadcast outlets to knowingly carry subliminal ads that are operating contrary to the public interest."

Is Ambient Marketing Stealth?

Because these marketing messages aren't always overt, some people consider ambient marketing stealth; however, to us, stealth requires deception and most ambient marketing is not deceptive. For example, you might not be consciously aware that you are receiving an ambient marketing message when looking at logo-emblazoned towels on a crowded beach, but yet, if you thought about it, there would be no question in your mind that Coppertone intends to promote their product by placing their message on a towel.

Why Is It Effective?

When properly executed, ambient marketing hits the customer at the time they are in need of your product. Take the banner-flying-over-the-beach example: the people who are likely to see the message are people who will probably be going to bars after they leave the beach. Barbie and Ken have had a lovely day at the beach. Now it's time to make plans for the evening. There are so many choices, but they've decided to go to the Kona Krab because they know this establishment offers a free appetizer with entrée. How do they know this? They saw it advertised on a banner flying overhead while they were soaking up rays on the beach earlier in the day. When ambient marketing is done correctly, it will entertain and sell products.

Ambient Marketing Via Sports

It's as American as apple pie and baseball. Ambient marketing messages are staples at your local ballparks. What stadium would be complete without ads covering practically every surface? Marketers who share target audience demographics with sporting events have been using this form of ambient marketing for years because it's a marketer's dream. There are so many ways to highlight your product: electronic billboards, tickets, programs, bathroom stalls, paper cups, snack bags …. The list goes on.

Community Sponsorships

Building goodwill among potential customers is one of the main tenets of marketing, and contributing to the community is certainly an ideal way to create positive vibes.

Naming Rights

Obtaining naming rights for community structures or locations seems to be gaining popularity—probably because contributing to something that benefits the community is a great way to boost your image. The premise is simple: your company donates money to help build or renovate a local park, bridge, stretch of highway, or any other structure and your company is incorporated into the name. So maybe you don't have the funds to help finance a community center renovation—don't despair. You might be able to provide services that would get you the desirable naming rights. Perhaps you own a concrete company. You could help create a much-needed walkway and have your sign posted nearby. You've got to believe that the people who've been doing without it will notice you and will look to you should they ever have need for your services. And because they're often overlooked by marketers, small-scale community efforts can generate significant benefits.

If you're a landscaping company, pitch in to help create a dog park. The investment for a project of that

> **Brainwaves**
>
> In late 2006, the Board of Directors of the Golden Gate Bridge District of the California Department of Transportation recommended a corporate sponsorship program for the bridge, as it has been losing money for several years. Wonder what those billboards would look like? Officials say whatever it is they decide, it will be done tastefully.

size would be much more manageable and your contribution would win the affections of a very grateful group of dog lovers. (And everyone knows pet lovers are a loyal group!) Look for groups that are struggling to accomplish a goal that would align with your offerings. Maybe you can provide just the resource they need to finish the job, all in return for the right to put your name on the finished project in some way. Keep in mind, too, that many efforts require multiple sponsors and those sponsors might be listed on a placard rather than incorporated into the actual name. That can be valuable, too!

Adopt Something

Adopting a playground or other recreational area is often as easy as looking up your local parks and recreation organization on the Internet. The New York City Department of Parks & Recreation has a formal Adopt-a-Park program whereby companies can adopt park benches, greenstreets (traffic islands planted with trees, shrubs, and flowers), basketball courts, or playgrounds for varying annual fees and levels of involvement.

Jamba Juice accepted the offer by contributing two playground associates for Chelsea Park in Manhattan, New York. According to the New York City Department of Parks & Recreation website, www.nycgovparks.org: "Jamba Juice and its commitment to promoting youth activity with an emphasis on fun made this adoption a perfect fit for both Jamba and Parks. The playground associates at Chelsea Park will be responsible for providing organized recreation to neighborhood children throughout the summer months as well as coordinating such events as the Officer Wilson Memorial Basketball Tournament." Learn more about this inspiring company at www.jambajuice.com.

The Adopt-A-Highway Maintenance Corporation (AHMC) started this type of sponsorship program and has been cleaning America's highways for over 15 years. From the AHMC website: "AHMC provides an opportunity for your company or organization to be recognized for sponsoring a section of highway. We do all the work and you get all the recognition!"

What will you get when you adopt a highway?

- ◆ Recognition from thousands of potential customers driving by your sign every day.

- ◆ A favorable and long-lasting image in the local community.

- ◆ Your company name displayed on America's busiest highways and interstates 24 hours a day, seven days a week.

Read more about this potential ambient marketing opportunity at the website www. adoptahighway.com

Hampton Inn & Suites increased its brand's visibility and community goodwill among families on road trips through its "Save-A-Landmark" initiative.

Brainwaves

Forget adopting the local library—can you believe entire towns have sold their naming rights? In 2000, the town of Halfway, Oregon, became the first official "dot com" city when it temporarily changed its name to Half.com in collaboration with new Internet startup, Half.com. In exchange, the town received $75,000 and 22 computers for the local elementary school. Half.com garnered worldwide attention, including a spot on NBC's Today Show.

How Far Is Too Far?

Seeing a tasteful corporate logo on a water fountain at the park or on your local baseball diamond is one thing but how would you feel about a company-branded elementary school? Commercialization in school has become a hot topic. Proponents say sponsorships provide much-needed funds without adding strain to taxpayers; detractors think schools should not be for sale to the highest bidder. And while everyone seems to agree that schools shouldn't be funded by alcohol or tobacco companies, there are some gray areas when it comes to what's acceptable. Highlands Elementary sponsored by Nike probably wouldn't be too objectionable but would Burger King High fly? Probably not. Take care in your sponsorships to make branding tasteful and appealing.

Unusual Marketing Media and Locations

When you think of marketing, dogs wearing billboards probably isn't the first idea that comes to mind. Check out the out-of-the-box marketing tactics in the sections that follow.

Dogs—Marketer's Best Friend?

Looking for the truly unusual? Consider advertising on dogs. Yes, you read it correctly. One such innovative company did just that. K9 Billboards used groups of trained dogs to market a variety of products. This method is noteworthy not only for its ingenuity, but also because it's interactive. Most people love animals, especially cute, well-behaved dogs. This is just what K9 Billboards was banking on. Potential customers are intrigued by the sight of a dog in a sandwich board (not really, it's more like a fitted jacket) and charmed by the dogs. Charmed enough to venture over to take a look and offer a quick chin rub. When customers approach, the handlers jump into action, offering product samples or coupons.

Here's the Buzz

Mascots are a great way to build brand recognition and create excitement. They're also a highly visible physical representation of your company, who can attend festivals, walk in parades, mill about among customers, and just generally attract attention. Sports teams prove that the concept works, as do icons such as the Pillsbury Doughboy, Tony the Tiger, the Keebler Elves, and of course, Mickey Mouse. If you're looking to create your own company mascot, there are a number of companies that can help you from concept to creation such as Sugar's Mascot Costumes (www. sugarcostumes.com) and Mascots & Costumes (www.mascotsandcostumes.com). Facemakers, Inc. offers three types of custom-made mascots: exact logo productions, product replicas, or you can choose to customize one of their existing designs.

Campus Laundry Rooms

Washboard Media is what NYC-based Encompass Media Group calls one of their nontraditional youth marketing programs that implements campus laundry room advertising. College-age students are notoriously hard to reach using traditional marketing methods. But they do have predictable needs, one of which is the need to wash clothes. And washing clothes is boring. So while these co-eds are a captive audience, why not give them something to read, such as a poster about your product? Encompass Media Group took advantage of this largely uncharted territory, explaining that they "purposely avoid the high-traffic, high-clutter locations where on-campus advertising commonly appears." Fashion, telecommunications, entertainment, automotive, and financial products sell well via this method. Encompass Media Group offers a variety of other types of nontraditional marketing methods including street teams, wrapped vehicles, and projection media. Check them out at www. encompassmediagroup.com.

Golfers 'R' Us?

Demographics suggest that golfers typically have high disposable incomes—maybe that's why there are so many new ambient marketing techniques that revolve around golf. Advertisements placed on the dash of the golf cart, on-screen advertising integrated into the golf cart's GPS system, and specialty wheel coverings that display advertising or tournament sponsorships. If your target audience includes golfers, you have a world of possibilities.

Booby Traps

Don't push yourself on the consumer. Know when to sell and when to back off. Today's consumers are inundated with marketing messages, and they aren't likely to embrace being marketed to while doing something they expect to be ad-free. While researching this book, we came across an article that detailed a patent for golf course hole advertising (patent number 6712714). We're happy to report that we couldn't find any examples of this actually in place. Hopefully it'll stay that way and golf advertising can stay where it belongs: on Tiger's cap or shirt sleeve.

Wall Murals and Floor Decals

One way to integrate into your potential customer's surroundings is by becoming one with the building. That's what floor decals and wall murals aim to do. Signature Graphics, Inc. is one company that creates such products. One notable example of their work is a Dove mural that was applied to a set of lockers at Bally's Total Fitness. Another company, General Formulations, creates floor decals called Traffic Graffic. Customers literally walk over your ad applied to the floor.

Advertainment

If you're looking for truly cutting-edge marketing solutions, look no further than Monster Media, headquartered in Orlando, Florida. They offer a variety of technology-driven "advertainment" marketing tools, many of which are surprisingly affordable. We spoke to John Payne, Monster Media President, to get the skinny on Monster's "advertainment" options.

"Advertainment is the integration of entertainment and marketing," said John. "It's a way to combat media clutter." Two advertainment options are GroundFX and WallFX, systems that project images onto the floor or walls that users can interact with using their hands, feet, or even their entire bodies. Whether it's sweeping Skittles away to reveal the logo or directing fish where to swim by stepping into their virtual pond, GroundFX and WallFX are captivating to both kids and adults. Monster Media has several standard effects that can be customized quite easily (and quickly) and exposure in a high-traffic location is very affordable—as little as $2,000 buys you an entire month. Monster Media has webcams on every system so they can monitor the audience interaction. "Clients can watch people's reactions to their ads," said John.

Monster Media will have 150 systems installed by November 2007 in a variety of locations—professional sports venues, mass transit stations, airports, and high-end Vegas hotels just to name a few. "Sports and entertainment venues are ideal because they have such a diversity of events," said John. They also have event-based marketing/mobile applications for short term marketing plans.

But GroundFX and WallFX are just the beginning. Monster Media also provides plasma-immersion technology. They recently completed a recruiting campaign for a transportation company. For under $10,000, the client had a system with interactive ads set up for a week-long trade show. "Offering something of interest to the trade-show participants really drew in the crowds," explained John. Of course $10,000 may seem like big bucks if you're on a shoestring budget but it's really a drop in the bucket when compared with the costs of traditional marketing and advertising.

Monster Media's interactive, motion-based systems can also be linked into Bluetooth promotions to create a truly memorable experience. "Consumers who pass by a plasma screen can text in to receive a discount or offer, or they might receive a text message offering them a chance to view a trailer," said John. All Bluetooth options are permission-based, meaning that users have to say yes or no to receive the offers. This prevents angering users who do not want to receive the text messages.

Beyond interactive technologies, Monster Media offers Turnstile AdSleeves, custom-fit wraps that fit around turnstiles at arenas or mass transportation entryways. The AdSleeves provide massive amounts of exposure as every person who enters and exits the venue has to pass through the turnstiles. Geico conducted a very successful turn-stile campaign in Chicago, in large part to determine if they wanted to invest more advertising dollars to expand their reach into that market.

What are John's suggestions regarding guerrilla marketing uses? "Marketing is a circular application," said John. "You have to hit people on all fronts." According to John, one area with great potential for making a high impact in guerrilla marketing is minor league baseball. "First of all, baseball hits a wide demographic. You've got kids, parents, grandparents—you name it," he said. "We recently conducted a campaign for a bubble gum product at 30 baseball venues. We had fully-integrated sponsorships—they were featured in PSAs both pre- and post-game and they had Turnstile AdSleeves so that all attendees would see your name as they entered and exited the venues. At the games, we hosted bubble gum blowing contests and we handed out samples at the concession stand. It was incredibly effective."

If you're interested in advertainment, check out Monster Media at www.monstermedia.net.

Partnerships

Who says you have to use one marketing method at a time? Why not combine strategic partnering with ambient marketing? Find a company that offers compatible services, strike up a marketing partnership, and leave promotional materials at each other's places of business. You own a health food store? See if you can leave some menus at a neighboring health club in exchange for allowing them to leave class schedules at your store.

> **Brainwaves**
>
> Rent or purchase subscriber lists from magazines that target your demographic for a direct mail campaign. Pick a specialized magazine and contact the magazine to see if you can access their subscriber mailing list. The more specific the magazine, the better!

Feel free to think beyond complimentary businesses and obvious partners. In 1999, Ask Jeeves (a question answering service at Ask.com) partnered with the Fruit Label Company and the California Apple Commission to label 15 million apples with AskJeeves labels. These labels which posed questions such as "Why is New York called the Big Apple?" and "How do I make homemade apple sauce?" were put on apples and distributed to grocery stores nationwide. This ambient campaign promoted apples and the new Internet service at the same time. What a very creative strategic partnership.

Creating Your Ambient Marketing Campaign

Here are some things to consider:

1. Keep it simple.

2. Make sure that it can easily be read from a distance, if necessary.

3. Consider the location when crafting your message. The length of your message should be based on how long the consumer will spend in this spot. For example,

an ad placed in an area where people might have to wait in a subway station or ride in an elevator could support a longer message. Something that is likely to be viewed in passing needs to be short and to the point.

Here are some questions to ask when choosing a location:

1. Does your target audience frequent this location?

2. Does this location lend itself to promoting your product? Is this venue appropriate for your company's message? For example, you probably won't want to advertise a restaurant that prides itself on its high-calorie, all-you-can-eat buffet at your local health club.

3. Will it be convenient for your target audience to buy your product? Can they buy it now?

It Worked for Them: Journeys Fitness and Wellness

Journeys Fitness and Wellness displayed the perfect example, not only of ambient marketing but many of the other concepts we've introduced in this book. Journeys is located in the Orlando suburb of Longwood, Florida and is owned and operated by husband and wife team, Kevin Laczko and Debbie Stickney. Kevin and Debbie opened their business in July 2004 after three months of preparation and planning. Kevin and Debbie wisely spent time deciding how they wanted to do business. Task #1 was developing a mission statement:

> "Journeys Fitness and Wellness, Inc., is committed to providing our clients with exceptional personalized fitness and wellness training while holding firm to strong moral and ethical values. We are dedicated to assisting and motivating each individual along their respective journey towards optimum fitness and wellness. Our ultimate goal is to equip clients with the tools and techniques for long-term body stewardship."

What does everyone say about real estate? Location, location, location. Kevin and Debbie set up shop in a small studio in a well-positioned shopping plaza just steps away from one of the highest ranked elementary schools in several counties (and just miles away from a top-ranked high school). Their close proximity to the school provides convenient access to two of the studio's target audiences—stay-at-home parents and students who want to enhance their athletic performance.

Off Site Promotions

To introduce themselves to the community they began off-site promotions at a local health food store and at several upscale apartment complexes located within walking distance. "We conducted a variety of free services such as chair massage, body composition analysis, blood pressure checks, and other health screenings," explained Kevin. "Of course, we'd have brochures and business cards on hand. Probably one out of 30 people became a client and the exposure was priceless," he said.

But those efforts alone weren't enough to really get things off the ground. Kevin and Debbie began advertising in local community circulars, and they took flyers door to door in the area.

Partnerships

They were on their way, but in order to expand they really needed more space. Their small studio was beginning to feel a bit limiting. (This is where things get really innovative!) Three months into business, they decided to partner with another personal trainer who wanted to move into the plaza—one who was well established in the community no less. By partnering with another trainer, Journeys was able to expand into a larger facility, and by combining their equipment, the trainers expanded the variety of their offerings. Today, they share the space, equipment, utilities—everything—and it works to both their advantages. They worked out a five-page agreement outlining how they would do business together and how they'd respect each other's existing clientele.

Sponsorships and Promotions

Over the last three years, Journeys has used a variety of ambient marketing methods in conjunction with the schools. They signed on as a partner with the elementary school. They provide health and wellness presentations in exchange for feature in the phone directory and placement of brochures at the entrance to the school. During back-to-school time, they offered free express chair massages to teachers and mothers. They've even stood at the corner during after-school hours handing out logo'd sports bottles, brochures, and coupons to drive business among the parent demographic.

For the high school, they offer certificates for free services to athletes of the month. They also have placement in football programs, baseball schedules, and sports schedule posters. They get many referrals from coaches and athletic directors at the school. Recently, they went the extra mile, purchasing a radio spot during the broadcast of the high school football game. Because he is a former University of Florida football player, Kevin's experience has proven to be a draw for up-and-coming football players. Also a former Army officer, Kevin makes the most of his background by conducting periodic Fitness Boot Camps in the area. "The boot camps provide variety for many of our existing customers and they're a great draw for people who want to get back with the program," says Kevin.

Customer Appreciation

From the beginning, Journeys has operated from a very customer-oriented frame of mind and nothing demonstrates that more than their Customer Appreciation Night. They offered food, a raffle, and other games and prizes to commemorate their first year in business. "We offer very personal services and we naturally develop strong ties to our customers," explains Kevin. "I think that leads to a high level of client retention. I try to make sure every customer we have knows how much we appreciate their business."

The Least You Need to Know

- ◆ Carefully consider your target audience before deciding on a location for your ambient marketing efforts.

- ◆ Community partnerships and sponsorships are one of the best ambient marketing methods available.

- ◆ A combined approach works best: use multiple ambient marketing methods to boost brand awareness.

- ◆ Ambient marketing methods are often off-the-wall attention grabbers.

Chapter 10

I Spy: Stealth Marketing

In This Chapter

- ◆ What is stealth marketing?
- ◆ Apparent, short-term benefits of stealth
- ◆ You've got a front row seat for marketing's new live theater
- ◆ Does it ever work? Or how you can use this power for good, not evil

Companies that don't have the time or money to wait for the world to discover them sometimes revert to deceptive means of promoting their product or services, called stealth, roach bait, or engineered marketing. But beware: stealth marketing can result in a backlash fueled by a media all too willing to pick up consumer alert stories.

Stealth Marketing

It's hard to believe that you might be interacting with people who might be paid to chat you up about various products and services. Yes, it's true. Human interactions are now for sale, at least in some circles.

What Is It?

Stealth marketing, often called undercover marketing or roach bait marketing, is a technique in which buying decisions are influenced by the use of subterfuge. The idea behind this strategy is to create buzz about a specific product using paid endorsers, the catch being that these representatives don't disclose that they've been hired for this purpose. Paying people to promote your product is a long-standing, commonly accepted marketing method. But it shouldn't be a covert operation; traditionally these campaigns have clearly indicated who was behind the marketing push. Consumers who fall for stealth marketing usually think they've witnessed a genuine endorsement, and when they find out they've been duped, they're typically not very happy.

How Did Stealth Marketing Begin?

Stealth marketing is not a new concept. One of the best early examples is how competitors of R. J. Reynolds Tobacco Company used negative buzz to scare people away from purchasing Camel cigarettes. It went like this: two people who happened to be standing in line together would spontaneously begin a seemingly random conversation talking about how they'd heard smoking Camels caused syphilis because many of the factory workers had the disease. The two "strangers" were actually paid to engage in these exchanges in high profile places where people might buy cigarettes.

How Does Stealth Differ from Guerrilla Marketing?

Stealth marketing is an innovative new way to connect with today's discriminating consumers. It can be done inexpensively, but it's sneaky and deceptive and is likely to only work in the short term. We all know that the ultimate goal of marketing is to increase sales, but if not done in an open and honest manner, it could have the opposite effect. Guerrilla marketing is unique, typically low-budget marketing. Guerrilla marketing methods (other than stealth) are not deceptive.

Brainwaves

Not all paid endorsers receive monetary compensation. They might receive payment in the form of free samples, coupons, or discounts. And not all recruited endorsers fall under the stealth category. Take for example, BzzAgent (bzzagent.com), a company founded in 2001 that is devoted to helping your company harness the power of WOM (word of mouth). Agents are recruited to try your product and asked to share their opinions. The agents are not obligated to push the product if they don't like it, and the company policy requires that they disclose their status as a working "agent."

Is It Legal?

Although there is no legal precedent relating specifically to stealth marketing, word of mouth advertising is covered under existing *Federal Trade Commission* (*FTC*) regulations. According to Section 5 of the FTC guidelines, "the Commission has determined that representation, omission, or practice is deceptive if it is likely to mislead consumers and affect consumers' behavior about the product or service."

Furthermore, in a staff opinion letter issued on December 12, 2006, the FTC announced that companies engaging in word of mouth campaigns where people are paid to endorse products must disclose this fact.

def•i•ni•tion

The **Federal Trade Commission** (**FTC**) is an independent U.S. government agency responsible for regulating methods of competition and advertising in America.

Why Is It Effective?

In our opinion, stealth marketing is not effective (unless your only goal is to generate immediate cash). But there are some who don't share our philosophy. They see nothing wrong with hiring good-looking people to sport their gear or spout the virtues of products and services on the Internet without disclosing the true nature of their relationship to the company, its product, and/or services. Others might even argue that stealth marketing is effective for exactly the reason we think it's unethical: because people don't know they're being marketed to. And it's true, for a while, stealth marketing sometimes works (again, if your goal is simply to make quick money). But problems arise when the public becomes aware of your scam.

Electronic Stealth Marketing

Because of its anonymity, the Internet is an open invitation for stealth marketing on a number of levels.

Stealth Blogging

With the growing number of businesses using blogs, it is not surprising that stealth marketers have infiltrated this medium by creating stealth blogs. Some companies are paying bloggers to promote their products, and put links to their websites on their blogs. These bloggers do not always disclose that they are being paid to do this.

Faux Bloggers Cause a Stir

Christmas 2006 wasn't the best of times for Sony. The viral marketing campaign engineered by their "consumer activation" agency didn't make their fans jolly. To promote Sony's PlayStation Portable, they created a fake YouTube video and faux blogs, all purporting to be created by young people desperate to get their paws on the new PSP. Unfortunately, they seriously underestimated the smarts of their target audience and numerous angry blogs resulted, calling the phony video/blogs transparent and insulting. Sony representatives apologized, but the damage was done.

Astroturfing

Astroturfing is one of the most obnoxious forms of electronic stealth marketing because it requires endorsement from not just one or two random influencers, but entire communities of people who are staged to appear as if they are a part of a grassroots effort—something driven by the people/public. (Get it? Astroturf is fake grass and astroturfing is fake grassroots.) Astroturfers *sneeze* on web surfers covertly through blogs, chat rooms, and forums. They pose as peers of the product's target audience, use the forum as a soap box to tout the virtues of the product, without revealing their connection to it.

def•i•ni•tion

Astroturfing is an orchestrated public relations campaign that gives the impression of being grassroots oriented. It gets its name from Astroturf which is, of course, fake grass.

McDonald's LincolnFry Hoax

The LincolnFry blog was supposedly a blog created by two people who were served a French fry at McDonalds that bore a striking resemblance to Abe Lincoln. They did two ads to support the blog which provided enough information, they hoped, to drive you to a website/blog, both of which were fictitious. But that's not the most unusual part of the story. The LincolnFry hoax was an homage to the "Virgin Mary Grilled Cheese" sandwich purchased by GoldenPalace.com for $28,000 off of eBay. After buying the sandwich, GoldenPalace.com took it on tour and then sold it on eBay with proceeds going to benefit charity. Interestingly, GoldenPalace.com also purchased the LincolnFry for $75,000. McDonald's donated the money to charity as well. While it appears the odd food stuffs did have a positive effect in raising money for worthy causes, we're not sure how much marketing bang for their buck McDonald's actually got out of the LincolnFry.

Live Stealth Marketing or Roach Baiting

It's unbelievable to imagine that we live in a world where seemingly genuine interactions with live human beings could be stealth marketing, but it's true. There are companies who pay actors to go about life pretending to love different products, solely for the purpose of making you buy one, thirst for one, or at the very least, talk about one to some other potential target. Yuck! Of course, any type of marketing that involves the phrase "roach bait" can't be good. Just read on and we know you'll agree.

Brainwaves

One of the most widely used forms of stealth marketing comes in the form of fake endorsements posted to blogs or message boards. You'd think it would be easy to get away with, considering the anonymity the Internet provides, but web surfers are amazingly good at sniffing out the faux influencers.

Roach Bait Marketing

Roach bait is an extermination method in which roaches are lured into a trap baited with poison. Roaches eat the slow acting poisoned bait, go back to their communities, and die. Then when the other roaches make a meal out of their deceased companion they die, too. In marketing, roach bait involves people (attractive people) who are hired to come into your social setting, talk about a particular product (engineering buzz), and then leave, hopefully infecting you and your buddies with the idea that you can't live without whatever they've been pushing. It might work like this:

A good-looking girl walks into a club and saunters up to the bar. When the expected "Can I buy you a drink," comes from Guy #1, she'll tell him she only drinks (insert brand of liquor here). On she'll move to Guy #2, to whom she'll repeat the endorsement. Maybe she'll go to another bar and on and on it will go until she's exposed her targeted number of guys to the covert endorsement. The fact that she's a *leaner* will never be revealed.

def•i•ni•tion

Leaner is the name given to people hired to promote products undercover and in person.

Here's another scenario: a new gaming company creates a new product and hires two guys to hang out in Starbucks, creating a fuss over the new gadget. Other people (of course) come over to check it out. Turns out the two guys were paid by the gaming company, but the stealth victims never knew they were interacting with paid actors.

Vespa Scooters

Vespa promoted its scooters via a stealth method, hiring attractive hipsters to ride around cities such as Los Angeles and Houston. This troupe of Vespa-riding beautiful people would appear open for interactions and were not surprisingly approached by people eager to get to know them. After exchanging some witty banter, the Vespa beauties would jot down their phone numbers for the happy recipients. Turns out, though, that the digits they offered weren't theirs but those of the Vespa dealership. Imagine how those people felt when they realized the encounter wasn't genuine or spontaneous.

Lights, Camera, Action!

Some roach bait techniques are quite elaborate. Some even involve scripts outlining how actors should behave and respond to various scenarios that might play out. Another could involve real collateral, as was the case with Beer.com. They created 50,000 bottle caps with their name printed on them, which they left strewn about bars in party destinations during spring break and Mardi Gras. Yet another outlandish example involved an actor who remained in character for 90 days straight while pretending to be a video game addicted 20-year-old who was losing his mind due to excessive game playing! The actor lived 24/7 as his character for 90 days straight before disappearing and causing conspiracy theory blogs to spring up all over the incident. Turns out the video game creator dreamt up the whole thing. That's quite an unbelievable investment of time and resources, all to convince people your deception is real.

Celebrity Confession = Stealth Marketing?

If you've ever wondered why some celebrities go public with their health issues, there could be one really great reason: somebody is showing them the money. When Kathleen Turner appeared on *Good Morning America* to reveal that she had rheumatoid arthritis, little did viewers know that she was paid by two drug companies to speak out about her illness and the drug that helped her. Another celebrity, this one a popular rock group's singer, went public with her fight with obesity and the solution she found: Inamed's Lap-band. Turns out she, too, was being compensated. Of course, it didn't take the major news networks long to wise up and they now ask about paid endorsements. But celebrity endorsement is still alive and kicking. Although it appears that Sally Field supports osteoporosis med Boniva simply because of its benefits (and maybe she does indeed love the drug), both television commercials and newspaper articles fail to note that she receives a paycheck from Roche.

What's Wrong with Stealth Marketing?

Word of mouth marketing or buzz marketing works because it comes from your peers and it is assumed to be someone's unbiased opinion. When a friend makes a recommendation, and you know there's nothing in it for them, it's incredibly powerful. And even if there is an incentive for them, if they're up front about it, they still maintain credibility. But when someone tries to mimic an authentic interaction, it's just trickery and nobody likes that.

The fake social marketing debacle isn't the first time Sony's creative marketing has rankled consumers. In 2005, Sony was revealed as the mastermind behind graffiti characters (suspiciously playing Sony's PSP) that were springing up in large urban areas. Angry e-mails from residents began appearing on the Internet. Rants against Sony were easy to find. One infamous post appeared on the technology site Popgadget, where a Lincoln Heights resident reportedly said "For some strange reason, I'd rather see my friendly local gang lay claim to that wall then have it given over to some crappy corporation and their urban marketing campaign." Harsh words, indeed. And a reminder that the public does not like to be taken for a fool.

> **Brainwaves**
>
> Technorati, the leading blog tracking site, keeps an eye out for splogs (spam blogs) and tries to keep their site as free from them as possible. They regularly clean house to rid their search results from these empty, deceptive blogs.

Another bright idea that could have used a little extra planning happened in 2006 when Chase bank branches in New York City projected the corporate logo onto the sidewalks in front of their doors. Local officials considered this sidewalk defacement and punished the company with fines until they stopped.

IBM and Microsoft both have similar examples with the IBM's Peace, Love, Linux campaign and Microsoft's "It's better with the Butterfly" campaign. IBM spray painted graphic images on the sidewalks of San Francisco and Microsoft pasted color butterflies all over Manhattan. Both companies were fined.

It's true that in our technologically advanced society, marketers must find new ways to reach potential customers, but riling city officials with offbeat marketing campaigns doesn't bode well for your future. Have a grand plan? Check out local codes before you get too far down the road.

The following are potential negative consequences of engineered buzz:

- You lose your credibility.

- People view you as dishonest and unethical.

- Once people realize they've been tricked, they may turn against you.

- If they're angry enough, they may begin negative word of mouth.

- Their negative word of mouth could spread like wildfire and kill your brand.

Your credibility and integrity are your most important assets, and they are hard to rebuild once they've been damaged.

Does Stealth Marketing Ever Work?

Sometimes, but generally only in the movies …

Some people have been successful at spinning the deception in their favor, either by outing themselves, or suggesting they intended to reveal the "secret" at some point. Case in point: *The Blair Witch Project*. This was an independent low-budget horror film that began stealth marketing before the movie was even released. Filmmakers began spreading the word around Internet chat rooms and message boards that the film was a documentary that had recently been discovered. Fan sites and people were buzzing like crazy wondering "Did three students really die making the film?" After the film's launch, the buzz continued with promotional materials further emphasizing that the film was a documentary. Around the time of the movie's release, another fake documentary, *Curse of the Blair Witch*, aired on television to further solidify the authenticity of the film's documentary status. In 1999, *The Blair Witch Project* became the highest grossing independent film—a record it held until 2002—raking in an estimated $248 million. Was it a success? In the short run, absolutely. But consider that the movie's sequel released in 2000, *Book of Shadows: Blair Witch 2*, grossed less than $50 million worldwide. Granted, with an investment of just $15 million, the film wasn't a flop. But it's a noticeable drop from the success of the first film.

Booby Traps

If children are the primary consumers of your products or services, don't even *think* about stealth marketing of any variety. Advocate groups and parents will not appreciate your attempts to deceive children, even if you are simply trying to be funny. When marketing to kids, it's more important to establish trust with parents.

The moral of the story: you might be able to win in the short run with stealth, but it's no great recipe for long-term success.

Unstealth Your Idea

Canon used stealth marketing to show off their new digital camera in 2003 by hiring people to pretend to be Japanese tourists. The couples would stop people to ask if they'd mind taking their picture. Of course, once people used the new camera, Canon hoped they'd see how great it was and they'd want one of their own. But the fact is, they didn't have to do this via stealth methods. It would have been just as easy to arm people with cameras and send them out on the streets to expose the public to the camera's benefits. They could have provided cameras to mothers—who takes more pictures than moms? Who better to share the message? It's unfortunate that they opted to go the sneaky route. Almost every stealth idea you can think of has an up-front application. Remember, as more and more of these stealth methods become public knowledge, people long to interact with people who are candid. You don't have to hide the fact you're selling something—just be creative and authentic.

"My Adidas"

In the '80s, rap pioneers Run-D.M.C. wrote a song about their favorite brand of sneakers, aptly titled "My Adidas." At one concert attended by an Adidas exec, Run-D.M.C. actually held their unlaced Adidas up in the air, enticing the crowd to wave theirs, too. Of course the exec loved it and Run-D.M.C. did end up with an endorsement deal, but that wasn't their intent. They didn't write the song because they were paid. They just genuinely liked Adidas shoes. Today, rappers *are* paid to mention brands in songs. Jay-Z was paid to mention Motorola. But other rappers insist their endorsements are organic, that is, they're just injecting a little dose of reality into their songs. (Much like Prince's "Little Red Corvette" which was not a paid endorsement.) It does seem to work, regardless of whether it's paid or organic. Artist Busta Rhymes' song, "Pass the Courvoisier," was reportedly an unpaid endorsement, yet sales of the liquor in the United States soared after the song's release.

> **Brainwaves**
>
> Where is the line between a curious marketing campaign and stealth marketing? Isn't getting people to "fall" for something a creative technique? Absolutely. But the difference between being clever and being stealth is in the reveal. Being creative requires a reveal at some point. Some time during the marketing message, even if only at the very end, the real company or motive must be exposed.

Ethical Issues

To determine whether your marketing idea is ethical or shady, the Word of Mouth Marketing Association (WOMMA) has a great Ethics Assessment Tool available on their website at www.womma.org. By answering their 20 questions, you're sure to stay firmly on the safe side of ethics.

Or you can try our quick and easy ethical evaluation method. Ask yourself, "How would I feel if this were done to me?" After all, it's wise to do to others as you'd have done to you.

The Least You Need to Know

◆ Stealth marketing is a dangerous practice.

◆ Healthy businesses are built on relationships; stealth marketing damages trust.

◆ The apparent short-term benefits of stealth marketing don't outweigh the risks.

◆ Don't do anything you'd feel uncomfortable about if it were announced publicly.

Part 3

To the Internet and Beyond!

Move over mass e-mail. Bye, bye static web pages. Podcasts, blogs, Bluetooth messaging, social networking, and other digital sharing techniques enable you to connect with millions of people as easy as 1, 2, 3. Crafting the right message? Now that might take some time and brain power.

11

Viral Marketing

In This Chapter

- ◆ Elements of successful viral marketing campaigns
- ◆ Methods of delivering viral marketing messages
- ◆ Using search engine optimization to feed the virus
- ◆ Viral marketing hot buttons

Viral is no longer a dirty word, at least when it comes to guerrilla marketing. Nothing illustrates this point better than the Diet Coke and Mentos experiment that got the founders of EepyBird.com on *The Today Show*. In little more than a year, more than six million people have viewed the experiment. You might say interest in viewing this experiment has exploded. Now the duo is joining forces with Blue Man Group and appearing on *The Ellen DeGeneres Show*. The priceless exposure continues. The moral of the story: make your message viral and there's no telling how many people you will reach.

What is Viral Marketing?

How great would it be if every one of your happy customers "sold" just one other person on your product or service? How about hundreds, thousands, and even hundreds of thousands? Viral marketing is a method of marketing whereby your message passes from person to person without your direct involvement. It's the technological equivalent of word of mouth. It's easy to see how growth is exponential. If you communicate with ten people and each of those people tells ten people and so on, within four generations your message will have reached more than 100,000 people. That's assuming that every ten people tell ten other people and that, of course, is the tricky part. Motivating people to spread your message is the central challenge of viral marketing.

Making Your Message Viral

Viral marketing works best when:

◆ It's quick and easy to pass along your message.

◆ Your solution is scalable.

MSN HotMail (a free web-based e-mail service from MSN) is a great example of the power of viral marketing. MSN used a very simple strategy: they provided free e-mail accounts to users and on the bottom of every outgoing e-mail they embedded a message inviting new users to claim their own free hotmail.com account. In just a year and a half they had more than 12 million users. Imagine how much they would have spent sending a direct mail piece to 12 million people. HotMail makes its money on upgraded email accounts that feature expanded storage capabilities, as well as advertising. As explained by *Metcalfe's Law*—with the addition of every e-mail account, the value of the existing e-mail account increases.

def•i•ni•tion

Metcalfe's Law is a term formulated by Robert Metcalfe which states that the value of a telecommunications network is the square of the number of users of the system. For example: a single telephone is useless, but the value of every telephone increases with the total number of telephones in the network. Why? Because the total number of people with whom each user can call, or receive calls from, increases with each added telephone. This theory applies to social networking sites as well.

Make the Message Easy to Share and Worthy of Passing On

As a kid you probably played the game "pass it on." To play the game, a group of kids would sit in a circle and whisper a message from person to person. By the time it was passed around the circle, the original message was often unrecognizable because it had been repeated incorrectly one or more times. The Internet makes instant communication fast and easy, but to reap the benefits from this form of marketing, you must ensure that your message is one that can be passed along easily and accurately.

Make the Viral Campaign Scalable

When you're deciding what incentive to offer to spark a viral campaign, make sure you're prepared to offer it to the masses, if necessary. Your viral marketing idea should be something that is adaptable to both small and large audiences. Whatever you decide, ask yourself, "Could I pull this off if 50,000 people wanted this tomorrow?" Keep in mind that even if you are only offering people the chance to view something online—that could still cost money. Consider how much traffic your existing bandwidth can take and investigate what it will cost to increase before attempting to spread your viral campaign.

> **Brainwaves**
>
> Offering something free or giving people an incentive to share your message helps drive viral marketing. If you don't have an incentive to provide for everyone, you can always give a really big prize to only a select few. The chance to win lifetime services, for example, will generate a lot of excitement even though only a few will win.

Ways to Deliver Viral Messages

Most viral marketing is accomplished using existing social networks both online and offline. These include e-mail, television, newspapers, live social networks, and YouTube. Here are a few others:

Pass-along e-mails—Anything you forward to your friends is technically considered a pass-along e-mail, but to make something viral it needs to have value. People will pass along your e-mail if they find it extremely compelling or entertaining, or because there's something in it for them like a special offer or free services.

Street teams—A street team is a group of unpaid fans that are asked to promote your product, usually in exchange for merchandise. Giving away free products to members of an existing social network can have a viral effect.

YouTube—This popular, free, video sharing website is the hottest trend in viral marketing. Often the YouTube videos are linked on various websites or sent via e-mail, so you can see the potential for widespread distribution.

Website links—Many viral campaigns begin simply as links on related websites that generate enough attention to be communicated en masse either verbally or through e-mail.

Types of viral marketing:

Booby Traps

Never exploit information obtained via a viral marketing campaign. Just because someone wanted to watch the funny video you posted on your website doesn't mean they want to receive your newsletter. Offer visitors the chance to sign up to receive your newsletter or other e-mail correspondence, but don't make opting-in a default.

- **Incentive-driven**—This involves offering something of value to motivate people to pass along your message.

- **Controversial**—The message you've created is so outrageous people feel compelled to pass it on for shock value.

- **Cause-related**—This is viral marketing that benefits a worthwhile cause. People pass it along out of a desire to contribute and be a part of something bigger.

- **Entertainment-based**—These are campaigns that are passed on because they are just plain fun or funny. These might be interactive quizzes, flash games, or even simply appealing imagery or copy.

The following are some viral marketing tips:

- Express an obvious truth that's gone unsaid. Say what everyone is thinking but nobody has had the guts to say out loud. Dove's Campaign for Real Beauty is a great example of this in action. (See the "It Worked for Them" section at the end of this chapter for more on the Campaign for Real Beauty.)

- Spin your message in an unexpected way. A recent article in a young women's magazine suggested highlighting your unusual attributes instead of camouflaging them (as is typically suggested in women's magazines). The idea that you should show off features (like skinny legs or a large behind) instead of hiding them is unique—which makes it a real attention-grabber.

◆ Be willing to laugh at yourself or your industry. Laughter is great medicine and people are prone to share something funny with their friends. Did you see the Superbowl ad where Britney Spears's soon-to-be-ex pokes fun at himself? It (almost) made us like him!

◆ Make sure you connect the dots. If you're able to grab people's attention, but they have no idea what your message is, you've missed the mark. Make sure you entertain and tie in your message. Don't be too cryptic. If your ad leaves people wondering what in the heck you are trying to sell, you've wasted your time and money.

◆ Keep it simple. Don't attempt to tell your audience the history of your company, list your mission statement, or explain company objectives. The viral campaign should simply pique their interest in you or your offerings. Point them back to your website for the nuts and bolts. Keep in mind: attention spans are short; your only goal in viral marketing is to get people talking about you and your product.

◆ Have realistic expectations. Creating a campaign that will become viral is a lot like trying to capture lightning in a bottle. Success in viral marketing is more art than science, so it may take more than one shot to hit the mark.

◆ Leave them wanting more. Curiosity is a powerful force. Everyone loves a secret.

Never include overt advertisement in your viral marketing efforts. The idea behind viral marketing is to create something so interesting that people naturally want to find out more. If you come on too strong, people will kill your viral effort by not passing it on. On the other hand, don't try to disguise the fact that you are marketing something. The viral campaign *should* communicate something about your brand, just not in a "sales-pitchy" way.

Rules and Regulations Regarding Viral Marketing

Internet regulations are currently evolving, but there are a few hard and fast rules to follow.

Tell the Whole Truth and Nothing but the Truth

Under the Federal Trade Commissions Act, advertising of any kind must be truthful and non-deceptive. You must have evidence to back up your claims and you cannot mislead customers in any way, either by false statements or omissions of relevant information.

Thou Shalt Not *Spam*

The CAN-SPAM Act of 2003 (Controlling the Assault of Non-Solicited Pornography and Marketing Act) provides that people or businesses who send e-mail with the primary purpose of advertising or promoting a commercial product or service must abide by certain rules. The CAN-SPAM Act means:

- Your e-mail cannot have a false or misleading header. Your domain name and e-mail address must be accurate.

- Your e-mail cannot contain a deceptive subject line. Your subject cannot be "Free iPod" unless that's what the e-mail content is about.

- Your recipients must have a way to opt-out. Unless you have an established relationship with the recipient, you must give them a method to get off your mailing list. The opt-out method you offer must remain available for 30 days following the date the e-mail was sent.

- Commercial e-mail must be identified as an advertisement and a physical postal address must be included.

def•i•ni•tion

Opt-in e-mail marketing is a strategy that allows your potential consumers to request to receive your product messages via e-mail, instead of receiving it automatically (like spam).

There are additional rules that apply to e-mail communications (including *opt-in e-mails*) and Internet advertisements. You can read more on the Federal Trade Commission's website at www.ftc.com.

Here's the Buzz

Pick a unique name for your viral marketing campaign—one that will place you high on Google and Yahoo! search results. To find something unique, do a Google and Yahoo! search before settling on a name. If your phrase returns 100 exact matches, it's not a good option. You want to select something that isn't already in use by someone else, as well as something that is already a commonly used phrase. Before the Heinz viral campaign, the phrase "Ketchup Against Tomato Cruelty" probably didn't return many hits. Ford Motor Company's "Evil Twin" campaign was less uniquely named.

Search Engine Optimization

If you repair clocks in the Orlando area, when someone types "clock repair Orlando" into Google, you want to be at the top of the list. That's the purpose of search engine optimization. Whether you're doing a viral marketing campaign or you're just rolling out a website, search engine optimization is an essential part of driving people to your website.

Search Engines

The list of available search engines is nearly endless. There are specialized search engines for categories such as: general, regional, news, answer-based, blog, medical, job search, geographic, business, comparison shopping, multimedia, and charity search engines. To keep things simple, we're only going to list the top engines from major categories.

- AskJeeves—www.Ask.com
- Google—www.Google.com
- Yahoo!—www.Yahoo.com
- Mamma—www.Mamma.com
- AOL Search—http://search.aol.com
- Windows Live Search (formerly MSN search)—www.live.com
- LookSmart—http://search.looksmart.com
- Lycos.com—www.lycos.com
- Netscape—http://channels.netscape.com

The Open Directory Project or www.dmoz.org is a search system that feeds Google, AOL, AskJeeves, Netscape, EarthLink, Lycos, and hundreds of other sites. It's a directory, created and maintained by web users, of web pages. The Open Directory Project is different from a search engine in that it does not display lists of web pages based on keywords, but instead lists web pages by category and subcategories. Open directory is different than search engines in that it does not use robots to comb the Internet looking for websites to list. Instead, real human beings sort through sites and list them manually, making the results more accurate. The Yahoo! Directory is another human-driven directory and it also lists by category, in addition to keyword searches. It offers two submission options: Standard (free) and Yahoo! Express (paid).

Types of Search Engine Optimization

When people search the web, they usually only look at the first 10 or so entries (the sites the search engine has ranked the highest), so you definitely want to be in that top 10. To optimize your web page so that it appears at the top of search results, you have to label it with keywords.

There are two types of *search engine optimization*:

◆ Organic SEO—Uses algorithms and targeted keywords to ensure that your website achieves top-ten placement in the major search engines. The challenge is that SEO algorithms are constantly changing and they aren't publicized so it's somewhat of a guessing game.

◆ Paid SEO—You can also pay for top billing in the search engines. Just be aware that you will likely be paying per click. Every time someone clicks on your site, you will pay a set amount, usually between 1 and 50 cents. There has been some controversy over pay per clicks as abuse of the system has allegedly occurred when users are paid to click on websites to inflate the costs. These days, clicks are generated per unique IP address, meaning that one person clicking multiple times will only generate one charge. Do any search on Google, and the websites that are featured in a narrow column on the right side, as well as the ones that appear at the top within the "sponsored links" area, are the paid SEO websites.

def•i•ni•tion _____

Search Engine Optimization (SEO) is the process of improving the traffic flow to a website by making it easy to find with search engines such as Yahoo! and Google. Websites that are well optimized appear higher in search results.

Search Engine Optimization Basics

There are a number of ways you can optimize your website. If you have time on your hands and you're short on money, you can even do it yourself. If you're short on time, you can buy SEO placement software or hire a consulting company that specializes in search engine optimization.

But before you attempt to do search engine optimization on your own, understand how pages are ranked. Page ranking is determined by a number of factors, and it varies based on the search engine. Here are the factors that determine your ranking:

- How many times does the keyword being searched for appear on your page?
- What percentage of the total words on your site does the keyword account for?
- How many sites are linked to your site?
- How big is your site and how often do you update it?

The percentage of total words on your website that your keyword represents is factored in to avoid ranking spam sites at the top. This means finding the right number of keywords is critical. Say you're a building contractor with the word "builder" listed on your site 100 times, and because of that you reach a number one ranking on Google. It could be that having "builder" appear 101 times would make Google consider you spam, and you'd be relegated to the bottom. You may have to tweak your keywords a bit before finding just the right ratio to get you placed at the top.

Do It Yourself SEO

To do search engine optimization yourself, you'll need to do quite a bit more research than we've provided in this book. It can be an in depth process, and there are many different approaches. To help you decide if you're up to the task, here are the basic steps:

- Find out where you currently rank using various keywords.
- Find out what keywords your competitors are using.
- Decide what keywords you want to use.
- Incorporate those words into your website source code.
- Submit your web page to the search engines.
- Repeat: edit the keywords and resubmit your page until you are at the top of search engine results for your desired keywords.

Many search engines pull information from other major search engines, so you don't need to concern yourself with every search engine that exists. Focus your attention on Google, Yahoo!, and Ask.com and you'll be well covered. AOL's search engine, for example, gets its search results from Google and the Open Directory Project. Keep in mind it may take weeks or even moths for changes to filter through the search engines.

> ### Brainwaves
>
> Even if you do not submit your website to search engines, you will eventually get listed. Major search engines have robots that continually navigate around sites based on keywords. They begin in one site, then visit pages that are linked to that site, then continue on around. But unless you submit your page, there's no telling how long you could wait for the robot to come visit your page.

SEO Software and SEO Placement Software

SEO software refers to programs that review the keywords associated with your website and help you generate additional keywords. SEO placement software addresses the other side of ranking, in that it looks at how many sites are linked to your site. Both can be used to boost your rankings. Search for "SEO software" or "SEO placement software" to find one of the many that are available.

It Worked for Them

Check out these companies who captured lightning in a bottle. They successfully implemented a viral campaign and are reaping the benefits.

Signature Advertising's Simon Sez Santa

Viral marketing doesn't get any better than showing off your skills while simultaneously entertaining your clients. One of the best examples of viral marketing we know was accomplished by our friends at Signature (SignatureAdvertising.com). Each year during the holiday season, the full-service marketing firm sends out a client gift that highlights their company's abilities.

Because Signature has an open door policy on fresh ideas—team members are encouraged to find innovative new things to offer clients—employees from the digital media department approached Chief Idea Officer, Charles Marshall, with a set of widgets they wanted to develop that they thought would be perfect for the holiday feature. "Go nuts," Charles told them, and the team was off and running. One of their ideas was a concept called Simon Sez Santa (www.simonsezsanta.com) whereby users could type in commands and Santa would accomplish the proposed feats (sing a song, and so on), much like Burger King's Subservient Chicken.

Keep in mind that Signature isn't a mega-agency like the one that pulled off Subservient Chicken. But size isn't everything. Accomplishing a viral campaign such as this would certainly show that they could play with the big boys. And did it ever! Their Simon Sez Santa turned out to be much more entertaining than the chicken ever was, and better yet, it communicated a message by demonstrating Signature's level of skill in their business arena.

> **Brainwaves**
>
> Burger King's Subservient Chicken (www.subservientchicken.com) was a clever viral marketing ploy that links to Burger King's "Have it Your Way" campaign. It allows users to manipulate the actions of a person dressed as a chicken.

Best of all, Signature didn't spend a fortune hiring talent and shooting the video—they used their own team and in-house tools. The Signature team brainstormed various commands and compiled a list of things they thought users might type in. Then, with no rehearsal and no script, Santa (played by IT Lead Jay Witherspoon) performed the various tasks on camera. "One of the commands was 'read a poem' and amazingly, Jay was able to recite one off the top of his head. He was incredible," said Charles.

Simon Sez Santa got out during beta testing. One of the developers asked a friend to try it out and it got passed around. Next thing you know, people were hunting down the site on the web. With no marketing, the video player had become viral in the best possible way, even more than Signature could have imagined. "We really only set out to entertain our clients and show them what we were capable of," said Charles. "We hadn't imagined that it would gain mass appeal." Day after day Signature had to up their bandwidth to accommodate the traffic. About.com featured the video as their humor site of the day and coolsiteoftheday.com showcased it on the day before Christmas Eve. Local papers and national publications picked up the story. The buzz flooded the Internet. All told, Santa got about 20 million hits before he went back to the North Pole.

The following year, there was no question that Simon Sez Santa would make an encore appearance. And being the innovative thinkers that they are, Signature found a way to customize the experience for their existing clients. If a client typed in their company name, Santa would offer a special customized greeting to their friends at that company. The second year out, Santa reached 60–70 million hits. Look for Santa to reappear this coming Christmas with some new bells and whistles.

Was it worth it? Charles Marshall says yes. "We definitely got new business as a result of Simon Sez Santa," he said. "Many clients who we'd previously told about our digital skills didn't really look to us for high-end media solutions until Santa showed them what we were capable of. Now, in addition to our Memphis office, we have satellite locations in Tampa and Atlanta and we've been named one of the fastest growing companies in Tennessee. Of course that's not solely due to 'Santa' but he sure helped get the message out."

Dove's Campaign for Real Beauty

Another sure-fire way to become viral? Speak truth that resonates with your audience. Nothing demonstrates this better than Dove's Campaign for Real Beauty (www.campaignforrealbeauty.com). The campaign takes aim at the fashion and cosmetics industry that all too often promotes unreal images of women, images that are damaging to girls' self-esteem and don't represent the target audience, which is not made up of supermodels. Dove features real women—even, get this, women over 50—in their advertising. Their slogan is "real women have curves," and they began the campaign as a "global effort that is intended to be a starting point for societal change and to act as a catalyst for widening definition and discussion of beauty." One of the most viral aspects of Dove's Campaign for Real Beauty is their Evolution Film that shows, through time-lapse photography, just how much effort goes into transforming a regular-looking girl into a Photoshop-enhanced perfect picture. They take viewers through the process of hair, makeup, and, finally, photo retouching. The regular girl is hardly recognizable from start to finish. Visit www.campaignforrealbeauty.com to see the full extent of their campaign efforts. Just keep in mind that ideas such as these are scalable. Truth is truth whether it's rolled out nationwide or throughout your city. Find a cause worth supporting and watch your customers line up to get on board.

The Least You Need to Know

◆ Creating a marketing campaign that goes viral is more art than science.

◆ Offer incentives to pass along the virus.

◆ Select the right keywords to keep you at the top of search engines.

◆ Be funny or outrageous to get people's attention.

There's a Place for Us: Social Networking Sites and Message Boards

In This Chapter

◆ How businesses use social networking sites and message boards

◆ Initiating conversation with customers via social media

◆ Free social networking sites and message board options

◆ Creating a presence online

Where can you find celebrities, Fortune 500 companies, and your local restaurant making "friends?" Stumped? Think MySpace. Social networking sites are just one portion of the rich market of consumer-generated marketing, otherwise known as community marketing or social marketing. No longer are these sites used merely to connect with friends or score dates. Businesses are jumping on the bandwagon and reaping big benefits.

What Is Social Networking?

Social networking began in 1995 with the introduction of a website called Classmates. com. On the Classmates.com website, registered users can find and connect with former classmates. From long-lost elementary school friends to old college room-mates, Classmates.com continues to be a thriving online community where users can post profiles, search others' profiles, send messages, and read message board postings. This virtual method of networking soon sparked other social networking sites like Epinions, and by 2005 there was a full-on craze underway.

Today, there are hundreds of social networking sites related to every topic under the sun. From the very general to the very specific, there seems to be a virtual community to suit every need. From JewishLoveMatch to Silicon Valley Pipeline to Catster, there is something for everyone. Most sites are free and only require the time it takes to set up a profile. Many also offer useful tools such as contact uploading, automatic address book updating, searchable/viewable profiles, the ability to form new links through "introduction services," and other forms of online social connections.

Here's how it works. To join the community a user must first create a profile. This might include some personal details about you, a short bio, photo, and what you're online to accomplish (networking, dating, meeting friends). Once you're in, you can search for people you already know or try to connect with new people who appear interesting to you. After that, it's just a huge referral service where you can connect with the friend of a friend and on and on. Talk about word of mouth! For businesses, exposure to product-friendly targeted audiences is the primary advantage of com-munity marketing. The thought behind this being that your *existing* customers in the community can "sell" your product to *potential* customers via this medium.

Comparing Message Boards/Forums and a Social Networking Site

With the introduction of numerous special interest social networking sites, distin-guishing between a social networking site and a message board can be difficult. And in reality, their use overlaps in many cases. You may even see the two terms used together: social networking message board. But strictly speaking, social networking sites place the majority of the emphasis on the profile or individual user's page. On a message board, the discussion is the main event. Social networking sites exist to con-nect people who may have many and varied common interests. Message boards are an evolution of Internet newsgroups that were popular during the early '90s, and they usually focus on a particular interest. Many television stations and bands have their own message boards.

If you need examples, check out http://forums.gardenweb.com/forums for an example of a message board. Check out www.linkedin.com for an example of a social networking site.

Read Your Customers' Minds

Beyond reaching people you might otherwise have never come in contact with, social networking sites and message boards give you the invaluable ability to read (literally), your customers' wants and needs. For years, companies have spent hundreds of thousands of dollars on consumer research in attempt to gain insight into what influences their customers' purchasing decisions—to discover what customers want, what they like and don't like about existing services, what they wish was possible, and what they prefer about your competitors. Social networking sites can provide this precious feedback in an easily accessible format (on your computer!). With the click of a mouse, you gain access to customers' innermost thoughts about you, as well as a variety of other topics that might help you fine-tune your products or services. Best of all, social networking sites and message boards afford you the opportunity to *respond* to their comments and give consumers what they really crave—genuine interaction and two-way conversation.

Booby Traps _____

No matter how enticing it seems, be sure you do more reading than posting when you participate in a social networking site or message board. Be a presence, but don't be a loudmouth. As in any other relationship, people like to talk about themselves a lot more than they like to hear about you. And too much selling may have the opposite effect on your customers. People are looking for an open forum of discussion, not an advertisement/commercial.

What might this look like in action? Imagine you run a dog grooming business and you read a post on the www.doggiechat.com message board praising your location and customer service, but expressing a desire to have the option of selecting the more potent tick-killing shampoo used by your competitor down the road. *Bam!* You can respond. Maybe this interaction inspires you to add to your product line, or maybe you have a good reason for not using the stronger shampoo. By posting a response, you can either educate customers about your choice of product (the stronger dog shampoo is harmful to dogs' health or the environment) or you can announce your expanded services (we're now offering spearmint shampoo!). Either way, you've responded directly to the customer, in plain view of other customers and potential customers. Connecting is what it's all about.

Here's the Buzz

Whenever you post on a message board or social networking site, be sure you fully disclose who you are. Providing your real full name, company, and title establish credibility. If you use a fake name, people may perceive you to be deceptive because you found it necessary to create a pseudonym. A clever screen name is fine, but be sure your real, complete company information is listed in your profile and with each and every post.

Why Is Community Marketing Effective?

People trust people more than they trust companies. And when people from a company interact with individual customers, it humanizes them and makes them more appealing. Consumers of today are generally distrustful of traditional marketing and advertising, so the closer you can get to a personal relationship the better. And what's great about the social networking model (in addition to the fact that it is free) is that by interacting one on one with just a few people, countless others observe this interaction. Even though they didn't directly interact with you, they can still share the experience and you can reap the benefits.

Here's the Buzz

When setting up profiles on different message boards and social networking sites, set up the same screen name whenever possible. People often visit multiple message boards and being recognizable gives you a leg up! This is another way to create a brand image for your company, your product, or your service.

Message Board/Forum Options

Message boards are referred to by many other names, including web forums, Internet forums, discussion groups, bulletin boards, discussion forums (as well as a few other combinations). Don't let it confuse you, it's all the same thing. Message boards and forums are communities in which your best customers become experts alongside you. It's not uncommon to see customers answering other customers' questions about your products/services on a message board. And because people often develop strong emotional bonds with other message board users, they often come back again and again, not only to discuss products, but also to connect with people they now consider to be friends.

Topics are most often divided into subcategories on message boards, making them a great way to cover a wide variety of topics in depth and in an organized fashion. As a business, you can do one of two things using message boards.

Intuit has one of the largest customer service oriented message board communities, which is hosted on its site at www.intuit.com/community. The boards support the company's various products: TurboTax, Quicken, and QuickBooks, as well as two forums for accountants and developers. By giving users a place to go and find immediate answers to questions both general and specific, Intuit decreases the strain on its human technical support team while simultaneously making its customers happier because they're more in control of getting the information they need. Best of all, the communities are open 24/7!

1. Become a member of an existing message board related to your field. For example, if you are a day spa, become an active member of a health and wellness message board. (Or better yet, be a member of several.) Start by answering people's questions, giving your expert opinion.

2. Create your own message board. If you are in an industry that requires substantial customer education, or one that is ripe with discussion topics, having your own message board may be the way to go. Having your own board also allows you to set guidelines to ensure the environment stays friendly.

Creating Your Own Message Board

Message board services broadly range from free, template-style services to paid services that are very robust and are much more customizable.

Free Message Boards

While there are many free message board setup services available, they require a moderate level of technical knowledge and are not easily customizable. They also don't provide the security or reliability of a paid service. In short, don't attempt this unless you feel confident about your level of technological skill, otherwise you could be headed for big-time frustration. If you want to give it a go and create your own message board, check out the following services that are free (or nearly free):

- Aceboard.net
- ActiveBoard.com
- Bestfreeforums.com
- BoardHost.com
- BoardServer.com
- Bravenet.com
- Conforums.com
- ezboard.com
- Forumhoster.com
- FreeForums.org
- GetFreeBB.com
- GoGetForum.com
- GreatBoard.com
- HWForums.org
- Hyperboards.com
- InvisionFree.com
- Jconserv.net
- LiveBoards.com
- MinuteBoard.com
- MyProBB.com
- Network54.com
- Onvix.com
- ProBoards.com
- RunBoard.com
- SuddenLaunch.com
- WebsiteToolbox.com
- WebringAmerica.com
- Yabbers.com

Before setting up your board, be prepared with a board name (usually between 3 and 20 characters), your username as admin, a category, and a description of your board. Be ready to create several topics to divide up your board content so things stay organized. And of course, you'll need to be armed with content you want to share. If you're an interior design firm, your topic headings might be "Completed Projects," "Upcoming Workshops," "Choosing a Style," "Budget Tips," and "Other Comments." When you launch, post either a short article about the topic as the first post, or enter a description of what's to come.

Hiring Someone to Create a Message Board

If you don't feel comfortable creating your own message board, it doesn't mean you have to abandon the idea of having one. Paid message board services often come in packages that contain various services and/or e-commerce tools, such as message board creation and community design, reskinning an existing board, hardware management, blog and chat capability, archiving services, board moderation (censoring language and keeping the community friendly), polling services, e-mail services, and much more. Expect a one-time set up fee that will vary based on the services you select and the size of your initial community. Monthly hosting and maintenance fees will grow based on the amount of users on the board. If you're interested in hiring a service, here's a great place to start:

- Invisionboard.com

- Lithium.com

- Xsorbit.com (also offers free and low-cost options)

Brainwaves

If you see a message board you like and want to find out how to create one like it, look for the "Powered by" box where you will find the company (whether free or paid) that created the board. Want to see an example? Check out the forum created by Lithium Technologies (www.lithium.com) for Playstation.com—http://boardsus.playstation.com/playstation. Scroll to the very bottom and you'll see "Powered by Lithium."

Social Networking Site Options

The more general social networking sites usually have specialty groups. Once you find a social networking site that best suits your needs, you can do one of two things:

1. Find a group related to your field. Within most social networks, you can find categories of groups or networks related to every topic imaginable. On MySpace, for example, categories of groups include business and entrepreneurs, computers, fashion, food, health and wellness, money and investing, pet and animals, professional organizations, and travel, just to name a few. And those are just the broad categories. Each of those categories can be broken down to even more specialized groups. If you offer accounting services, look under the money and investing category, and then dig down to find the group related to your field of expertise. Under money and investing, you'll find groups related to real estate, small business, stock, and so on. It may seem like a lot of layers, but these specialty groups are pretty easy to find and join. And keep in mind, many people and businesses are members of more than one social network. Just be sure you don't sign up for more than you can manage.

2. Start your own group, network, or club. If you don't find a group that suits your needs, you can create your own. The process varies by site, but you'll need to answer a few questions before getting started:

❏ Under what category will your group be listed?

❏ What group name will you use?

❏ Do you want your group to be open to the public or by invitation only? (Hint: you want yours to be public!)

❏ Will you allow members of your group to post images?

You'll also need to submit a short description of your group's purpose.

The following is a list of popular business-focused social networking sites:

◆ LinkedIn (linkedin.com)—LinkedIn is a community of more than nine million people from 130 industries. Basic LinkedIn business networking services are free, but they also offer enhanced services for a fee, including tools to find sales leads, new career opportunities, business partners, and industry experts.

◆ Ryze (ryze.com)—Ryze offers a free networking-oriented homepage and free access to special networks related to your industry, interests, or location. Ryze also offers paid services that give you advanced search capability. Ryze has 250,000 members in 200 countries.

◆ Soflow (soflow.com)—In Soflow you can set up your personal contacts and join "clubs" of professionals. The basic service is free, but you can purchase premium services including targeted advertising to members and press release posting, in addition to other tools to help increase your chances of connecting with the right people.

◆ Business Entrepreneur Networks (bizpreneur.com)—This network is great for small businesses and entrepreneurs. In addition to finding business contacts, you can search for funding, employees, and articles on business start ups.

◆ Tribe (tribe.net)—Tribe is an online community focused on connecting people to get things done. Tribe is not 100% business focused, but is centered on finding resources, particularly in larger cities.

◆ XING (xing.com)—XING (otherwise known as OpenBC) is an online community with a directory of business contacts and much more. XING members are able to find professional contacts and opportunities through its unique discovery capability and advanced contact management tools. XING manages tens of millions of member-to-member connections using 16 languages and all industries, with "real world" events held around the world.

◆ Ecademy (ecademy.com)—Based in the UK, this site is particularly useful for making international business contacts. In addition to networking, Ecademy offers business-building resources as well. Users have the option to purchase a limited or full membership. Ecademy has approximately 95,000 registered members.

Creating a Presence

Social networking site or message board? General or special interest? Before you decide where you want to set up camp, start by doing a Yahoo! and Google search on yourself. Whether you know it or not, people may already be talking about you. If they are, then that's where you should start!

Your Profile

Give special attention to the profile you create—it is vital to your success in using a message board or social networking site. Fill it out completely and invest the time it takes to make it great. Never, ever begin posting with just a shell of a profile. An incomplete profile says to other users: "I want to network with people for my purposes and I can't be bothered with telling you who I am." It's akin to crashing a party. And besides, the profile is your virtual business card. Be sure it paints the best possible picture of who you are. Put your best foot forward and don't go "live" until you've got your profile buttoned up.

Booby Traps

Don't use your company logo as your photo. It only makes people wonder what you look like, and what they imagine is most likely worse than reality. Unless you are selling something directly related to beauty or good looks, people don't expect you to look like a supermodel. The point of using a social networking site is to establish a personal connection and a visual of what you look like is essential to viewing you as real.

The following are some social networking site/message board rules and etiquette:

◆ Don't send out "friend" invitations without first introducing yourself. Sending invitations to people who have no idea who you are makes it appear you are desperate or disingenuous. Or selling something.

◆ If you read a negative comment about your product or service, keep defensiveness in check. Even if the post is outwardly hostile and clearly inflammatory, simply answer point by point and calmly explain your point of view. If you are in the wrong, give a sincere apology and explain how you'll ensure the issue is not repeated. Being defensive makes you sound guilty.

◆ Be very selective with your endorsements. Before you recommend a colleague, be absolutely sure that they can deliver the quality expected if called upon by your "friends."

> **Brainwaves**
>
> Don't make the mistake of thinking that the only comments that merit a response are the negative ones. Make your presence known online by thanking customers for posting their positive experiences. Tell them how much you appreciate them sharing their experience and you're sure to turn a pleased customer into a die-hard fan.

The Wave of the Future: Integrated Social Software

The use of social networking is likely to expand as companies figure out how to leverage the tools. Social networking can be used internally for project management purposes and to create a sense of community within an organization. Evidence IBM's announcement that they've developed the industry's first platform for business-grade social computing, called Lotus Connections. When it launches, Lotus Connections will offer an integrated bundle of social network tools such as blogging, bookmark sharing, user profiles, and other features that help business people exchange ideas and connect with experts across their organization.

It Worked for Them

Social networking can breathe new life into lagging businesses, or it can open up a whole new world of customers previously inaccessible.

"Weird Al" Yankovic

In July of 2006—after 12 albums and nearly 30 years in the music business—"Weird Al" Yankovic ventured into the digital universe. "Weird Al" told CNN that he had "kind of written off the chance of ever having another hit single, since record labels weren't really releasing commercial ones," but through the use of iTunes and a MySpace page (www.myspace.com/weirdal), "Weird Al" Yankovic achieved his first top 10 album and his first top 10 single. Yankovic manages his MySpace.com page himself and has personally added each and every friend, which now totals nearly half a million.

J.P. Morgan Chase

Through an agreement with Facebook, J.P. Morgan Chase gets to promote its credit card loyalty program directly to its target audience—college students. Facebook is a social networking site for colleges, universities, and now high school communities. By pairing up with Facebook, Chase is able to run banner ads throughout the social networking site that invite users to join a group page of people who want to learn about or sign up for Chase's new "+1" credit card. For referring other friends, users earn points which can be cashed in for various college-oriented prizes such as DVDs. The group page also includes tips on credit and spending. The company has also hired a force of "student influencers" to generate buzz and drive traffic to the Facebook group page.

The Least You Need to Know

- Before deciding where to create a presence, do some research to see if there are any social networking sites specifically related to your field of expertise.

- You can join more than one social networking site.

- Be sure to fill out your profile completely before posting online.

- You have to take the good with the bad. If you someone has posted something negative about your product or service, look at it as an opportunity for growth, and apologize when necessary.

Chapter 13

Social Marketing with Blogs and Podcasts

In This Chapter

- ◆ Blogging to create buzz
- ◆ Blogging basics for the nontechnical
- ◆ Best blogging benefits
- ◆ Podcasting basics

There's more to social marketing than social networking sites and message boards. Blogs, podcasts, and wikis are another way you can let the outside world into your little universe. (Don't panic: we'll define all these cyber terms as we go.) It's a big world, but technology is making it smaller and smaller. And it's easy to see that the inside scoop is what society seems to crave. Just look at the proliferation of reality TV shows, and you'll see that with each passing year, our society becomes more and more voyeuristic. People seem to really desire to know more about what life is like for other people. No, this doesn't mean you have to post a picture of yourself in your underwear. It just means you need to make a genuine connection so that readers can get a glimpse into your personal experience and inner thoughts.

What Is Social Marketing?

Social marketing is a catch-all term used to describe various methods of online communication. Blogs, message boards, podcasts, social networking sites and wikis—they're all social marketing.

Blogs

A blog (short for weblog) is a user-generated, online diary that allows readers to post comments on the material written by the author, otherwise known as the blogger. Blogs can be public (available to any websurfer) or private (made available only to those the blogger accepts or who subscribe). Blogs are subscribed to by readers using an *RSS feed*.

Blogs can be written by anyone, but the best bloggers are very knowledgeable about their subject material and have a flair for writing. But beware: blogging is not for the faint of heart. Blogs require a serious time commitment, both to write the blog and to manage user comments (and respond to those comments, and back and forth). Writing an effective and useful blog requires focused attention and a thick skin is recommended. You must truly be committed to authentic communication in order to be a successful blogger. And because the blogging environment is a community where bloggers comment on other bloggers, you'll need to devote some time to reading other blogs in order to be relevant. If you're still interested, read on …

def•i•ni•tion

An **RSS feed (Really Simple Syndication)** is a data format used to publish digital content such as blogs, news feeds, or podcasts that are updated frequently. Users can check their RSS feeds at any time to see if content has been updated.

Why Do Blogs Work?

Blogs work because you are, in essence, telling your customers that you will meet them on their playing field. By putting your thoughts out there and allowing customers to talk back to you, you've engaged in a level of communication that is deeper than the packaged messages they typically get from businesses. Hopefully, these exchanges lead to greater understanding. And hopefully, greater understanding will ultimately lead to more sales!

Reasons to write a blog:

◆ Establish your credibility

◆ Enhance communication with your customers

◆ Give customers an inside look at your business

◆ Create an authentic culture

◆ Announce and discuss changes

◆ Boost interest in what you have to offer

Before you get started writing, remember this valuable piece of advice: don't write anything down that you don't want printed in the newspaper. That's an old adage we live by that bears repeating: don't write anything down you don't want printed in the newspaper. What you write in a blog exists forever, so be sure you take this seriously. The point of your blog should be to establish your credibility as an expert, and educate customers about aspects of your business that they may not be familiar with.

> **Brainwaves**
>
> According to Technorati (www. technorati.com), an Internet blog search engine, there are more than 55 million blogs in the blogosphere (all blogs that exist on the Internet). And that number doubles every six months.

Blogging Hosting Services

The vast majority of blogs are created using free or paid blog hosting services such as:

◆ Blogger (www.blogger.com)

◆ LiveJournal (www.livejournal.com)

◆ Wordpress (http://wordpress.com)

◆ TypePad (www.typepad.com)

◆ Moveable Type (www.moveabletype.com)

◆ Vox (www.vox.com)

◆ Xanga (www.xanga.com)

Many other options exist—in fact, there are too many to name them all. If one of the above doesn't suit your needs, just search for "blog hosting service." You can also host your own blog, which gives you the benefit of having a dedicated URL with your own blog name, in addition to having your own e-mail that is much more professional than a Yahoo! or Hotmail account. If you have a relationship with a developer, or you have your own IT person on staff, ask him or her about setting it up. If you don't have a server but you are interested in learning more about hosting your own blog, find an individual or an agency that specializes in web development.

Here's the Buzz

Linkback (sometimes called Trackback, Pingback, or Refback) is a method that allows blog authors to receive notification when somebody links to one of their documents. For example, if someone comments on your blog in their blog they might provide a link to yours. A linkback allows you to be notified that someone has linked to your blog, which is important because it allows you to read and respond to bloggers who are talking about what you've written. Linkbacks allow you to keep track of what's going on that relates to you in the blogosphere.

A ping is an alert sent out to let blog readers know that a blog has been updated. The alert comes via RSS or Atom feed and is delivered directly to the desktop of people who have opted to receive the feed. Most blog authoring tools are set up to automatically ping one or more servers every time a new blog is created. Many bloggers also use ping services such as Ping-o-matic (pingomatic.com) to reach an even wider audience.

Linking in Blogs

When writing a blog, it is customary to link to information you've referenced in your blog. This allows users to delve further into the topic if they so desire. This boosts your credibility as a blogger because it demonstrates that you have done your homework and aren't misrepresenting the topic you are addressing. For example, at gadgetell.com, a blog that covers tech reviews, news, and other related things, blogger Doug Berger wrote a blog about their migration from "a customized installation of WordPress to ExpressionEngine." Users who do not know what WordPress is can click on the word and they are taken to http://wordpress.org, where they can read all about WordPress.

Anatomy of a Blog

There are many different parts to a blog, and not every blog contains all of the possible parts. Here's a list of some stuff you might find when browsing various blogs.

- ◆ Blog entries (also known as blog posts)—The most current blog entries are displayed at the top. *All* blogs have blog entries.

- ◆ Links inside blog entries—Within blog entries you will find links to websites that give more info on the topics the blogger writes about.

- ◆ A *blogroll*—This is a list of blogs that are of interest to the blogger.

- ◆ *Permalinks*—URLs that ensure resource information remains permanently available.

def•i•ni•tion

A **blogroll** is a list of blogs or other resources that the author finds relevant to the subject. Users who opt in are voluntarily signing up to receive e-mails that go out to large lists. Opting in happens when users give their permission to be included on a mass e-mail list.

Many blogs contain **permalinks**, or permanent reference points. These permalinks are URLs that allow the blog entry or other outside source to be viewed even after the source has been archived.

- ◆ Past blog posts—Many bloggers have a list of other posts they've written. This list could contain their most recent posts or posts of particular relevance to their blog topic. The list can be named anything they choose. It could be "recent posts" or "what it's all about," or "other stuff." Regardless of what it's named, it's a list of blog entries they've written in the past.

- ◆ Links list—Unlike links that are within a blog entry, this is a list of links to other websites that the blogger finds relevant. Often these are links to other organizations' websites or bloggers who have common interests.

- ◆ Comments—A blog isn't a blog without the ability for readers to post comments about what the blogger has written. That said, not every blog will have comments because, let's face it, some blogs are boring and there's nothing readers want to say about them. If there are comments, they could be listed via a link at the bottom of the blog entry, or they might appear in a list to the side of the entry.

◆ Archives—Past blog entries are usually organized by month and year and are accessible somewhere on the page.

◆ Subscription via e-mail—This allows users to enter their e-mail addresses so they can be notified via e-mail when the blogger writes something new. Many blogs don't have this feature and instead only allow subscriptions via some type of syndicated feed.

◆ E-mail list subscription—This is a separate area where users can opt in to the blogger's e-mail list to receive news from the blogger that is outside of the blog entry.

◆ Syndication—This is a method of subscribing for blog updates via an RSS feed.

◆ Blogs that link here—This shows all the blogs that are linked to the blog you are reading.

Comments

The reader's ability to post comments about what a blogger's written is a defining feature of a blog. Feedback is the name of the game here, and true personal interaction is required. If users cannot post comments to a blog, you could be damaging your reputation more than you are helping it because you will be considered inauthentic. After all, if you're only going to communicate in one direction, it would be easier to post your message on your website. This doesn't mean you can't put a system in place whereby you review comments before posting them, but you do need to be sure comments are reviewed and posted quickly, otherwise readers will question your censorship. What draws people to blogs is the promise of open and free communication. If it feels staged, you lose credibility.

Booby Traps _____

If you moderate the comments posted on your blog, understand that you must allow the negative comments along with the positive ones. A blog's only value is authentic two-way conversation, and if you aren't prepared to deal with someone disagreeing with you publicly, then a blog is not the direction to take. Keep in mind that if you do refuse to post a blogger's comments, he or she is likely to go blog about you somewhere else anyway. Wouldn't it be wiser to have them blogging where you at least have a chance to retort?

Why Do Blogs Work?

Just like the other social marketing methods, blogs work because today's consumers are tired of being fed marketing messages. They are smart, savvy folks fully capable of making their own decisions if given all the facts.

For a business, the purpose of a blog should be to enhance your credibility and to give your customers a peek behind the scenes. Successful blogs are both informative and amusing to read. They are updated on a fairly regular basis, although this can vary based on the quality of a blog. While small- to medium-size companies might use blogs to spark an interest in their brand by engaging in meaningful discussion, more established brands most often use blogs to enhance a connection with a distant audience they've lost touch with. And remember, blogs are personal and are written by human beings. Having a "company-written" blog doesn't enhance connection, because it doesn't humanize you. Also important: whoever is writing the blog should identify himself or herself. You can have several people from a company contributing to one blog, as long as each blogger is identified.

> ### Brainwaves
>
> Several forward-thinking executives have gotten in on blogging, which is still a very new form of communication. Bob Lutz, Vice Chairman of General Motors, writes a blog and he's just one of several GM executives who blog at the GM FastLane Blog (fastlane.gmblogs.com). Blogs written by CEOs or company leaders work wonders to break down barriers between the consumer and the corner office.

Blogging benefits:

- Because they aren't sent through e-mail (they use RSS feeds), blogs bypass spam filters.

- At times, the blogosphere reports ahead of the national media, and it is being increasingly viewed as the place to go for up-to-date, first-person accounts of current events. That was the case with the horrific tsunami in Thailand. Bloggers who were on site sent pictures and descriptions as the disaster unfolded.

- Blogs give you a soapbox on which to make your case. You can speak in depth on a specific topic. In fact, it's really best to stay focused on a particular topic. Whatever your expertise is, share your knowledge about that specified topic.

◆ Blogs have been credited with enhancing the excitement surrounding a live event. Whether it be an internal company meeting or a public event, blogs can get people revved up and energized for an upcoming in-person gathering. Gameworld Network actually featured live blog coverage of a Nintendo Press Conference in Toyko. Minute by minute bloggers reported details of the press conference, giving readers nearly instantaneous access to the live event.

Blogs Create Customer Loyalists

The companies that use blogs to generate authentic interaction with their customers undoubtedly find that these people become their biggest fans and advocates. Wouldn't you rather do business with a company that you feel a personal connection with than one you don't? The fact is, many people admire those who are not afraid to speak the truth publicly, whether they agree with them or not. To many, the mere act of honest conversation is more important than the minor details of your product differentiation.

Tagging

Tagging is a system whereby bloggers can label and retrieve data using tags, or keywords, they assign to other blogs, web pages, photographs, and other web content. The point of tagging is to make stuff easier to find and share. There are several tagging systems.

◆ Flickr (flickr.com)—A service that allows users to tag images using keywords of their choosing.

◆ Del.icio.us (del.icio.us)—Users bookmark sites and tag them with descriptive words.

◆ YouTube (www.youtube.com)—A tagging system for video files.

◆ Technorati—A weblog search engine. Blog posts are tagged either via blog software that supports categories and RSS/Atom feeds, or via code written into the body of your post. Technorati pulls images from Flickr and video files from YouTube.

Why Tag?

One simple reason: because with each passing day, more and more information is created and posted on the Internet. By marking web content with various labels, the content is classified for other users to find. Also called social bookmarking, tagging is increasing in popularity as people on both sides of the blogosphere are realizing the benefits. Tags allow blog readers to mark, store, and retrieve web content. Conversely, tags allow bloggers to categorize their own content and feed the tags into alert services, which then notify users that an associated blog exists. Technorati, for example, is a service that allows users to search blogs for content of interest to them. Many other online services are beginning to see the advantage of tagging. Amazon.com, for example, is beginning to use tagging by pulling the 100 most frequently used words in a book (excluding common words like "of" and "it"). These words are then displayed as a tag cloud and users can click on the tagged word and see all sentences using that word displayed. This is called tagging in a concordance feature.

Uses for tags:

◆ Subscribe to tags via RSS that are related to your brand or industry.

◆ Detect trends by viewing the most popular tag.

◆ Tag your blog or other web content at one of the tagging sites described here. Create your own tag if an appropriate one does not already exist.

◆ Post press releases to your blog and tag them individually, in addition to the tag for your entire blog.

Here's the Buzz

Web 2.0 is a new catch phrase. It was coined in 2004 by O'Reilly Media, in collaboration with MediaLive International. They used the phrase Web 2.0 as the title for a series of conferences. The phrase encapsulated the idea that there is a second generation of web-based services that emphasize collaboration and sharing among users. This second generation includes social networking sites, wikis, communication tools, and folksonomies (user-generated taxonomy for categorizing web content). Since the initial Web 2.0 conferences, the Web 2.0 catch-phrase took hold and is now cited nearly 10 million times by Google alone.

It Worked for Them

There are a variety of ways to measure blogging success—monitoring the number of visitors and comments, how many link requests you're getting, how many feed subscriptions you're receiving—the list goes on and on. In Chapter 22 we'll delve into the precise measurements, but for now, let's take a look at these obvious success stories.

Stonyfield Farms

Stonyfield Farms began blogging in 2004 to continue to connect with its already loyal customer base and to increase awareness about its yogurt products, as well as general health issues. It seems to be working. Stonyfield Farms has two blogs that are visited thousands of times each day. Its blogs center on two topics: children's health and organic farming. The "Baby Babble" blog is written by Stonyfield Farms employees who have children. In the blog they discuss a variety of topics that relate to children's development—not strictly those related to yogurt. Its other blog, the "Bovine Bugle" is written by Jonathan Gates, an organic dairy farmer in Vermont, one of the many farmers whose milk products are used to create Stonyfield Farms yogurt products. Interestingly, in his blog, he just discusses his day-to-day life and is obviously not restricted to blogging about things related to organic farming—one blog is centered around making boxes for barn cats, another recounts a recent skiing adventure. This method is incredibly effective when it comes to connecting with readers. If Jonathan wrote only about organic farming, it would make him seem very one-dimensional, and therefore less appealing.

Brainwaves

Adobe used blogging and podcasting in a unique way to announce their new Creative Suite 3. In March 2007, via a PR blog, Adobe revealed that Adobe Creative Suite 3 would be announced on March 27, 2007. Even though it was only a preannouncement, the blog immediately generated buzz. It was picked up by other bloggers and spread around the blogosphere. Adobe Creative Suite 3 didn't ship until spring, but the blog enticed users to join in for a live webcast and podcast detailing the product's features and configurations.

The Yankee Blog Swap

Unhappy with the capabilities of traditional blogging platforms, RSS Pieces, Inc., a blog hosting and publishing company based in Cape Coral, Florida, built its own patent pending blog platform called "Diachronics." It performs search engine optimization on content using RSS syndication tools and podcasting technology "for guaranteed increases in search engine results." Soon after a Realtor friend contacted RSS Pieces to create a blog and it identified a niche market need—a blog solution for the real estate industry. Thus myRealtyBlog was born.

In late 2006, Mary McKnight at RSS Pieces, Inc., had the brilliant idea to do a Yankee Swap (traditionally a gift exchange party game) with a few of her closest real estate friends. Next thing she knew, many serious contenders in real estate were interested in participating. Two of the biggest names in real estate blogging—Zillow.com and Redfin—got involved and the first annual Yankee Blog Swap was underway. The swap brought together 32 of the most influential real estate bloggers who agreed to be randomly selected to swap blogs for the day. This was a win-win situation for everyone involved—it generated new networking opportunities and exposure to a wider audience for the bloggers; for readers, it increased the knowledge base and depth of information provided. Today at www.yankeeblogswap.com real estate bloggers can come to participate in swapping events, or they can submit their names for guest blog spots. What's even more genius about the idea is how much buzz the swap created for RSS Pieces!

Podcasts

A podcast is a media file distributed via the Internet for playback on mobile devices and personal computers. Podcasting is offered via subscription, meaning users opt to hear the podcasts, either for free or for a fee. Simply put, a podcast is a prerecorded solo session, similar to a recorded radio show, in which the podcaster determines the subject matter or content.

A podcast can vary in production size and budget. It can be a monologue delivered by glancing at your thinking points, or an entirely scripted presentation. They vary in the size and cost of production based on the number of people participating. A solo performance or conversation between two people could be recorded using minimal equipment and set up, while a musical performance by many would require extra microphones and a mixer or other equipment.

What are a podcast's practical applications? Because many people listen to podcasts as informative entertainment, if you are the expert in a field and you feel comfortable discussing your topic, you can educate people on a topic related to your business. For example, if you are a landscaper, you might create a podcast about gardening, explaining how and when to plant certain shrubs or flowers.

If you're looking for an example of podcasting, Whole Foods offers a slew of them on its website (www.wholefoods.com). For its broadcasts, it enlists the help of various experts. They cover a wide variety of topics including:

- Cast Iron Cookware and Catfish
- The Buzz on Honey

♦ All About Chocolate

♦ All About Tea

♦ All Multivitamins Are Not Created Equal

♦ New Year's Entertaining and Holiday Green Mission Tips

Creating a Podcast

Podcasts usually require a bit of technical knowledge to accomplish, and you may need to purchase additional equipment or software for your computer. You'll need a microphone, which can be built into the computer or attached separately, and some sort of podcasting software such as GarageBand or Audacity. New iMac computers have a built in microphone, which will save you the cost of that piece of equipment. iMac computers also come with iTunes, which is a great program that allows you to listen to and organize your songs and podcasts. Windows Vista offers Windows Media Player 11 including MTV's URGE music service (in the United States only).

Podcasts are shared in MP3 format. You can share your thoughts, discuss your future plans, have a panel discussion, sing a song, or put on your own audio play. You can be the star of your own *American Idol* show! There are no limits to what you can broadcast. It doesn't have to be a sound-stage quality show, but if you are recording multiple people, make sure the audio is properly recorded. If you aren't showcasing your own musical ability, you can choose prerecorded music, or some other kind of soundscape. Just be careful not to misuse commercial music or impinge on copyrighted material.

If you're still confused, you can give yourself a crash course in podcasting, either by reading in-depth descriptions of podcasting elements for yourself at podwagon.com, or by viewing paid online tutorials at schoolofpodcasting.com. Or you could probably just ask your nine-year-old nephew.

Here's the Buzz

Select specific music or sound effects that will be identified with you and your podcast. It's an easy way to brand yourself and your product.

Why Podcasts Work

Podcasts allow listeners to receive your message at the time when they are most receptive—namely, the time they pick to listen! Because they are portable, users can download your podcast and take it with them to listen to at their leisure. Whether

10 minutes or two hours, your podcasts should be enjoyable and informative. By their very nature, podcasts are also personal, because people can hear your voice inflexions and intonations. It's another way to connect with your customers. Podcasts should be no longer than 45 minutes and no shorter than 10 minutes.

It Worked for Them

FX Network's new show, *The Riches*, featuring Eddie Izzard and Minnie Driver on FX Network, is using podcasting in a truly unique way (fxnetworks.com/theriches). If you're a fan, you can visit their website and go to the community section, where you'll find fan podcasts. After filling in your pertinent info (name, e-mail, phone number, and so on), you can indicate that you'd like to be included in fan podcasts. The system then calls your telephone, where you are offered the ability to record your message (and re-record if you mess up). Fans can either leave general messages to be added to a list of fan podcasts, or they can record an interview question for Eddie Izzard, Minnie Driver, or another cast member.

The Least You Need to Know

- Blogging is a relatively new form of communication that is gaining popularity very quickly.

- There are many places you can begin blogging for free.

- Blogging requires a significant time commitment.

- Blogging can be very effective at creating a bond with your target audience.

- Podcasts are effective because listeners can tune in when it's convenient for them.

- Because podcasts are one-way communication, they're best used when you have lots of information to share from your expert perspective.

14

Somebody's Watching Me: Mobile and Proximity Marketing

In This Chapter

◆ What's your number? Mobile marketing

◆ Proximity marketing basics

◆ Bluetooth technology and devices

◆ Getting people to opt in

It's 8 A.M. and you've just sat down at your desk with a cup of coffee. You open up your e-mail to see what lies ahead for the day, when you're bombarded by 34 unsolicited messages offering you everything from college degrees to things that would make a sailor blush. Sound familiar? It's the onslaught of e-mail spam, and it affects everyone with an e-mail account. It's estimated that more than 90 billion spam messages are sent every single day. When you receive spam as a result of where you live or something you've purchased, do you ever feel like someone is watching you? What if you received the same amount of spam every day, but it happened every time you turned on your mobile phone?

We all know that e-commerce is a growing field with new online retail outlets popping up daily. With so many Americans online for a substantial portion of the day, it makes sense that marketers have shifted their focus to online marketing, often with great success. Marketers are always looking for the newest thing. So, what's next?

Mobile Marketing

The term mobile marketing refers to marketing on a mobile device—usually a telephone or a personal digital assistant (PDA)—not to be confused with a public display of affection (although, some people do love their mobile devices!). It's hard to put an exact number on it but there are somewhere between 2 and 2.5 billion mobile phones worldwide. That means that approximately one-third of the world's citizens own one. In the United States alone, an estimated 200 million people own and use mobile telephones. The prevalence of mobile phones in eastern and western countries and developed and less developed countries is a marketer's dream.

Mobile marketing first popped up in Europe and Asia where *SMS* messaging gained popularity in the early 2000's. Since then, the popularity of SMS messaging has grown exponentially. It is still most popular in Asian countries, followed by European countries, and lastly, the United States. It is gaining popularity quickly Stateside, however, albeit more slowly than the other locations.

def•i•ni•tion

SMS stands for short message service, a technology which allows users to send a text message via their mobile telephone or PDA. The message must be less than 160 characters. Most often, SMS messaging is used between individuals.

Note to readers: There is another kind of mobile marketing—the kind where your marketing efforts are mobile, meaning they travel from place to place. This kind of mobile marketing is the kind you receive on a mobile device.

It's Your Choice

Mobile marketing generally refers to marketing using SMS messaging. Because mobile phone numbers are currently not published in a public directory, marketers have had to develop schemes in which the consumer voluntarily "opts into" the promotion and initiates the contact with the marketer. In doing so, they give their mobile contact information to the marketer. An example of this is an advertisement in a fashion magazine for a popular laundry detergent. The advertisement features photographs and fashion tips from a well-known celebrity stylist in Hollywood. To receive more tips from the stylist, the user sends an SMS message to the number published in the ad. In turn, she'll receive weekly tips from the stylist and (surprise, surprise) promotions from the detergent company. Because the user gave the detergent company her contact information in exchange for something the customer perceived to be of value, the customer opted into the promotion and chose to receive future marketing content from the detergent company.

When mobile marketing was first introduced, it was heavily criticized as being yet another type of electronic spam. However, it has quickly become accepted and assimilated into today's digital culture, particularly in Europe and Asia, although it is growing in the United States. Today, several hundred million marketing SMS messages are sent out every month.

The following are types of SMS mobile marketing campaigns:

◆ Promotional Communication (Pull Campaign)—Like our laundry promotion example, this type of mobile marketing "pulls" the consumer in with some kind of promotion. It works like this: customers are given a number to text to receive information or enter a contest. The customer initiates the contact with the marketer.

◆ CRM—Using mobile marketing to offer your best customers enhanced service or an extra perk is called a CRM, or customer relationship management, mobile marketing campaign. An airline might send frequent passengers updated flight information, or a restaurant could offer a coupon for a free appetizer to people who have dined there more than three times.

◆ B2E—This stands for business-to-employee. This type of marketing is primarily internal. It's a great way for a company, large or small, to make announcements to their employees or facilitate promotions and contests.

◆ Outbound (Push Campaign)—This is the direct mail version of mobile marketing. In a push campaign, a marketer sends SMS messages to all the contact numbers in his or her database. Push campaigns are the gray area in mobile marketing. They have the most potential to be regarded as spam.

Who's Using Mobile Marketing

In the fall of 2005, Dove launched its successful "Campaign for Real Beauty," showcasing photography and video of women of all ages, races, shapes, and sizes. In addition to the campaign imagery, billboards in New York and Los Angeles also provided a number that passersby could key into their mobile phones to vote on their favorite graphics and photographs. The votes were tallied and results were transmitted and broadcast in real time on a huge screen in Times Square. Leaving no stone unturned, Dove also incorporated social marketing methods by inviting consumers to visit the Dove website to speak their minds in online discussions of the meaning of beauty. This highly successful campaign garnered tons of media attention and was responsible for a huge boost in traffic on the Dove website.

Only for Teenagers?

Don't be fooled into thinking that mobile marketing is reserved for an exclusively younger demographic, although they do certainly make up the majority of SMSers. In the Spring of 2007, drug manufacturer Pfizer used a mobile marketing campaign to promote Lipitor, a popular cholesterol-lowering prescription medication used by 26 million Americans, primarily middle-age. Pfizer cleverly cultivated buy-in by placing posters that advertised coupons for trial drugs in doctors' offices. To receive the drugs, patients had to call a phone number and request coupon delivery to their mobile phones. The coupons were sent exclusively via digital methods, although they could be redeemed at any pharmacy. Pfizer wisely set up the promotion so that patients had to initiate contact with it; therefore, any messaging from Pfizer could not be seen as unsolicited junk mail. (And now it has contact info for future promotions.)

Pharmaceutical and cosmetic giant Johnson & Johnson targeted a younger audience using mobile marketing during the 2006 MTV Video Music Awards. During the show, it broadcast an advertisement urging viewers to text in to be entered into a contest to win a trip to the 2007 MTV Video Music Awards. In addition, entrants received a coupon for a free trial of Acuvue contact lenses. 70,000 viewers responded to the advertisement for the contact lenses. Not a bad return on investment if you ask us.

It's important to note that in all three of these examples, the consumer actively chose to receive the marketing content. Having the consumer opt in is what differentiates this type of marketing from spam.

Who Called Whom?

There is mobile spam out there. Some companies are giving out mobile phone numbers they receive from customers or worse yet, they're selling them. There is a distinct difference between effective, permission-based mobile marketing and mobile spam. A 2006 study by the Associated Press and AOL reported that 35% of mobile phone owners use text messaging and that 18% of mobile phone owners have received unwanted text messages. The Mobile Marketing Association (MMA) requires that all SMS marketing be permission-based and opt-in; however, not all marketers follow the rules.

Keep in mind that unlike e-mail, the majority of mobile device subscribers pay a separate charge for SMS messages sent and received. That means that subscribers are being charged for unsolicited SMS or spam messages! How infuriating is that? In 2006, there was a case brought by UCAN against large wireless carrier Sprint PCS involving sending subscribers SMS advertising content and subsequently charging them for it. The case was settled with Sprint agreeing to stop sending unsolicited advertising messages to subscribers. Nothing could turn a potential customer away from you faster than asking them to pay for something they don't want. That's why it's always good to send to people who have opted in and to send them something of value.

Follow the Rules

Always follow the rules when it comes to mobile marketing. If you're unsure of the guidelines, here are a few resources to check out:

- ◆ Utility Consumers' Action Network (UCAN)—A consumer group that exists to monitor mobile spam. For more information on this group, visit its website at www.ucan.org.

- ◆ Mobile Marketing Association (MMA)—An international industry group devised to promote mobile marketing. It has established guidelines for mobile marketers with the intention of regulating the fast-changing and expanding field. Find guidelines and other information at www.mmaglobal.com.

- ◆ Interactive Advertising Bureau (IAB)—An organization created to promote and regulate Internet advertising. The IAB's website, www.iab.net, offers a host of resources.

Pros and Cons of Mobile Marketing

Does mobile marketing sound appealing to you? Here are the pros and cons so you can make an educated decision.

Pros:

◆ Inexpensive—Marketers do have to pay the SMS charges associated with sending messages, but compared to many other methods of advertising, the costs are relatively small.

◆ Frequency—Mobile marketing campaigns allow companies to "touch" their consumers with relative frequency. If the consumer opts in and chooses to receive content from the marketer, then the marketer can send frequent content and stay at the top of the consumer's mind.

◆ Database building—In order to receive any content from a company, consumers have to give the companies their mobile phone numbers. Once a company has those mobile numbers, it can build a database with them for future marketing and promotions.

Cons:

◆ Limited usage—While SMS messaging is growing in the United States, it still has a long way to go until it is as widely used as other forms of communications. While it is definitely possible to target older audiences, on the whole it's a younger, more urban demographic that is fluent with the technology. (That fact is constantly changing, though!)

◆ Spam factor—Even if you initiate a pull campaign and your targeted customers choose to give you their mobile number, if you send them too much content or messages that don't offer enough value, as time goes on, the consumers eventually forget they "opted in" and they view your messages as spam. Be careful.

Proximity Marketing

Imagine walking through the mall, and as you approach The Gap, you receive a message on your mobile phone for a coupon for 10% off any purchase that day at the store. Sound like something from the futuristic movie, *Minority Report*? Or think about being at a rock concert, and while you're waiting for it to begin, you receive an SMS message on your PDA with a link to an interview with one of the band members. Coincidence? No. It's *proximity marketing*.

def•i•ni•tion

In a nutshell, **proximity marketing** refers to geo-targeted advertising and marketing using Bluetooth technology. Proximity marketing is a new, cutting-edge medium that is currently only practiced in limited areas. You may not have heard much about proximity marketing (sometimes called location marketing), but you will in the future. We guarantee it.

What Is Bluetooth Technology?

Bluetooth Technology enables electronic devices to connect and sync with each other wirelessly within a short range using a small, embedded radio transmitter and receiver. The earliest application of this technology was wireless communication between a hands-free headset and a mobile phone. Using a Bluetooth adapter, your computer can "talk" to your printer and other devices wirelessly. Common Bluetooth-enabled devices are mobile phones, digital cameras, digital media players, PDAs, and computers. Bluetooth operates on low power and a high frequency which means there are no proven negative side effects resulting from long-term exposure.

Bluetooth was developed by the Bluetooth Special Interest Group, backed by IBM, Motorola, Nokia, Intel, and Microsoft, and hundreds of other member companies. Their goal was to develop a wireless technology that would allow different devices from different companies to exchange data. Imagine if you had to use a Nokia device to sync your Nokia phone with your headset, and an HP device to sync the information on your laptop to your PDA. You would spend your life juggling myriad electronics!

According to the Bluetooth Special Interest Group, at the end of 2006, there were 1 billion Bluetooth-enabled devices worldwide, with 12 million shipping each week. So, while we're not seeing too much Bluetooth marketing right now, with this kind of growth, we will be soon!

So How Does Bluetooth Work with Marketing?

Each Bluetooth-enabled mobile device has a unique identification code—like a PIN number—that allows it to be identified and connected to other devices. Certain companies that specialize in proximity marketing have developed servers that can detect when a Bluetooth device is within a certain range (500 feet, 100 feet, and so on). When the device is in range, the server checks the ID code and sends relevant information to the device. So, let's say that Anna is walking down a busy street. When she gets within 50 feet of John's Coffee Shop, she receives a message on her Bluetooth device asking if she'd like more content and coupons from John's. At this point, she can either say "no" and continue right by John's or she can opt in and receive the content.

The server is very small and runs off standard power. It can be plugged into an Ethernet or WiFi connection to be accessed remotely.

One of the most appealing aspects of Bluetooth marketing is the variety of content that can be sent. Depending on the capability of the user's device, it can receive ring tones, video, static images, coupons, bar codes, and games. And that's just for starters. The possibilities really are endless, depending on the mobile device's screen and capabilities.

Can You Turn Off These Messages?

In order for a server to recognize the ID code of a device, the user must have the device switched to "discoverable." If the user does not wish to be found, he or she can simply turn their Bluetooth to "invisible" and they will be invisible to marketers. So, Anna could choose to have her Bluetooth device set to invisible, in which case John's Coffee would never detect her in range to send her information and she could stroll down the street completely undisturbed. Many users are not aware this setting exists, which is one reason proximity marketing is gaining popularity. As people discover how to "become invisible," marketers will have to place a lot of focus on offering something so valuable that people will want to keep themselves discoverable.

Here's the Buzz

Bluejacking refers to unsolicited messages sent via Bluetooth to mobile devices. Usually a "bluejacked" phone displays a text message that the user doesn't know how he or she received.

It Worked for Them: Coldplay

Every day mobile marketing and proximity marketing campaigns are gaining in popularity.

In 2005, the popular band Coldplay was getting ready to debut its third album.

Coming off the wild success of the first two albums, its label knew that the launch of *X&Y* had to be splashy and memorable. The label approached Filter UK to coordinate a massive Bluecasting campaign in London to build buzz for the upcoming release. Filter installed large television screens in several busy London Underground and train stations. The TV screens promoted the album, playing clips of songs, cuts from music videos, and interviews with the members of the band. The screens encouraged commuters in the area to switch their Bluetooth devices to "discoverable" so they could receive more content about the album launch. If they did so, when they were within 100 meters (roughly 300 feet) of the television monitors, they received a message on their device asking if they would like to receive more Coldplay content. If they opted in, they received more video and audio footage from the new album.

The servers detected 87,000 unique Bluetooth devices, out of which an astounding 13,000 opted to receive the Coldplay content, which included music clips, photographs, and video. That's a 15 percent return rate—pretty incredible for direct marketing!

The Coldplay case is one of the largest and best-known case studies but many other companies have used Bluetooth proximity marketing.

Bluetooth Marketing Benefits

There are a lot of benefits to Bluetooth marketing. Some of the more obvious ones are:

- **Cost effective**—After the initial investment for the server, a company can send limitless messages for a very low cost. Perfect for a guerrilla marketer's budget.

- **Ability to target very specific markets**—Bluetooth servers have the ability to build a profile of users over time and continued usage. Consequently, marketers can develop very specific messaging to different consumers

- **Right here, right now relevance**—Because the Bluetooth messaging is almost instant, there is no delay for marketers to publicize their message. Marketing messages can hit a consumer right at the moment he or she is in the spot to make a purchasing decision. With Bluetooth marketing, you can almost guarantee that your targeted customer is geographically near you.

- **High-tech factor**—Because proximity marketing is still fairly new, there is an element of surprise built into it that isn't in many marketing media. Consumers haven't been exposed to much of this marketing and when they first are, there is a "wow" factor that is hard to achieve with today's jaded consumer.

◆ **Viral element**—Because Bluetooth users can easily share information with each other, it's more of a possibility that they'll share marketing content that is sent to them. This kind of viral spread can only help a marketer!

◆ **Direct mail for out of home**—Today's digital communication world means that no matter where you are, you can be in touch—with your office, your family, and with marketers. E-billing has largely replaced paper billing; e-mail has largely replaced mail. It stands to reason that there will be a new substitute for the popular direct mail. Proximity marketing delivers a solution via which marketers can target consumers who are out of their homes. And, with less paper wasted, it's better for the environment!

◆ **Multi-tasking with your wireless device**—Worldwide, more and more people have wireless devices on their person at all times. Multitasking has become a part of our culture, whether we like it or not. Increasingly, our multitasking devices are Bluetooth enabled. Proximity marketing gives consumers a forum in which to use their wireless devices in different ways.

Drawbacks to Proximity Marketing

Along with all the benefits of proximity marketing, there are some drawbacks as well. A few of those are:

◆ **Is it spam?**—Even though users have the ability to opt in and out of receiving content, marketers' initial contact with targets is unsolicited. Many Bluetooth users may want their mobile devices set to "discoverable" so that other users can detect them, but they may very well not want to receive solicitations which they may find annoying. This annoyance variable is always a concern with any kind of unsolicited direct mail.

◆ **Consumer backlash**—Just like with SMS mobile marketing, too much contact with a consumer can get annoying and people can feel like they're being interrupted in their daily lives. Be mindful of how often you target people.

◆ **The Big Brother effect**—There are people out there who just don't want to feel every move they make is being tracked. Messages should be worded carefully so that customers don't feel watched or stalked!

◆ **Not everyone has Bluetooth**—Although the number of Bluetooth users is growing quickly, there is still a limited number of people who use it. Because of this, there's a limited market for this type of marketing. It's certainly likely that the number of users will continue to increase at a rapid pace; however, technologies have a lifespan, and it's hard to tell how long Bluetooth will be a hot commodity.

Booby Traps

We hear horror stories about hackers on the Internet all the time. Well, guess what? Now hackers have found a way to get into your Bluetooth device. Any device set to "discoverable" can potentially be hacked into by someone with the know-how and lack of scruples to do it. They can then steal calendar and contact information and anything else you may have stored. So be careful what you store on your Bluetooth device, and consider your environment before having your device set to "discoverable." Although "bluesnarfing" is pretty rare, it's out there and could be on the rise.

I Want Bluetooth, What Do I Do?

Many computers, mobile phones, and PDAs come with Bluetooth functionality already installed on them, and in this case, you're ready to go. If your phone is Bluetooth enabled, all you have to do is buy a headset, something you can get fairly inexpensively from your wireless carrier. Once you've purchased the hardware, there are no additional charges beyond your standard minute plan to use the Bluetooth. If your computer has Bluetooth capability, it should pick up on other Bluetooth devices you have if you go through the detection mode.

If you have a device that is not Bluetooth enabled and you wish to install Bluetooth, you just need an adapter, which you can get from any major electronics retailer.

How to Make It Work

The most successful proximity marketing campaigns deliver something of value to the consumer. Consumers are far more likely to be receptive to unsolicited marketing if they're getting something of value. Take the Coldplay case study as an example because it produced unprecedented positive feedback. Commuters in London were offered exclusive previews of the upcoming album if they participated in the marketing effort. They perceived the content not as advertising, but as a benefit to them.

Some of the most important things to remember with this type of marketing involve basic common courtesy. Remember:

◆ **Be mindful of your environment**—There are times when proximity marketing is appropriate and there are times when it's not. The last thing you want to do is annoy any potential customers, so be careful about when and where you use it.

♦ **Ask permission**—Before you send people information, get their permission. It will only backfire if you don't.

♦ **Give and take**—If people are willing to let you contact them via Bluetooth, give them something that's worth their while. An advertisement with no special promotion, coupon, or tip isn't. Self-centered marketing can cause consumer resentment.

> **Brainwaves**
>
> Do you have a new product or service that you could give customers a "sneak preview" of before its regular launch? What about piloting something new with a select group of customers? People love to be the first to know, so this is a great way to build some excitement about what you have to offer.

With mobile phone usage and ownership growing rapidly worldwide, and consumers spending more time away from their home or office connected wirelessly, the allure of proximity marketing will continue to grow. There are threats and pitfalls with any type of marketing, but those seem to be outweighed by the large number of benefits. In the end, consumers will decide if the coupons, promotions, announcements, and information are relevant enough that they don't mind feeling like someone is watching them.

The Least You Need to Know

♦ You must send valuable content when you send mobile marketing messages or use proximity marketing.

♦ Ask permission before you send messages of any kind using Bluetooth.

♦ Mobile marketing sends text messages to large groups wherever they are. Proximity marketing sends messages to people within a geographical area.

♦ People have to pay to receive text messages so use restraint in the frequency of messages you send.

You've Got Mail: E-Mail Marketing

In This Chapter

- ◆ Rules of e-mail marketing
- ◆ What makes e-mail marketing work?
- ◆ eNewsletter writing and publishing
- ◆ Getting around spam filters

Can you imagine your life without e-mail? If the answer is no, you're not alone! Our world is becoming increasingly digitized and people are spending large portions of their days in front of computers. More and more people are relying on e-mail as their primary form of communication. In fact, studies have shown that the more influential and connected people are, the more frequently they use e-mail to communicate and stay in touch with people. That means that there are millions of e-mail users out there whom you can target for your business! If you haven't taken the plunge into e-mail marketing—or at least dipped your foot in the water—there's an ocean of possibilities awaiting you.

Effective E-Mail Communication

Whether you enlist the help of a bulk e-mail service or you do it yourself, your e-mail campaign can't be successful if people don't open your e-mails. That's why priority number one must be creating a message that will compel recipients to open it. Fortunately, a lot of information has been gathered on the topic.

Many people get upwards of 100 e-mail messages each day. The faster they can tell what your message is about, the more likely they are to prioritize it and read it. Using a topic-specific subject line also helps readers find your e-mail if they need to refer back to it. When you make someone's life easier, they appreciate it.

Beyond being honest, be crystal clear. Don't try to hide the fact that you're promoting something. If your e-mail is deceptive in any way—no subject, a fake "reply," a friendly greeting implying it's someone the recipient knows—the chances are high that it may be deleted before it's even opened. In fact, many e-mail users are so vigilant about spam, that they may report your message to their e-mail server. If that happens, all future messages from you could be blocked. So don't be shy about who you are and what you're sending. Just make them an offer they can't refuse. Here's how:

> **Good e-mail marketing:**
>
> From: Paul's Pizza
> Subject line: Special offers this week at Paul's
>
> **Bad e-mail marketing:**
>
> From: Paul
> Subject: Hope to see you soon.

Booby Traps

To be in compliance with the CAN-SPAM Act of 2003, all e-mails must have: a valid "from" address, the ability for users to unsubscribe or opt out, the physical mailing address included in the e-mail, and a descriptive "subject" line. In addition, all unsubscribe requests must be processed within 10 business days.

Paul, pizza parlor owner, may indeed "hope to see you soon" (preferably in his restaurant ordering a lot of pizza) but he isn't straight up in conveying that. From his message, the e-mail recipient and future customer could be confused into thinking that Paul is a long lost friend contacting him after 25 years. Imagine how irritated he'll be to open the e-mail and realize that Paul isn't an old friend but someone trying to sell him a pizza.

The following are rules for effective e-mail marketing:

◆ **Get in the address book**—Spam filters are the enemy of every e-mail marketing campaign. One way to avoid being snagged is by getting into recipients' address books. Use every opportunity to remind users to white list your ISP and/or add your e-mail to their address books.

◆ **Be professional**—Unless you're instant messaging your buddies, avoid abbreviations. Not everyone is familiar with the latest slang. It's also best to avoid smiley faces or other emoticons. Take the time to check your spelling and make sure your message makes sense.

◆ **R-E-S-P-E-C-T**—Write in a respectful and friendly manner and remember the magic words—please and thank you. Pay attention to the tone of your e-mail. You do not want to come across as angry and demanding.

 Here's the Buzz _____

If you are unsure about whether the tone of your e-mail is appropriate, have a friend or colleague read it. Without the help of body language and voice infliction, your tone can often be misinterpreted. Better safe than sorry.

◆ **Be succinct**—Unless you are writing a friend to catch up, e-mail is not the time for lengthy ramblings. Be polite, but get to the point quickly.

◆ **Include a call to action**—If you want your reader to answer a question or address an issue, be sure to say so. Don't expect that they'll automatically understand your thinking on next steps without spelling it out.

◆ **Don't cry wolf**—If your message isn't urgent or of critical importance, don't flag it as high priority.

◆ **Don't shout, please**—Using all caps (uppercase letters) is understood to be shouting. It's also hard to read. Follow rules of netiquette.

◆ **To whom it may concern**—Whenever possible, use the recipient's name. The more personal your message, the less likely it is to be viewed as spam.

◆ **Avoid attachments**—Many people refuse to open anything with an attachment for fear of contracting a computer virus.

◆ **Who are you?**—Always include a digital signature at the bottom of your e-mail. Different e-mail programs have different ways you can do this, but it's a quick and easy way to make your messages look professional. It also allows people to have all your information at the tip of their fingers, so they don't have to hunt around for your phone number or address.

An example of a good e-mail signature:

John Lovett
Project Manager
Acme Corporation
1234 Industrial Way
City, State, 12345
(123) 456-7890 (phone)
(123) 456-9900 (fax)
(123) 234-5678 (mobile)
www.acmecorporation.com

eNewsletters and Other Valuable Content

One way to use e-mail marketing with internal or external audiences is through an eNewsletter. eNewsletters are one of the best methods of e-mail marketing, because you're delivering something of value and you're helping customers get to know who you are. They are a great way to deliver timely information.

Booby Traps

Buying a copy of an e-mail list is not recommended, because most lists of value are not for sale. Think about it: anyone who will sell this information likely has an overused list of people who are getting spammed. And if a company is willing to sell the list to you, they've probably sold it to others who are already abusing the list, making the chances of your message getting through even less likely.

Building Your E-Mail List

Hopefully, you have a database of existing customers that includes an e-mail address field. If you don't, start creating one today. This can be as simple as asking people to fill out a contact card the first time they come in or even placing a fishbowl on your counter with a sign that says "Drop in your business card to be added to our e-mail list." Other ways to collect e-mail addresses include:

◆ Ask current customers to provide friends' e-mail addresses

◆ Ask website visitors to subscribe to your eNewsletter mailing list

◆ Ask for e-mails at every point of customer contact: on the phone, in the store, on sales calls

◆ Provide a guest book at trade shows and other industry events

◆ Rent a list (owners of e-mail lists send a message to their user base on your behalf)

Be sure to let people know when they provide their e-mail address that you would like to contact them via e-mail with special offers or other useful information. If people decline, you can always verbally assure them you will not sell their e-mail address to any second party.

Get creative with your e-mail lists. If you own a boutique in a college town, see if you can hire an undergraduate who will give you lists from various groups with which she is associated—her sorority, classes, and so on. Alternatively, if you own an art gallery with expensive paintings, why not see if you can wrangle contacts from the local country club directory? Think of people you know who could benefit from a similar list to yours. Maybe you could share contacts to create a larger combined mailing list.

> **Brainwaves**
>
> In your first e-mail communication, remind people why they are receiving your message. "You received this message because you are a valued customer of Your Business Here. From time to time we send out discounts and other important announcements. To be removed from our mailing list, click here." This should put users who are prone to report e-mails as spam at ease.

Publication Frequency

Your e-mail newsletter should be sent regularly. Believe it or not, people will begin to expect it. If your publication is too irregular, it seems unprofessional and lacks credibility.

How often you publish your newsletters is entirely up to you. Daily Candy, a city-specific update about new restaurants, shops, and cultural and entertainment events is published every day. Its content is so timely that it has to be. Of course, it's unlikely that you'll need to publish a newsletter every day, but what about sending one out weekly or monthly? Always consider the return on your investment. It will take time to create a quality newsletter.

Content

What's the most important part of your eNewsletter? Your first thought might be that appearance is most critical; however, by far, the most important aspect of your newsletter is the content. A beautiful eNewsletter may catch someone's attention once, but if there's nothing there of value, you won't retain your readers. Keep in mind, too, that flashy, design-heavy e-mails aren't really recommended anyway. Finding something that looks the same no matter what e-mail client you are using is difficult. The way something appears in an AOL e-mail may look different when viewed through a company e-mail account. The degree of skill required to make things render properly in various e-mail programs is the very reason many companies opt to hire dedicated e-mail marketing companies to create and manage their e-mail marketing campaigns.

Select Your Editor

Are you going to write and create your newsletter or have someone else do it? Chances are, if you're a smaller operation, doing it yourself is the most cost-effective and logical way to go about it. If you're not comfortable doing your own newsletter, think about hiring someone else to do it for you. Maybe someone you have working for you has a hidden talent for writing and is just waiting for a chance to use it. You might have a friend who loves to write who could help you with it in return for discounted services and/or merchandise. Figure out from the start how you want to go about the actual writing process. You want your newsletter to sound consistent and have a single style that carries from issue to issue. This will help to brand your newsletter to your readers.

The following are tips for a successful newsletter:

◆ Make sure your message is relevant and appealing to your audience.

◆ Use an intriguing subject line—as we mentioned earlier, readers are more likely to open an e-mail from a marketer if the subject is clear and appealing.

◆ Make sure the "from" field is clear and has a name. It shouldn't just be a generic name like admin@abcorp. It can be as simple as From: Acme Corporation. If it isn't from a specific name, it can look like spam.

◆ Proof all the copy in your newsletter. It looks careless to send a message that contains typos, especially if it's going to customers and potential customers. Have someone else look at it as well. It's hard to proof your own work because your eyes jump over the familiar copy.

◆ Check all your links. Make sure you test all links to ensure they're functioning correctly. Technology can be tricky and just when you think it's your friend, it bites you!

◆ Let people know they're being added to a mailing list when they provide their e-mail address. Explain that you'd like to send them special offers or other useful information via e-mail. Be sure to let people know you will not sell their e-mail address to any second party.

◆ Include your contact information in every e-mail. If readers want to ask you a question, it shouldn't be hard for them to find you.

◆ Make unsubscribing easy. No matter how fantastic your newsletter is, there will always be people who just don't want it.

◆ Make the most of your subscription feature. If people subscribe to your newsletter, collect as much info as you can. You don't need to know their height and weight, but wouldn't it be nice to know their names and mailing addresses—not just their e-mail addresses?

◆ Don't take yourself too seriously. No matter what the topic, there's always room for a little humor or lightheartedness. If you send a newsletter weekly, why not include a tiny blurb about movies opening that week? Writing in a conversational tone can also work wonders in differentiating yourself from the competition's stiff and boring eNewsletter.

◆ Outline your goals. Figure out what you would like to achieve with your e-mail marketing campaign. Is it more sales, increased website traffic? Keep your goal in mind when writing your e-mail copy.

◆ Be timely. Because of the instantaneous nature of e-mail—people get it immediately and it sits looming in their inboxes until they open it—messages should be timely.

◆ Make your e-mail graphically appealing but simple. You'll want the primary draw to be your clever copy, not mind-boggling graphics that either won't display properly or will take forever to download. Your e-mail should stand out when recipients open the message, but simple is best. If your e-mail looks too busy and too chock-full of content, it will overwhelm readers and they're likely to save it for later. E-mails that are saved for later often turn into e-mails that are never read at all.

◆ Include clear calls to action or intriguing headlines. That means more than just "click here to learn more." Call your readers to action using motivating phrases (50 percent off all orders today) or intriguing verbiage such as, "Top Ten Reasons …".

◆ Make it user friendly. Navigation should be easy to read and find. Just as users should be able to opt out of receiving your newsletter easily, they should also have the capability to subscribe other users, forward the message, ask questions, and contact you or your support team.

◆ Offer a text-only version of your e-mail that doesn't contain all the whistles and bells. Different e-mail programs respond to incoming messages differently. Some e-mail programs just won't open up complex HTML tags. Additionally, some companies have very sensitive servers that block a lot of HTML.

◆ Use descriptive text. In the same vein, always use descriptive text to accompany any graphics you include. The text can replace the images for readers who cannot download images due to their e-mail servers. You don't want anyone to miss out on something crucial due to technical difficulties!

◆ Give them a reason to read. What's in it for them? At the end of the day, the overarching purpose of your e-mail marketing campaign is to promote a product or service you can provide. You know it and so do your readers. At the same time, even though they know you're selling something, they do expect something of value. This could be information, contests, promotions, or discounts.

How many e-mails have you received with grammatical, punctuation, and spelling errors that would make your fifth-grade teacher cringe? For some reason, people often think that because "it's only an e-mail," they can be more casual than if they were composing a more formal written business correspondence. Boy, are they mistaken! Keep in mind that you are communicating without the aid of tone and emphasis, making it even more important that your words are clear. In the middle of a busy workday, the last thing someone wants to do is decipher a cryptic message. Error-ridden e-mails absolutely affect the way people view you and your company.

The Dreaded Spam Filter

People have become more and more savvy about spam over the past few years. Most people have spam filters set up in their personal e-mail accounts and almost all companies do. Because these spam filters can be hard to get around, you should provide information on your website about changing spam filter settings. Many times, users simply need to verify your domain name to allow you to send them messages. In other cases, they may have to adjust settings in their e-mail program. You should become familiar with the settings in common e-mail programs so you can provide basic technical support if your subscribers need it.

RoverMail

Until fairly recently, there has been a noticeable void in e-mail marketing products geared toward the needs of small to mid-size businesses. Choices were limited. If you wanted to be able to develop and distribute your own e-mails, to minimize costs, you had a couple of choices at two very different ends of the spectrum. First, you could use an inexpensive online e-mail marketing tool typically offering poorly designed templates, very little customization, and limited campaign tracking. Second, you could purchase custom software that could cost in excess of $15,000.

"Guerrilla" businesses often need something in between. RoverMail fills the void. It's a new, niche product created by our friends at a boutique marketing firm, RedRover Company, LLC. Their product gives you:

◆ A professional-looking e-mail template—something that doesn't look cobbled together or poorly designed

◆ The ability to develop and distribute your own HTML e-mails without knowing complex web design programs

◆ Comprehensive e-mail campaign tracking

◆ An affordable tool with small upfront charges and little ongoing cost

RedRover's RoverMail is an e-mail marketing tool developed specifically with small to mid-size businesses in mind. The tool offers the functionality of very expensive, high-end e-mail marketing software on a "guerrilla" budget. Set-up costs range from about $1,000 to $1,500 and ongoing charges are as low as $75 per month.

For more details about RoverMail, visit www.redrovercompany.com, click on Services and then RoverMail.

It Worked for Them

Harbor of Health, a medical clinic and fitness center in the Memphis area, had been using e-mail marketing tools for some time before they discovered RoverMail. They'd initially opted for e-mail marketing because they needed to educate potential customers about their innovative healthcare services, offerings that were new to the Memphis market. While direct mail certainly has its benefits, it can be costly for a start-up business. Because their services weren't familiar to their target audience, Harbor of Health needed to feed potential customers little bits and pieces of information at a time, making direct mail unaffordable on a large scale. E-mail marketing was a good fit, not only due to cost, but also because the company's primary target audience is known to frequently use the Internet and e-mail—affluent females generally under 50.

Harbor of Health used e-mail marketing to supplement its direct marketing efforts. They sent direct mail only to residents in close proximity to the facility and used e-mail to affordably get the word out throughout the entire city. This combined approach allowed them to get more for their marketing dollars.

Steele Ford, Harbor of Health's Executive Director, explained: "Before RoverMail, we would only send one HTML e-mail campaign per month or two for cost reasons. While the results were positive, the e-mails had to be custom-designed and manually published for us each time and that was costly. We had to manage opt outs on our own and tracking was limited. Now, RoverMail does most of the work for us and it's much more affordable. Plus, the tracking allows us to monitor how successful a campaign is so that we can modify our approach before the next one. RoverMail allows us to work smarter, not harder. Finally, an e-mail marketing tool with the small business in mind."

The Least You Need to Know

- Never try to trick people into opening your e-mail.
- Using an informative subject line is essential for success.
- eNewsletters are a great way to deliver valuable content to your target audience.
- E-mail marketing can be an affordable complement to other marketing efforts.

Part 4

The Nuts and Bolts of Guerrilla Marketing

Cool new tools are fine and dandy, but you have to go about marketing in a methodical way. And what if your product isn't as fun as mixing Diet Coke and Mentos? Do you still have a chance? Absolutely. With a little thought and ingenuity, you can turn ho-hum into hot.

Chapter 16

Who Am I, Anyway?
Analyzing Your Situation

In This Chapter

- Guerrilla marketing: is it right for you?
- Evaluation of traditional marketing you've used
- Assessing your customer base
- Balancing traditional tools with guerrilla tactics

Can you boil your product or service down to a short, plain-spoken *positioning statement*? Are you able to identify a highly targeted audience? Do you know the profit margin on your product or service? Do you have passionate employees or brand advocates willing to champion your guerrilla marketing efforts? Are you comfortable taking a few risks? If you answered yes to most of these questions, then you're ready to try the guerrilla approach to growing your business.

def•i•ni•tion _____

A **positioning statement** is a concise statement conveying the benefits of your product/service offering. It's what your brand stands for. It provides the blueprint for the marketing of your brand.

Guerrilla Marketing Essentials

Whether you're doing guerrilla marketing or traditional marketing, you first need to know where you stand. A little research is in order. Here are some things you need to know:

◆ Who are your competitors?

◆ Why should your customer buy your product instead of the competition's?

◆ What are your advantages: location, price, broader distribution, innovative product, and so on?

◆ What are your weaknesses: location, lack of customer awareness, no track record, and so on?

You should be keenly aware of how you stack up in the marketplace so that you can take advantage of the factors that are in your favor. These are things you may want to feature in your guerrilla marketing.

In addition, by recognizing your weaknesses, you can be prepared to overcome prospective customers' objections. Carefully consider each downside and brainstorm ways to offset them.

A Simple Message

We talked in Chapter 2 about the need to talk about your product in a way that clearly states what the benefit is to the customer. Being able to quickly and succinctly communicate the *value proposition* for your product or service is the foundation of guerrilla marketing. Why? Because the beauty of unconventional marketing is in its simplicity. If it takes you 10 minutes to explain your product or service, then more traditional one-on-one business development may be more appropriate than guerrilla marketing. With guerrilla tactics, you're either relying on the public to serve as your sales force, building awareness of your product or service through word of mouth, or you're counting on the average Joe grasping your message in mere seconds.

Well-Defined Target Audience

Guerrilla marketing is most efficient when it's highly targeted. Take the example of an investigative services firm that targets law firms. Instead of taking the traditional marketing approach of cold calling law offices or sending out direct mail, this firm opted to create its own "referral program" by slipping its business cards into law books at the courthouse library. The steady stream of lawyers and their support staff using these reference materials saw the cards and assumed that other attorneys used the investigative firm. This gave the investigative business *third-party credibility* and generated more calls than they could handle.

def•i•ni•tion
> A **value proposition** is how you will differentiate your company from your competitors.
> **Third-party credibility** occurs when someone not formally associated with you or being paid by you endorses your product. The thinking behind a third-party endorsement is that the source is objective and rendering an honest opinion.

Know Your Profit Margin

We talked in Chapter 1 about your need to make a profit, defined as the difference between your cost of goods sold and your revenue. In more specific terms, you need to know the *profit margin* for each of your products. So you know how much you are making.

Be sure to avoid this pitfall when navigating through the guerrilla marketing jungle: know your profit margins for each product or service with relative accuracy *before* you market. Entirely too many small and mid-size business owners are unable or simply haven't dedicated the time to determining profit margins by product or service line.

While guerrilla marketing can often be significantly less expensive than more traditional marketing channels, it is always dangerous to select a marketing strategy without first knowing your budget. And to get to your budget, you must first know your margins. When calculating your margins, be sure to include the cost of your resources. While guerrilla marketing is known for its low out-of-pocket costs, these strategies can often be labor-intensive. If you need to hire additional labor to deploy your guerrilla plans, then this added labor cost should factor into your margin analysis. And even if you plan to use existing resources, consider the *opportunity cost* that may be involved in taking them away from other revenue-generating activities.

My father used to say that you get what you pay for. The first rule of business is that if you're not growing, you're dying. So while it's logical and natural to try to keep your costs down, keep in mind that you do have to spend some money to make money. Trite wisdom aside, it pays to regularly invest in building your business.

def•i•ni•tion

Profit margin is your measure of profitability, it is calculated by dividing your net income by the revenue the product generates. Taxes and expenses should be subtracted from the net income before calculating the profit margin. Profit margins are expressed in percentages and the higher the profit margin, the better.

Opportunity cost is the value of the activity that you are forgoing so that you can participate in an alternative activity—the value of the next-best alternative that must be sacrificed. It's the potential amount of money lost for each day an opportunity is delayed. If you dedicate an employee to a day of guerrilla marketing activities in lieu of that employee's typical on-the-floor sales activities, the opportunity cost is the amount of sales that the employee would have likely generated had he/she been selling that day.

Your Guerrilla Marketing Team

With guerrilla marketing, you're often trading off the need for a big advertising budget for more unconventional feet-on-the-street tactics. These "feet" are most effective when they're attached to more than just any old warm body. If you have employees or brand advocates who buy into your unconventional guerrilla tactics and who are willing to actively champion your cause, you will dramatically increase your probability of success. Two ways to gain that buy-in: (1) make it fun, and (2) offer performance incentives. Performance incentives are the financial motivation to complete specific activities. Performance incentives should be tied to measurable activities. They can be offered to your employees or to brand loyalists and influencers who've volunteered to help champion your cause.

Assessing Your Situation

When my sister was a youngster, she entered a swimming contest to raise money for charity. She convinced our dad to give her $5 for every lap she swam. Because Stacy hadn't really been practicing much, Dad assumed she couldn't swim too far. Wasn't he surprised when she presented him with a slip of paper signed by the coach indicating she had completed 100 laps! He was $500 poorer, but pretty proud that she had done such a superb job.

People who undertake plans without looking carefully at the current situation run the risk of spending their dollars in the wrong place, or spending too many dollars on lackluster results. As you plan your guerrilla marketing efforts, first consider what your current situation is.

Calculate the Benefits of Your Past Marketing Efforts

Take a quick assessment of the traditional marketing strategies you've tried. Include everything from printing fliers to placing newspaper ads to, well, whatever you've done to promote your business.

Have your efforts paid off? Calculate at least a rough *return on investment* (*ROI*) for each of these strategies. Determining your ROI is just a matter of comparing new sales generated as a result of a specific marketing effort to the cost of advertising and providing the product or service.

If this is your first time calculating ROI, here's an easy formula:

1. Determine the total cost of your advertising investment for a specific marketing effort. For example, if you spent $750 on printing and postage for a direct mail campaign and your offer was a $10 gift card, of which you gave away 25, your total investment would be $1,000.

2. Calculate the amount of net revenue associated with that investment. Let's say, for example, that your direct marketing effort generated $10,000 in new product sales and the cost for you to deliver that $10,000 in products was $4,000. Your net revenue was $6,000.

3. Calculate your ROI by dividing the net revenue by the total investment: Net revenue = $6,000 divided by $1,000 = a 600% ROI.

def•i•ni•tion

Return on investment (ROI) is a performance measure used to evaluate the efficiency of an investment or compare the efficiency of a number of different investments.

If you're unable to measure the effects of your traditional marketing, put away your checkbook and stop spending marketing dollars. There are too many marketing opportunities available that will allow for such measurement to waste your time on strategies that you can't measure.

If you *are* able to measure the result of your traditional marketing strategies, but find that you're barely breaking even (or worse yet, are in the hole), guerrilla marketing may be for you. While some guerrilla marketing tactics can be fairly resource intensive, the capital requirements are typically minimal.

> ### Brainwaves
>
> When handing out coupons featuring a special product offer at a local event, be sure to code the coupons by guerrilla marketer. Retain the redeemed coupons so that you're able to determine sales generated and ultimately the ROI by each individual guerrilla marketer or sales representative.
>
> When advertising a special offer that can be purchased online, be sure to use a sub-page of your website for tracking purposes. For example, instead of promoting your standard www.mycompany.com address, feature www.mycompany.com/freebie so that you can track orders placed as a result of your guerrilla marketing tactics.

Are Your Customers Susceptible to Guerrilla Marketing?

Before beginning a guerrilla marketing campaign, give some thought to the receptiveness of your customer base to this type of strategy. It's not for everyone. Are your targeted customers highly conservative? Would they find unconventional sales and marketing tactics disconcerting? If the answer is yes, you have an uphill battle, one that could be too costly to win. Consider testing the waters with a small group of prospects first, before you wade all the way in.

Balancing Traditional and Guerrilla Tactics

An appropriate mix, or balance of traditional and guerrilla tactics, is typically the most successful approach to growing a steady stream of prospective customers. Why? Because different products and services necessitate different marketing strategies. More importantly, no two customers are alike. They respond to different types of marketing, making a blended approach ideal.

It's quite a generalization, but typically, younger *target demographics* are more open to unconventional marketing tactics. An older demographic might find guerrilla marketing to be intrusive or inappropriate, responding more positively to straight-forward, clearly identifiable marketing programs.

def•i•ni•tion

Target demographics are the common characteristics of prospective customers in which you are focusing your marketing efforts. Your target demographic may very well change by product/service line. For example, the target demographic for the iPod is tech-savvy urban youth that come from a fairly high-income household.

Real World Example

Here's an example of what a very simple, balanced traditional/guerrilla marketing plan might look like. Let's say you are marketing a new floral shop that focuses on weddings.

The following are traditional marketing elements:

◆ Yellow Pages advertising

◆ Bridal magazine inserts

◆ Sponsorship of a local bridal show

The following are guerrilla marketing elements:

◆ Hold wedding planning seminars, sending invitations to those listed in the paper as newly engaged. Invite guest speakers, including an area caterer, an event planner, a travel agent, and an invitation supplier. Kick off the seminar with tips for selecting floral arrangements and selecting a florist. Hand out materials about your floral shop and wedding packages.

◆ Send congratulatory flowers to the newly engaged featured in your paper.

◆ Partner with an area jewelry shop. Ask them to hand out coupons to their male customers buying engagement rings. The coupon would be good for a free bouquet of flowers that the bachelor can give to his would-be wife when he proposes. When the coupon is redeemed, ask the customer to complete a card with contact information, the anticipated date of the proposal, and so on, to allow for follow up.

How Much Should Your Campaign Cost?

You are the only one who can determine what you can afford to spend to market your product or service. Common sense will guide you to a degree. You certainly don't want to overdo it. That's why it makes sense to try things on a graduated basis to see how they pay off before you jump in with both feet.

One way that advertisers measure the cost of a campaign is in cost per impression. This is a formula for comparing the total number of targeted customers you are able to reach with your marketing message.

Here's how it works. If you spend $1,000 on a newspaper ad in a trade publication that is distributed to 10,000 subscribers who are in your targeted audience, then your cost per impression is $.10. To take this analysis one step further, if the annual value of a new customer is $500, only two of your 10,000 impressions need result in a sale in order to break even.

Understand that just because you send something to 10,000 people doesn't mean they'll all see it, much less pay attention, much less buy your product as a result. Measuring impressions merely tells you how many people are on the receiving end of the item and therefore could see it. The real trick is in measuring how many people take action as a result. That's a much more meaningful number.

The Downside to Using Guerrilla Marketing Tactics

Like any marketing strategy, the guerrilla approach has its drawbacks. If your audience is vast—as in an entire city—the guerrilla approach typically won't work as well. That's why they call it mass marketing. It's for the masses. When you spread the cost per impression across a vast audience, more traditional mass marketing, such as TV or radio, becomes much more affordable. Guerrilla marketing is intended for a highly-targeted audience. It's most often too labor intensive for anything more. Guerrilla marketing is also often more effective in *B2B* (business-to-business) marketing than *B2C* (business-to-consumer) marketing, because there is more profit to be made per prospect, making the time investment worth it.

def•i•ni•tion

B2B marketing is the marketing of products or services from one business to another. For example, if you own a janitorial services company, your target market is other businesses in need of your cleaning services. **B2C marketing** is marketing directly to consumers. Grocery stores market directly to consumers, as opposed to other businesses.

The Least You Need to Know

◆ Calculate your profit margin before beginning guerrilla marketing.

◆ Guerrilla marketing is most effective when combined with traditional marketing methods.

◆ Find some way to track your guerrilla marketing efforts so you can tweak your plan as you go.

◆ Don't give up too soon: some forms of guerrilla marketing take time.

Chapter **17**

"You Talkin' to Me?" Assessing Your Target

In This Chapter

- ◆ Consumer groups that influence message diffusion
- ◆ Impact of gender
- ◆ Generational differences
- ◆ Companies devoted to targeting groups

What's interesting to one person is boring to another. What one person finds funny might be stupid to someone else. There's no question that marketing messages are interpreted differently based on the person they're presented to. Fortunately, most groups have common views and beliefs that tie them together. Identifying the traits of your target audience is a key element in crafting an effective guerrilla marketing campaign.

Consumer Groups That Influence Message Diffusion

Understand how information about your products and services gets disseminated among prospective customers, and you'll enjoy greater efficiency with your guerrilla marketing efforts.

It is widely believed that there are two steps in the process of *message diffusion*. Opinion formers who are active media users, interpret messages and content for lower-end media users. These opinion formers are trusted sources within their area of expertise. While equally important to the success of your brand, early adopters, the market majority, and laggards have less direct media exposure and take their cues from influencers.

def•i•ni•tion

Message diffusion is the process of gaining market acceptance for your product or service.

Opinion Formers, Mavens, and Influencers

Also called influencers, opinion formers are highly tuned to all forms of media. If you're a baseball fan, you'll recognize the name Bob Costas as an opinion leader for America's pastime—baseball. When the steroid scandal first plagued Major League Baseball, fans across the nation took cues from Bob Costas about what was fact or fiction. The same rules apply to the adoption and acceptance of products and services. If you're looking for the latest good book, you might turn to Oprah as an opinion leader.

Here's the Buzz

Unsure who your brand's influencers are? The easiest way to get to the bottom of it is to ask your current customers who or what influenced their buying decision. Was it an article about your company in the paper? Or an entry on a local blog about your product? Or a vocal member of an organization in which they're affiliated? (See also Chapter 5 on influencers.)

If you're seeking a good flick to rent, an influencer might simply be the sales representative at your local Blockbuster who seems to have seen every movie ever made at least twice. Influencers aren't necessarily highly paid celebrities (although some celebrities are certainly influencers)—they simply have more exposure to, and understanding of, media within their area of specialty.

Influencers, by definition, indirectly affect or sway others. They are mavens (experts) in a specific area and wield great power to promote or destroy your brand. Where possible, it is wise to involve key influencers in product development or refinement. Not only is their feedback valuable, but this type of interactivity can also encourage early advocacy efforts.

Early Adopters and Evangelists

An early adopter embraces new products or services before others. They serve as evangelists who will enthusiastically advocate for your company once they're believers. They are more open to the latest, greatest technology than the market majority or laggards, and they tend to have fairly high disposable income to allow purchases early in a product lifecycle, often when the price is at its highest. They are typically well-educated, popular social leaders. Early adopters make up only 10–15 percent of the population. (You know these people: they're the ones who have the new product before you even knew it existed.)

Market Majority

The market majority waits until they've seen their early adopter friends and neighbors try a new product or service before buying themselves. They are generally not big risk takers. They tend to be deliberate, traditional, and somewhat skeptical. They have less disposable income, which in part is what drives their pragmatic behavior. This group has many informal social contacts that they rely on to provide input into potential purchase decisions. They go on *Consumer Reports'* website and evaluate products based on tried-and-true methods.

Laggards

Laggards are very slow to accept new products and services. They have a fear of debt. They have little exposure to mass media and are less comfortable with technology than the other groups. They are primary influenced by a small group of neighbors and friends who serve as information sources. Traditional mass-media marketing efforts often don't drive purchase behavior from this group. Impulse buys are not a reality in their world. Even if they have plenty of disposable income, they are not likely to spend it thoughtlessly. They typically consider themselves frugal, even though others might view them as penny-pinchers.

Impact of Age and Gender

Understanding the fundamental differences in how men and women of different generations process information can make or break your guerrilla marketing efforts. Let's take gender for starters.

Gender Marketing

Women tend to process much more detail than men. Men want the most basic message in the fastest possible way. They don't have time to listen to lengthy debates about the virtues of various products. Men primarily seek strength in advertising images, and women seek beauty. To grab a man's attention in advertising, use bolder images, and with women, offer additional detail to feed their over-working minds. It's also important to note that women look for the "catch" and tend to be less trusting of an offer. Women feel the need to buy and hoard. Can you say shoes? In comparison, men want to understand how things work—the mechanics of it. They want the bottom line quickly.

Marketing to Women

Marketing to women should be transparent, not overtly feminine. Show that you're sensitive to the needs of this market and that you're taking it seriously.

When determining what role gender marketing will play in your guerrilla efforts, be sure to consider not only who the decision maker is for your product or service, but also whether or not there is an influencer. Oftentimes, the influencer holds the *real* purchase power. Just ask Home Depot. They learned that for their products, the influencer was often, surprisingly, the woman in the household. While women made up 50 percent of their sales, they learned through market research that women also had great influence over purchases made by the men in their households. Further research uncovered that women tend to think about home improvement in terms of outcomes vs. products, so Home Depot smartly began building room vignettes in their stores to appeal to this female purchasing behavior. Additional cosmetic changes designed to appeal to female purchase preferences included brighter store lighting, a higher décor-to-raw-product ratio, and less cluttered stores. Other changes were offering "do-it-herself" workshops and training staff to ensure that each customer has all of the tools and materials needed to finish a project. Most women will tell you that a pet peeve is having to make multiple trips to pick up additional supplies forgotten the first time. Multitasking women find this terribly inefficient, and they welcome tips from sales representatives who "get it."

Brainwaves
Gender-based marketing is tricky. Get it wrong, and you can offend your target group. It's a risk you can't afford not to take, however, as women begin to gain more and more consumer buying power. A great way to ensure that your marketing is appropriately gender-focused is to rely on a balanced team of men and women decision makers on your marketing execution team.

To assess how savvy you are at gender marketing, take this quiz. Review the list of attribute pairs that follow. Indicate which of the characteristics in each pair is common to females (F) or males (M). The answers can be found at the bottom of this page.

Male or Female?	Characteristics
1a. ❑ M ❑ F	Collective perspective—they are groupies
1b. ❑ M ❑ F	Individual perspective—they are more solitary in their decision making
2a. ❑ M ❑ F	Maximizing approach to shopping
2b. ❑ M ❑ F	Prioritizing approach to shopping
3a. ❑ M ❑ F	Bare bones preference for messaging
3b. ❑ M ❑ F	Preferred message approach—"the works"
4a. ❑ M ❑ F	Prefer connections
4b. ❑ M ❑ F	Prefer competition
5a. ❑ M ❑ F	Ability to deal with many subjects simultaneously (prefer products that make their juggling easier)
5b. ❑ M ❑ F	Single-minded (prefer to deal with one subject at a time)
6a. ❑ M ❑ F	Plain spoken/direct
6b. ❑ M ❑ F	Expect advertisers to be one step ahead of what they're thinking
7a. ❑ M ❑ F	Responsible for about 85 percent of buying decisions
7b. ❑ M ❑ F	Responsible for about 15 percent of buying decisions
8a. ❑ M ❑ F	Prefer to warm up to a product—a nonblaring message
8b. ❑ M ❑ F	Don't mind a straight-forward sales approach
9a. ❑ M ❑ F	Convenience is key
9b. ❑ M ❑ F	Practicality is key

continues

continued

Male or Female?	Characteristics
10a. ❑ M ❑ F	Seeking products that align with their family-oriented needs
10b. ❑ M ❑ F	Seeking products that align with their social and work-related needs
11a. ❑ M ❑ F	TV is the favorite form of media
11b. ❑ M ❑ F	Internet is the favorite form of media
12a. ❑ M ❑ F	Most popular subjects they seek out through media: sports, games, and electronics
12b. ❑ M ❑ F	Most popular subjects they seek out through media: news, weather, finance, and games
13a. ❑ M ❑ F	Prefer to "see it (in person) to believe it" before buying
13b. ❑ M ❑ F	Use other forms of media to learn about websites that they can in turn visit to make their real purchase decision
14a. ❑ M ❑ F	Great loyalty to a few, select websites
14b. ❑ M ❑ F	Less online loyalty
15a. ❑ M ❑ F	Comfortable spending time at work on the Internet related to nonwork activities because of the work they do during nonwork time
15b. ❑ M ❑ F	Tend to better divide their time—work at work and personal after hours
16a. ❑ M ❑ F	Make up 30 percent of new business start-ups
16b. ❑ M ❑ F	Make up 70 percent of new business start-ups
17a. ❑ M ❑ F	Majority of corporate purchasing agents and managers
17b. ❑ M ❑ F	Minority of corporate purchasing agents and managers

(1a) F (1b) M; (2a) F (2b) M; (3a) M (3b)F; (4a) F (4b) M; (5a) F (5b)M;
(6a) M (6b) F; (7a) F (7b)M; (8a) F (8b) M; (9a) F (9b)M; (10a) F (10b) M;
(11a) M (11b)F; (12a) M (12b) F; (13a) M (13b) F; (14a) F (14b) M; (15a) F (15b) M;
(16a) M (16b) F; (17a) F (17b)M

Generational Marketing

The Me Generation. Millennials. Gen Y'ers. What does it all mean? There is no clear cut answer. Generational experts have labeled and defined the generations in a variety of ways, and the start and end dates of each generation are widely disputed. Despite these disparities, the most commonly referred to generation categories and time spans are:

- Matures (Silent Generation)—Born before 1946 (62+ as of 2007)

- Baby Boomers—Born between 1946 and 1965 (ages 42 to 61 as of 2007)

- Generation X (Me Generation, MTV Generation)—Born between 1966 and 1982 (ages 25 to 41 as of 2007)

- Generation Y (Internet Generation)—Born between 1983 and 2000 (ages 7 to 24 as of 2007)

- Generation Z (Millennials, New Silent Generation)—Born between 2001 and today (ages 6 and younger as of 2007)

Don't get caught up in the exact time span for the generations. What's more important are the general differences in purchase behaviors between the groups. The three generations that garner the largest purchasing power are Baby Boomers, Gen X, and Gen Y. You probably have a pretty good feel which groups are your target audience already.

Tips for Marketing to Baby Boomers

The Baby Boomers were the first of the generations raised on television. Baby Boomers define themselves in many ways by their music. Keep in mind, the defining event of the Baby Boom group was the Vietnam War, and that played a huge part in shaping the political views of this generation. When guerrilla marketing to boomers, here are some tips to keep in mind:

- Make sure that you're offering a product or service that has a good perceived value. While this generation is not necessarily seeking the cheapest alternative, they are looking for good value.

- Baby Boomers are not blindly brand loyal. You must continue to earn their loyalty throughout your interactions with them by providing good value and excellent customer service. On the plus side, even if they've been with your competition for some time, they're willing to change if you present a good case for your product or service. Sell a Baby Boomer on the convenience or practicality of your product and you have yourself a new customer.

◆ Baby Boomers don't respond well to scare tactics. Instead, inspire them to buy. The "act now," or "limited time offer" approach will turn them off.

◆ Don't underestimate the Baby Boomers when it comes to technology. Many are very tech-savvy, and even those who weren't initially on the bandwagon have since recognized its benefit and jumped on. The Internet is becoming a common vehicle for Baby Boomers seeking product information. Don't assume that because they didn't grow up with computers they don't know how to use them. This is a sharp group.

When marketing to Baby Boomers, be sure your packaging, your advertising, and your signage are easy to read. This means making type sizes bigger and using simple fonts. It also requires that you avoid dense copy placement and make sure you have enough white space. Baby Boomers don't like to be reminded that they are aging. Making your materials hard to read is the most efficient way to do just that.

Here are a few other things to keep in mind with Boomer marketing:

◆ Travel is important to Baby Boomers. Adventure and experience are hot topics among this crowd.

◆ Don't market to Boomers using 20-year-old models. If you're selling to Boomers, feature Boomer-age images. Show them you embrace who they are.

◆ Build personal relationships to set your company apart from the rest. This appeals to the Boomer market.

◆ More than six million Baby Boomers are already grandparents, and that number is expected to quadruple during the next 10 years. Extended family is important to them.

◆ This is the generation that questions the status quo and resists authority. Appealing to their rebel side is always an option.

◆ Baby Boomers tend to be quite open to buying on credit in lieu of saving.

◆ Throughout their lives, Boomers will continue to focus on continued education and growth. Showcase the enlightening aspects of your product to gain interest. Placing emphasis on self-actualization can be very effective when marketing to boomers.

◆ Baby Boomers tend to buy things because they need them versus buying things because they want them. Practicality is appealing to many.

Brainwaves

When you're communicating with Baby Boomers, be particularly sensitive to characterizing them as "getting older." Focus instead on their life experiences. Consider the Ameriprise Financial commercial featuring Dennis Hopper, for example. In it, Dennis is sitting on the beach discussing retirement. He talks to boomers who are now entering this phase of life, reminding them that "the thing about dreams is—they don't retire." He paints a picture of active retirement, not sitting-in-a-rest-home retirement. When advertising to this generation, never use words such as "senior," or "older," or even worse— "elderly." Instead, talk to them person to person, not company to "targeted group." More than most, Baby Boomers are not a homogenous group. Their interests are many and varied. Always keep in mind, many Baby Boomers feel they are in the prime of their lives.

Marketing to Gen X

Gen X'ers are a generation who grew up on computers. They're highly tech-savvy and are very comfortable with online shopping. They are also very accustomed to getting information via the Internet. When the first wave of tech tools began to spread, they were at just the right age to receive (and embrace) the message. While future generations have had no choice in embracing technology, Gen X'ers have chosen it as a way of life.

Internet Marketing is Highly Effective for Gen X

The Internet is perhaps the most effective channel through which to communicate with Gen X. The Me Generation thrives on the speed, excitement, and discovery of e-commerce. They consider themselves to be early adopters of the latest social marketing methods. Gen X'ers are self-reliant. They will be able to navigate through your website very well on their own if your site is well structured. When marketing to Gen X'ers, your page needs to be visually appealing. It should load quickly (or they will

def•i•ni•tion

Gen X is also called the Me Generation or MTV Generation. These are people born between 1966 and 1982. They are ages 25 to 41 as of 2007.

abort and go to another site). Copy must be succinct, and the site navigation should be intuitive. Fail to heed these instructions and there's a good chance a Gen X'er will lose patience and they may never come back to your site.

The following are some tips for marketing to Gen X'ers:

◆ This generation has been saddled with recessions. They have not really had the opportunity to enjoy the kind of shameless consumerism that Gen Y enjoys.

◆ They are highly discriminating in their purchases and have very little brand loyalty.

> **Brainwaves**
>
> The MTV Generation spends money on things that make life more fun and interactive. They are more loyal to product form and function than to product name and brand. (This is true with one exception: brand loyalty comes into play for Gen X'ers when it comes to items that are culturally relevant. Nike shoes versus a no-name sneaker, for example.)

◆ To appeal to Gen X, show them how others are using your product or service and how purchasing it will allow them a sense of belonging.

◆ Gen X'ers buy because they want it versus need it.

◆ This generation prefers lists and bulleted information. They don't want to wade through pages of words just to get to the price or benefits. Put it all out front to reach a Gen X'er. They want the bottom line.

◆ Gen X'ers are the first real multitaskers. Just watch an X'er surf the web or use an instant messaging service. Not only can they walk and chew gum at the same time, but they can design a website while doing it, too!

◆ Gen X'ers are pros at filtering advertising. They don't even see web banners any more, they fast forward through commercials. To reach this audience, too marketers are forced to integrate their advertising into core web information or entertainment.

◆ Gen X'ers adore product and service customization. Companies like Hilton Hotels, Dell Computers, and Levi's Jeans are capitalizing on this trend. One-size-fits all is a turnoff for most X'ers.

◆ People in the Gen X generation often work to live versus live to work. They want to see the light at the end of the tunnel where they are soon able to work fewer than 40 hours a week. They are not defined by their occupation. Appeal to their quality of life instead of drive to succeed.

◆ Talk to X'ers respectfully, recognizing that they are intelligent and individualistic. While a skeptical generation, if you can remove this skepticism, you may have a customer for life.

◆ X'ers love to become part of the marketing. Remember the Doritos Super Bowl commercials where customers produced the ads? This is an X'ers dream—to show off their talents before a national audience. Try to create friendly competition on a local, regional, or national level. The ideal prize? 15 minutes of fame and recognition. Use your loyal X'er customers to market to others. They'll eat it up.

> **Brainwaves**
>
> User-generated ad campaigns, like the Doritos example mentioned, are ad campaigns where the company encourages viewers to submit ads they've created. The best few are usually featured on a website, with the top creation airing during some high-profile television event.

Marketing to Gen Y

This generation is the Internet generation. They may remember life without the Internet, but most don't. *Gen Y* will significantly outnumber Gen X within the next ten years. This is a generation of people who, for the most part, have not known hard times. They are the first generation where consumption is a way of life. This group often buys what they want, when they want it, without much restraint.

Things to keep in mind when targeting Gen Y:

◆ This group is used to consumerism on demand. They order movies when they want them. They buy music online when they want it. This generation is even more impatient that Gen X'ers. Think your page needed to load fast to grab a Gen X'ers attention? It needs to be nearly instantaneous to keep the attention of a member of Gen Y.

◆ This generation is very tuned in to TV and Internet advertising. More so than Gen X, who've tuned it out.

◆ Generation Y is perhaps the most culturally diverse of all generations. This makes it difficult (and dangerous) for marketers to put them into a neat box of likes and preferences.

def•i•ni•tion

> **Generation Y** is the Internet Generation or "Millenials." Generation Y includes people born between 1983 and 2000. They are ages 7 to 24 as of 2007.

◆ This is an independent generation that is resistant to labels.

◆ Gen Y'ers are savvy about marketing and don't want to be talked to as if they are "know nothing" teenagers. Viral marketing has proven to be effective with this group.

Companies in the Business of Targeting These Groups

Is all this knowledge just TMI (too much information)? Take heart. There are companies who are in the business of reaching different market segments.

BzzAgent, LLC

Thanks to the barrage of social networking websites like MySpace, on-demand movies, TV, and music, the mass media world has become quite fragmented. It's a new world where consumers are in control of messaging. People spread their own advertising messages about their personal experiences with products or services through word of mouth.

As an alternative to mass media, Dave Balter founded a company called BzzAgent in 2001 with a vision of harnessing the power of this word-of-mouth advertising. He aspired to create an online community that would allow consumers to experience new products and services first-hand, naturally relay their experiences to their social networks, and then document their word-of-mouth conversations as input to marketers. This feedback is used to make product and service enhancements. It's also the beginning of a grass roots marketing campaign. Marketers have the ability to quickly generate trial among influencers. And they can target the participating influencers (called agents) by a variety of demographics. It's essentially controlled, measurable word of mouth.

> **Brainwaves**
>
> As of early 2007, BzzAgent had over 250,0000 agents (or influencers) in its network and is growing by about 4,000 members per week. The company has completed more than 250 word-of-mouth programs since opening its doors in 2001.

Proctor & Gamble's Tremor Teen Buzz Marketing Unit

Tremor is a marketing service designed to generate word-of-mouth marketing among teens. Tremor appeals to teens who want their opinions to be heard and valued by companies that market to them. Through Tremor, teens are exposed to products from a variety of industries, including fashion, beauty, entertainment, and food. Teens get to take part in the creation and launch of products and ideas that serve their age group. Companies obviously benefit by the exposure to their target audience and participating companies often provide free samples to the Tremor Crew members in the hope that they'll make a hit. Teens who are interested in joining the Tremor Crew sign up to try various products provided by participating companies.

The Least You Need To Know

- Consider your audience's gender and age before crafting your marketing message.

- There are very real differences between generations.

- Your marketing message should be designed to match the interests of your audience.

- What's appealing to one age group or gender could be offensive to another.

18

Choose Your Weapon: Which Form of Guerrilla Marketing Is Right for You?

In This Chapter

- ◆ Assessing your situation
- ◆ Defining your marketing goals
- ◆ Matching your tactic to your audience
- ◆ Methods that work for everyone

If you're selling the latest technological gizmo but you're marketing to retirement communities in Palm Springs, you're probably wasting your time and money. This chapter reviews the do's and don'ts of guerrilla marketing.

Guerrilla Marketing Plan

Many people find value in creating highly detailed marketing plans that include extensive demand forecasting and in-depth analysis of every possible angle. If you're one of those, you can find more detailed information on marketing plans throughout the book. There is also a wealth of information online to assist in creating a truly comprehensive marketing plan.

We, on the other hand, take a more instinct-based approach to getting things done. Without a doubt, some planning is essential and there are things you simply must know in order to plan an effective marketing campaign. Nobody would suggest you begin marketing without first assessing your customer base, your competition, and the general market landscape. But we suspect that because you are reading this book, you're probably more like us: you want to get the nitty-gritty information so you can hit the streets running. After all, no amount of market analysis can capture that intangible "it" factor that makes things a success. Sometimes things that work on paper won't fly in the real world, and sometimes the most unlikely ideas work like magic. Here are some thought-provoking questions to help you develop your guerrilla marketing plan.

Questions related to your competition:

- Who are my nearest competitors? How many are there?
- What are they doing that's working?
- What are they doing that's not working?
- How are they marketing their products/services currently?
- What are the similarities between my offering and theirs?
- What are the dissimilarities?
- Is there an unmet need that I can fill? Do they fill a need that I don't fill for my existing customers?
- What makes me different from my competitors? What are the unique features of my product?
- Will my competitors soon be offering new products/services or opening new locations? Are they in a decline?
- Is there something they're offering that I'm not? Is there an obstacle to overcome?

Compare your product/service to your competition, including price, product features, service, marketing methods, and sales channels.

This set of questions will help you determine where you stand against your competitors:

◆ Is demand for this product or service growing or declining?

◆ What are the primary and secondary markets for my product/service?

◆ Who are the decision makers who drive purchasing for this product or service?

◆ Are there any social or cultural issues I need to consider when marketing this product or service?

◆ Are there laws or regulations affecting how I market this product or service?

◆ How large is my potential customer base? Where are my customers coming from demographically speaking?

◆ How long do I expect to keep a customer? Is there a life cycle to my offering? Is my product seasonal?

◆ How many new customers do I need to stay afloat?

◆ How invested are customers in their existing provider?

◆ What motivates them? Money, convenience, luxury, health?

Marketing Goals

Before you decide what marketing technique to implement, think about what you're hoping to achieve through your marketing efforts. Here are some possible goals:

◆ Increase business among existing customers

◆ Increase foot traffic—get people in the door

◆ Get (x) number of new customers signed up

◆ Revive interest in an existing product/service

◆ Launch new product/service

◆ Boost product/brand awareness

◆ Get people to try product/service

◆ Drive people to website

◆ Increase website conversion rate

Ask yourself:

◆ What is my end goal? Is there a percentage increase I need to achieve?

◆ What will I consider a success for each guerrilla marketing tactic. (For example: trade show attendance, two business contacts = success. Blog, one lead per month = success.)

Again, before you outline your plan, it's essential to know where you are going. Different goals require different tactics. Guerrilla marketing outreach efforts are helpful for gaining new clients but deepening your relationships with existing customers would be best addressed with customer service enhancement and recognition programs (guerrilla-style, of course).

Matching the Right Media with Your Product

Here are some questions to provoke thought about the type of media that might work best with your message and audience.

◆ What kind of message is your target audience likely to respond to?

◆ How many times does your target audience need to hear your message before they are inspired to act on it?

◆ Where will your audience be and how can you capitalize on that? When are they most likely to be receptive to your message?

◆ How will your message be best remembered (how should it be delivered)?

◆ What is your budget?

◆ Will your budget allow you to continue to keep reinforcing this message? Frequency = sales.

Applying Your Message

Okay, you've prepared your guerrilla marketing message, now where do you want to apply it? Here's a recap of the guerrilla marketing methods we've outlined in this book. Check the ones that interest you and get ready to go bananas!

❏ **Website.** This is a must for every business these days. Whether you do it yourself or hire someone, if you don't have a website, get one.

BEST BENEFIT: It's the price of entry into the game.

DRAWBACK: If poorly done, it can damage your reputation, so do it right!

❏ **Flyers**. Flyers can be effective for a wide range of people. Hand them out at events, on campuses, or distribute them door to door in neighborhoods close to your business. People with a high level of disposable income are not as likely to respond to flyers.

BEST BENEFIT: You can reach lots of people in a targeted area. Including a coupon can increase foot traffic to your business.

DRAWBACK: Flyers can be viewed as tangible "spam" and turn people off. They're not environmentally friendly as many go to waste.

❏ **YouTube Video**. Typically a good fit for arts and media-related fields. Film makers, musicians, video production companies, ad agencies, and not-yet-famous actors/actresses have been known to use YouTube to gain publicity. Many companies are now using YouTube as a way to extend the life of their television commercials. If you've got a great TV commercial, be sure to post it on YouTube!

BEST BENEFIT: If you hit it big, you're sure to become viral. Particularly effective if your target audience is under 30.

DRAWBACK: If your video doesn't gain notoriety, you'll have no return on investment. Risky investment of time.

❏ **Pass-along E-mail**. Pass-along e-mails cast a wide net. The key is creating an e-mail that is valuable enough people want to pass it on. Offering something free or at a discount motivates people to pass it on.

BEST BENEFIT: Effective at driving people to your website. Plus, you have a chance of becoming viral.

DRAWBACK: You could end up in the junk mail box. Mailing lists can get out of control.

Booby Traps _____

When attempting any marketing effort that has the potential to become viral, be aware of bandwidth restrictions. If your pass-along e-mail begins drawing people by the thousands, you may need to purchase a higher bandwidth quickly, and that can become expensive. Make sure you've planned ahead for this scenario so you'll be able to deal with it quickly should it happen.

❑ **Customer Survey.** If your primary goal is to get new clients, this might not be your best bet. Customer surveys are best for strengthening your relationship with existing clients. Indirectly, surveys may educate customers about products/services you offer of which they might have been unaware.

BEST BENEFIT: Surveys show your customers you are interested in their feedback. Easy way to stay on top of shifts in customer satisfaction.

DRAWBACK: None! It's always good to ask your customers' opinions. Knowledge is power!

Booby Traps _____

It is illegal to conduct sales efforts under the guise of research in most countries (including the United States). Sales or solicitation is not permitted in any form. The way customers learn more about your products is simply in the reading of the survey questions, not in any direct effort on your part.

❑ **Testimonials.** Particularly powerful if they come from well-known or trusted figures. Testimonials can be especially effective as a means of highlighting specific aspects of your business that are hard to describe in any other way. The more detail you provide about your source the better. Generic first-name testimonials are less effective because they give the appearance that they could be manufactured. Also, the more quantifiable the data, the better.

BEST BENEFIT: Testimonials are useful for all sorts of promotional materials and, of course, they're free.

DRAWBACK: Use of generic testimonials like "they're fantastic" seems canned and disingenuous. If the person giving the testimonial is unknown, her opinion may have little impact.

❏ **Blog**. Well-suited for businesses who have a majority of their target audience online. Blogs are great for showcasing little-known aspects of your business. They're ideal for deepening your relationship with existing customers. You need good writing skills to be a real player in this arena. They are inexpensive but time intensive.

BEST BENEFIT: Blogs can show off your clever and interesting personality. They have the potential to create customer evangelists. They are immune to spam filters.

DRAWBACK: They're a serious time commitment and require some writing chops. You also need to have a strong ego to withstand people disagreeing with you via blog comment posts.

❏ **Podcast**. Podcasts are quickly becoming an alternative to radio broadcast. They're great for sharing how-to information and can be used to provide free expert advice to a large group. Your target audience would need to be fairly tech-savvy. Once initial equipment is purchased, they're very inexpensive.

BEST BENEFIT: Because they're short, they appeal to those with short attention spans. Listeners usually tune in from start to finish, meaning information doesn't have to be repeated. Because they're new, they possess a certain novelty that intrigues those interested in new technologies. They are personal and offer a great way to connect with customers.

DRAWBACK: Podcasts aren't widespread yet. You need some technical knowledge to record and post them.

❏ **Proximity Marketing/SMS Mobile Marketing**. Great for driving foot traffic and/ or website traffic. Can deliver content like coupons, games, video, audio, or text files. Currently best suited to the under-25 crowd but as the use increases (if you're offering something truly valuable), popularity should rise. These are best used to support other marketing efforts, not as a stand alone.

BEST BENEFIT: Mobile marketing is increasing in popularity; it will likely become the next big thing in marketing. It also has the high-tech factor that appeals to many of today's jaded consumers.

DRAWBACK: If you don't offer something people consider valuable, you can be viewed as a nuisance. The majority of mobile device carriers charge subscribers for SMS messages.

❑ **Influencer Marketing.** Great for reaching activist or trendsetting audiences. Whatever form of guerrilla marketing you use, you will (hopefully) employ influencer marketing.

BEST BENEFIT: If you can get the right people talking about you, your marketing efforts are nearly free! Once it's underway, it doesn't require a lot of your time and effort—the influencers all around you will do the lion's share of the work.

DRAWBACK: None! What's not to love about people influencing people to buy your stuff?

❑ **Celebrity Endorsement**. Great for raising brand or product awareness or boosting brand credibility. More effective for targeting women.

BEST BENEFIT: *Borrowed equity*—by aligning yourself with a popular celebrity, you reap benefits, too!

DRAWBACK: If the celebrity is caught doing something salacious, you suffer the backlash, too.

def•i•ni•tion

A celebrity endorsement can be **borrowed equity** because it transfers some of the celebrity's "equity" to the product, giving the product qualities it might not have had otherwise. For example, if Angelina Jolie endorses a certain brand of lip gloss, that lip gloss becomes "sexy" by its association with her.

❑ **Product Placement**. Placement in a major motion picture would require a very high-end product. Placement in independent film can be very low cost, possibly even free. Best used for products that have broad appeal or those that are trendy. It must be easy to identify the product's use without description.

BEST BENEFIT: Product placement gets your brand in front of lots of people on a more subconscious level, and movies have a long shelf life.

DRAWBACK: Viewers may not notice.

❑ **Product Seeding**. Ideal for trendy or little known products/services. Fairly inexpensive and has the potential for large rewards.

BEST BENEFIT: You have the potential to become the next "it" product or service.

DRAWBACK: You will probably have to give away lots of product to unqualified prospects in order to have a chance of hitting your mark.

❏ **Stunt Marketing**. Stunts are typically used to create brand visibility. They can be expensive or inexpensive, depending on the scale.

BEST BENEFIT: It can garner serious media attention. After all, shock sells.

DRAWBACK: It can backfire in a seriously public way. Stunt marketing does not appeal to all audiences.

❏ **Product Sampling.** If your product is new to the market or it so greatly exceeds the experience provided by your competitor's product, sampling may be a match for you. Remember to have the product on hand to sell.

BEST BENEFIT: People get a chance to experience your product. You might reach customers you could never convince with words.

DRAWBACK: You can irritate people if you're too aggressive in offering samples.

❏ **Trade Show Event.** A trade show booth gives you access to a highly targeted audience, and it allows you to meet customers, competitors, and suppliers in person. Trade show booths are often coupled with contest or promotional items.

BEST BENEFIT: People have opted to be there and are interested in your industry. Trade shows also offer the opportunity to demonstrate your product in ways that may not be possible via other marketing channels.

DRAWBACK: Creating an effective booth can be both a challenge and heavy expense. Not for the faint of heart.

❏ **Mall Carts or Kiosks.** Good for seasonal products and for product sampling. Great for items that are likely to be impulse buys or those that are hard to find. Great place to offer free evaluations.

BEST BENEFIT: Malls offer lots of consumer traffic. Kiosks are generally less costly than opening a brick and mortar type business and lease times are often shorter.

DRAWBACK: It can be physically demanding and time exhaustive.

❏ **Open House/Launch Party**. Plan on spending a moderate amount of time and money planning and hosting an open house. Open houses are a fantastic way to generate excitement for a new product, to introduce yourself if you're new in the neighborhood, or just boost foot traffic if you don't typically get a lot of walk-ins.

BEST BENEFIT: Open houses and launch parties allow you an unprecedented opportunity to mix and mingle with customers, creating emotional bonds.

DRAWBACK: It isn't guaranteed that people will show up. It's also hard to break away from conversation if one person begins monopolizing your time. Be sure to have take-aways for others in case that happens.

❏ **Event Sponsorship.** Sponsoring events gives you a big bang for your buck. You get positive brand awareness; target marketing; and possibly a promotional tie-in, coupon distribution, or product sampling. You could even conduct a demo or contest on site. Cost for sponsorship varies based on your level of involvement, the type of event, and the number of event attendees. A local 5K race is likely under $500.

BEST BENEFIT: Sponsorship increases your standing in the community and creates goodwill. It's also a way to contribute to a cause.

DRAWBACK: Sponsorships can blend into the background.

❏ **Posters in Unusual Locations.** These are best used to reach college-aged audiences.

BEST BENEFIT: You can often be the only advertiser in the area. It's an uncluttered medium.

DRAWBACK: It's becoming more and more popular, so it may not be uncluttered for long.

❏ **Movie Screen Advertising.** Products/services that have broad appeal benefit from movie theater advertising. Because of the quality of film, take care to create an extremely slick ad.

BEST BENEFIT: Recall seems to be relatively high among this type of advertising. They're usually affordable and you have a captive audience.

DRAWBACK: You typically don't have control over what movie your ads precede.

❏ **Banner Ads.** Banner ads can reach a variety of demographics based on the sites you select. Effective banner ads usually have a call-to-action such as "click here for …" or "40% Off Now." The typical banner ad size is 468 pixels wide by 60 pixels high.

BEST BENEFIT: Standard size eliminates the need for customization. Even if people don't click through, you've gotten your logo in front of people, increasing brand recognition.

DRAWBACK: Click-through rates for banner ads are trending down. Many people have an aversion to banner ads.

Booby Traps

When creating a brochure, leave out information that is likely to change. Give broad strokes and save the in-flux data for your website so you can change it quickly and without incurring a huge expense.

❏ **Fly-By Airplane Banner/Skywriting**. Aerial advertising prices start at $500 and go up to $50,000+. Effective at reaching a large group of people in a highly noticeable way. Best for targeting people at beaches or sports events. If you have a call to action, even better.

BEST BENEFIT: You're sure to catch people's attention. The sky is the ultimate in uncluttered ad space!

DRAWBACK: It's expensive.

❏ **Sports Team Sponsorship**. Sports team sponsorships can be as small as your local high school football team to a NASCAR sponsorship—the choice is yours. These are great for endearing yourself to a particular community.

BEST BENEFIT: You reach a wide demographic. Lots of different types of people come to games.

DRAWBACK: Even though they represent a wide demographic, the audience often draws from the same group of people over and over.

❏ **Logo Items**. Giving away novelty items/promotional items can be a great way to build brand awareness. And of course, everyone loves free stuff! Best items to pick are unusual and entertaining or useful. Our company, Spellbinders, Inc., sent out mini lava lamps at Christmas time last year. Our clients are still raving about them and they aren't just being polite—when we visit their offices, we see them on display!

BEST BENEFIT: If you choose wisely, your logo is in front of your customer for a long time.

DRAWBACK: If you pick something less than appealing, it will end up in the trash.

❏ **Strategic Partnership**. When you have a limited budget, partnership can be a great way to extend your reach.

BEST BENEFIT: Two heads are better than one. Together, you can afford to do things neither could do alone. Partnership marketing allows you to make use of additional distribution channels.

DRAWBACK: Be careful not to partner with a business that could overshadow you. Choose different, but complimentary, products or services and those that are similar in size.

❑ **Customer Appreciation Night**. Expressing your gratitude for their business can turn happy customers into full-fledged brand loyalists. Appreciation events are wonderful for developing stronger relationships with existing customers.

BEST BENEFIT: "Thank you" is an extremely powerful phrase. People love to feel appreciated, so there's a high probability that your event will create some customer evangelists.

DRAWBACK: You aren't likely to get new customers from this practice. Ask for an RSVP so you can accurately gauge attendance and ensure a good return on investment.

❑ **Customer Appreciation Program**. Some form of customer appreciation is recommended for all businesses.

BEST BENEFIT: Boosting spread of word-of-mouth methods. People who feel appreciated are more motivated to talk about you.

DRAWBACK: Because it can be large or small, there's really no drawback to customer appreciation programs. Just don't start anything you can't continue.

❑ **Social Networking Site Participation**. Social networking works best for those products that have a computer-savvy target audience. It's a great way to differentiate your product by providing the genuine interaction that today's consumers crave.

BEST BENEFIT: Provides a forum where existing customers can sell your product to others in the community.

DRAWBACK: Only viable if your target audience is comfortable communicating via the Internet. Time investment is not worth the benefit if you don't have a large audience already participating in the social networking site.

❑ **Create Your Own Message Board**. Message boards work well for products or services that require some degree of consumer education or those that might intrinsically spur discussion.

BEST BENEFIT: Creates a sense of community and drives more traffic to your site. Can become a hang out place for your target audience.

DRAWBACK: Time intensive to manage. Requires an administrator/moderator to monitor what's posted and keep materials up to date.

❏ **Participate in Existing Message Board.** Easy way to start a conversation about your product. Allows you to become an expert in your field.

BEST BENEFIT: Gives you insight (in the form of feedback) into your customers' wants and needs. Could save you a bundle in research costs.

DRAWBACK: Could require quite a bit of research and reading before you find applicable posts to respond to.

Here's the Buzz _____

Writing or responding to letters to the editor is an easy way to get your name in front of newspaper readers—if your letter stands out. Sharing your opinion allows you to expertise yourself in a way that's totally free. Just be sure to align yourself with a positive topic that will benefit the community. Don't just carp or complain.

❏ **Press Releases and Media Alerts**. Writing and submitting press releases to newspapers and magazines is a great way to garner publicity, and people are more likely to believe what they read when it comes from an unbiased source then they are paid advertisements.

BEST BENEFIT: Free and often easy as many journalists have space that needs filling in their publications.

DRAWBACK: To be successful, your product must be something that the target audience of the publication would buy.

❏ **Barter**. If you have goods or services to trade, consider bartering.

BEST BENEFIT: Can increase your customer base, help conserve cash, and provide the means to get rid of excess inventory.

DRAWBACK: Must have a product that someone is willing to barter for.

❏ **Street Team**. If you have a large following of product loyalists, gather them together and send them out to spread the word.

BEST BENEFIT: Very inexpensive way to get your information out to the masses.

DRAWBACK: Not all products can inspire the type of devotion this stunt requires.

❏ **Reciprocal Linking**. Reciprocal linking is a mutually beneficial arrangement for companies with similar or complementary target audiences.

BEST BENEFIT: Can increase your website traffic and search engine rankings. Free.

DRAWBACK: Can reflect badly on you if the company's websites that you provide links for aren't relevant and up to date.

❑ **Opt-In E-Mail Newsletter.** Anything that subscribers must opt in to receive will be welcomed by readers.

BEST BENEFIT: eNewsletters can help build your client list as people recognize your expertise. They're a source of free publicity and are very effective at driving people to your website.

DRAWBACK: You must have knowledge about something that people are interested in learning more about. Could prove difficult if writing does not come easily to you. Requires an investment of time on a regular basis.

❑ **Customer Reward Program.** Rewarding your customers (with coupons, prizes, or points for prizes) for their patronage is a way to ensure continued satisfaction and brand loyalty.

BEST BENEFIT: Allows you to identify your best customers, track their buying habits, and reward their loyalty.

DRAWBACK: Can be cost prohibitive.

❑ **Customer of the Month.** Picking and honoring a customer of the month is another great way to reward customer loyalty.

BEST BENEFIT: Effective means of thanking your best customers. Helps build and cement customer relations.

DRAWBACK: Really no drawback. Anything that inspires loyalty is likely to have a positive impact on your bottom line.

❑ **Contest or Sweepstakes.** People love being offered the chance to win a prize, and it's a great way to thank your loyal customers.

BEST BENEFIT: Can help build brand awareness and drive traffic to your site. Effective means of gathering customer information.

DRAWBACK: The laws regarding contest and sweepstakes for your particular state will need to be researched.

Tactics That Create Goodwill

Some guerrilla marketing methods are doubly beneficial. Those that provide some benefit to the community are definitely win-win.

❏ **Cause-related Viral Message**. Cause-related viral messages lend instant credibility to your company.

BEST BENEFIT: Allows people to feel good about buying your product. Can differentiate you from your competitors.

DRAWBACK: Not a good fit if your target audience is not outspokenly socially conscious or "green."

❏ **Partner with Local Schools.** Entering into a partnership with an area school lets the community know that your company is socially responsible.

BEST BENEFIT: It's an investment in the community and the families of your employees. Enhances your corporate image.

DRAWBACK: Your product must be something that the school would be eager to be associated with.

❏ **Donate to Charity.** Donating your goods or services to a charity event is a great way to promote goodwill and build awareness of your company.

BEST BENEFIT: The event you are sponsoring will often announce your sponsorship and allow you to promote your company on all their printed materials and possibly on signage at the venue.

DRAWBACK: Can be expensive.

❏ **Free Seminars or Consultations.** Want to be known as the expert in your field? Free seminars are an excellent way to highlight your knowledge in your field. Very inexpensive with the potential for significant benefits.

BEST BENEFIT: Being recognized as an expert builds credibility. You'll benefit from increased visibility. In many cases, you'll become better known than your competition. It's basically free advertising.

DRAWBACK: Free seminars can be time consuming, although once they're developed, the time invested is reduced. You must take into account the opportunity cost.

❏ **Adopt Something (Highway, Playground, etc.).** When you need to demonstrate commitment to the community, adopting something like a highway or a playground is a perfect fit. Ideal for landscaping companies or community related organizations.

BEST BENEFIT: It's fairly permanent, and being associated with a public service enhances your image.

DRAWBACK: You have to provide ongoing clean up and maintenance, so it's not a one-time cost.

❏ **Support-a-Beach Impression.** Obviously, this is only effective if your target audiences go to the beach.

BEST BENEFIT: Impossible to overlook. You're contributing to a worthy cause—helping eliminate litter on beaches.

DRAWBACK: As the day goes on, your beach impressions fade away.

The Least You Need to Know

- ◆ Before you pick your guerrilla marketing tools, take a look at what your competition is doing.

- ◆ Figure out who your primary and secondary audiences are and pick guerrilla marketing methods that will speak to them.

- ◆ A combination of innovative and traditional marketing tactics works best.

- ◆ There are some tactics that work across all demographics.

Message in a Bottle: Creating and Spreading the Word

In This Chapter

◆ Writing your tagline and elevator speech

◆ Creating your website

◆ Motivating your guerrilla marketing team

◆ Creating your guerrilla marketing materials and applying your message

You've identified your strengths, you've determined your target audience, and you've figured out what type of guerrilla tactics you want to use. Now it's time for the heavy lifting. Time to put the parts together and make them fly.

Craft a Meaningful Message

Lack of a meaningful message is, without a doubt, one of the most common downfalls of so many well-intentioned marketing efforts. People often invest oodles of time figuring out with whom to communicate and then little or no time is given to the actual content message. Thousands of dollars are spent on websites and then copy is just slapped on the page without thought to how compelling the words themselves are. It's easy to lose sight of how critical the message itself is. If you're implementing several different guerrilla marketing tactics, you probably have a number of elements to write. Let's start with the basics.

Your Tagline

First, think of the one thing you want to communicate. If you could only tell a prospect one thing about yourself, what would it be? Trying to cover too many bases is where you lose people. Come to terms with the fact that you will not be able to impart everything about yourself in one simple statement. Instead focus on the one thing that differentiates you from the competition and showcase that.

Example: when Tom's of Maine introduced its toothpaste, it knew it was competing with giants. Getting people to switch over to its toothpaste by using a sales pitch already touted by Colgate and Crest was unlikely. After all, why should someone switch to Tom's of Maine toothpaste when what they currently use already fights cavities, prevents plaque, kills bad breath, and so on? Tom's execs must have asked themselves, what's the one thing we want to communicate? Tom's of Maine opted to focus on the one unmet need in the market. It highlighted the natural aspect of its brand.

Brainwaves

Taglines can be descriptive (explaining your business) or emotional (creating a feeling for or about your business). Taglines are particularly helpful when your business name doesn't make it obvious what you're selling.

A great example of a descriptive tagline is Kinko's "Our office is your office." "Like a good neighbor, State Farm is there" would be considered an emotional tagline.

Your Elevator Speech

Earlier in the book, we touched on the concept of an elevator speech, but to recap: an elevator speech is a short description of what you do, one that could be recited in the length of time it takes to complete an elevator ride. The idea is to come up with an engaging but brief response to the question, "So what do you do?" You want something better than "I'm a lawyer," or "I own an organic produce market." Every time someone asks you what you do and you offer a lackluster response, you've missed an opportunity. Bottom line: no matter what guerrilla marketing strategy you employ, you need an elevator speech.

Before you get started writing your elevator speech, consider that you may need more than one. A highly targeted elevator speech is more effective than a one-size-fits-all. Identify your three most important target audiences and create an elevator speech for each.

Start by jotting down answers to the following questions: Who are you? What do you do? Who do you do it for? What's the benefit in working with you?

> **Brainwaves**
>
> Tinsel Town's version of an elevator speech can be seen in the movie *Working Girl.* Melanie Griffith's character explains how she came up with the idea she just pitched while, literally, riding up to the boardroom in an elevator.

Once you have answers to these questions, string them together and edit down. Eliminate and combine phrases as needed. Your goal is to keep it short, otherwise it sounds memorized. Shoot for 60 words or less. Remember, focus on what's in it for the customer. Tell them the benefit, not the process you take to create the benefit. What does this sound like? Something like this:

"I'm Tom. I own an organic produce market in the neighborhood. I partner with local growers to provide fresh, nutritious foods for locals who desire to live a healthier and more globally conscious lifestyle."

That one is 34 words. Here's another, shorter elevator speech:

"I'm Dhara. I'm an investment banker. I help my clients save money so they can retire early."

Or how about "I'm Caroline. I'm a hair stylist. I help women look and feel beautiful."

Be sure to use real-world language when writing your elevator speech. Avoid jargon phrases like:

"I'm Arnold. I help people leverage their skill sets to enhance their job performance and maximize their career paths."

Every word of your message needs to be power-packed. The more useless the words and fluff you use, the faster your audience will tune you out. Need an example of how this works? Look at the following sample sentences and see which works best.

- When you're facing a challenge, often the best approach is to simply do the task at hand.

- Just do it.

Less is more when it comes to creating a message that will reach your target audience.

And now that you've got your elevator speech (or speeches depending upon your audience) ... memorize it. Say it in the shower. Practice it on people you run into, even if they aren't potential customers. Practice makes perfect!

Writing Your Website

Before we get into writing, we have to touch on website design, because the two are inextricably intertwined. Before you assemble the parts you think should be on the site, surf around and look at your competitors' sites. What are they offering? What works well? What seems to be missing? Make a list of the must-have items you will include.

If you're working with a developer to create your website, he or she will help you organize the content on your site. Once you've provided the overview of what you want to communicate on the site, the developer will probably ask you questions that may prompt you to add additional information or features. After you've gone through this process of discovery, you can expect the developer to give you a *wireframe*. The wireframe will help you figure out where you need to write content.

def•i•ni•tion

Wireframe is a basic visual guide, similar to a flow chart, that illustrates how users will navigate around a website.

What if you aren't working with a developer? Perhaps you're creating your website on your own. What then? The key is to make the user experience intuitive, meaning that stuff on your site should be where people would logically look for it. If you're unsure whether you've created an intuitive site, ask a friend to take it for a test drive. Things should be labeled in clear, understandable ways using visual clues to help guide them along.

Point of View

From what point of view will you write? Will you talk directly to the audience, or will you write about your business as an outside person? Once you pick a point of view, stick with it throughout the site. Most websites are written in either first or third person voice.

- First person—Writer is narrator. Pronouns used are I, me, my, mine, we, our, and ours. Using first person tends to set a warm tone.

- Third person—Commonly used in research papers and business reports. Typically considered more "business-like." Pronouns include he, she, him, her, hers, his, it, its, they, them, and their.

One idea per paragraph is a good rule of thumb to keep things simple on your website. Copy on websites is typically much shorter than for printed materials, primarily because looking at a computer screen can be tiring on the eyes, and because people who are surfing the web have a short attention span.

Easy on the Eye

Many website visitors leave a website within seconds of arriving. You have precious little time to make a first impression. Keep your visitors longer by making your site appealing and easy to read. Here's how:

- Break up copy using bulleted lists and subheads.

- Use a simple typeface.

- Don't overuse bold, underline, and italic (or worse yet, all of the above)—never use shadow.

- Make type large enough so that it is easily readable (even for people who are over 40).

- Make sure type and background contrast for readability.

- Don't put too much copy on the front page—it overwhelms the information.

- Put important content above the fold, in other words, where a reader can see it without having to scroll.

Many studies show that people read websites differently than printed materials. They are more likely to scan web content instead of reading it word for word, as they might a printed piece. If you want people to read your website, keep it simple.

Avoid Vague Claims and Meaningless Words

Over generalized claims to fame: You know this type of message. They're the ones that claim to be the "leader" or "most popular" or even "top ranked," without any substantiation. If you are top ranked, cite exactly who ranked you tops. If you're the most popular, tell your audience with whom. And if you're only ranked number one among an extremely small subset of the population, then you should think of something else to hang your hat on. We're not saying it's worthless—being rated number one by a publication with a small circulation is worth a mention somewhere on your webpage, but it's not your marquis message. If you've won the J. D. Power & Associates Award, that's a headline. You ranked number one on the annual survey conducted by your city's daily newspaper? That's a fairly substantial claim. Other words and phrases that have been overused to the point of being meaningless are:

- World class
- Premier
- Revolutionary
- Quality
- Professional
- Cutting edge
- Industry leader
- Powerful
- Valuable
- Ultimate

Many of these are fine words, but they've become words that people skip over to get to the real message. Instead focus on the benefits of your product or service versus the competition. Need help? Try out ThinkMap's Visual Thesaurus (www.thinkmap.com/visualthesaurus.jsp). This affordable and useful tool can help jumpstart your writing efforts.

Editing Down

The more you edit down, the better your copy will be. You can almost always find ways to say things in a more concise manner. More complicated is not better. Some common phrases that can be turned into one word:

Common Phrase	Replacement
Provided that	If
At the present moment in time	Now

Common Phrase	Replacement
The majority of	Most
Facilitate	Help
In order to	To
Being that	Since
Utilize	Use
So as to	To

Phrases to Skip

Many phrases aren't even necessary. They can be eliminated without replacement because they are superfluous. Here are a few:

◆ We are pleased to announce

◆ The fact that

◆ On a daily (or monthly or annual) basis.

Common Writing Mistakes

These writing tips apply to a website, brochure, flyer, or any other collateral you create. First, there are some rules that are steadfast. Here are a few:

◆ Spelling. This is, of course, the most cardinal rule. Feature a misspelled word in your marketing piece and you can just kiss the customer goodbye. If you can't pay enough attention to get your own stuff typo-free, why should customers trust you with whatever it is you want to do for them?

◆ Contractions and Possessives. These are errors that will not be picked up by spell check because they aren't misspellings. "It's" is a contraction for it is. "Its" is a possessive. "Their" is a possessive while "they're" is a contraction for they are. Same for "your" and "you're" and "whose" and "who's". Make sure you've got it right. A good tip to remember is that possessive pronouns never have apostrophes.

◆ Singular and plural issues. If you refer to a singular person, make sure you use "he or she" later in the sentence. Multiple people can be referred to using "their." What doesn't work: "First, the customer gives us their …" is incorrect.

"First, the customer gives us his or her ..." is correct. Another example: "The company has been experiencing growth in their ..." is incorrect. "The company has been experiencing growth in its ..." is correct.

◆ Effect and affect. Effect is a noun that means a result or consequence. Affect is a verb that means to influence. Effect can be used as a verb that means to bring into being. Wrong: "Using our product will effect your bottom line." Right: "Using our product will affect your bottom line." Wrong: "The e-mail marketing campaign had the desired affect." Right: "The e-mail marketing campaign had the desired effect."

◆ Principle versus principal. Principal is an adjective meaning ranked first in importance. Principle is an underlying law or the basic way in which something works.

Break the Rules

Break free from your fourth-grade grammar teacher; it's okay to break some rules. There are hard and fast rules (see the common writing mistakes just mentioned), but writing in a reader-friendly and appealing way often requires an out-of-the-box writing style. You'll notice incomplete sentences in this book (and in many best sellers, too).

One of the best ways to overhaul your writing style is by switching from the passive voice to the active voice. Active and passive voice refer to the relationship between the verb and the subject. It's all about structuring your sentence. The subject should be doing something instead of having something happen to them or it. For example, instead of saying "The sales flyers were made by the first shift team members." Instead, write: "The first shift team members made the sales flyers." Another example: "The survey was taken by participants," would be more powerful if stated as: "Participants took the survey." The order of your sentence should place the person or thing doing the action before the verb. For more writing tips, check out the book *Woe Is I* by Patricia T. O'Conner.

Here's the Buzz

A must on every website is an "About Us" page. The "About Us" page tells visitors who you are and what your unique selling proposition is. As apparent as the nature of your business may be to you, it might not be as obvious to others. Failure to include this customary feature can leave visitors confused.

Make It Easy to Spread the Word

A key element in every guerrilla marketing campaign is making it easy to spread the message. After all, word of mouth is guerrilla marketing's best friend. When you create your website or any other guerrilla marketing material, keep in mind how easy it is to pass on to others. This could be as simple as a "tell a friend" feature on your website that allows users to send information via a simple click and e-mail entry. Supercharge your "tell a friend" efforts by making the shared info contain a discount.

Example: "Click here to send a friend a 20 percent discount on his or her first order!" Another important way to make it easy to share your message is by providing contact information (and when you are able, hot links) in all your communications. Customers who want to refer someone to you don't want to have to hunt your info down. Make sure your contact info, URL, links, and tagline are on every communication piece you create.

Giving your brand advocates materials like flyers, brochures, coupons, business cards, or downloadable PDF files can help them spread your message, too.

Here's the Buzz

One of the best ways to make your guerrilla marketing message easy to share is by giving your influencers an interesting talking point, something that is easy to recount to another person. Remember Gary's Uptown Restaurant and Bar? He gave people an easy to share talking point: bald people eat for free on Wednesdays. What's easier to share than that?

Motivating Your Guerrilla Team

Everybody wants to know what's in it for them. Even if people love you, a little incentive never hurts. In fact, offering rewards to the people who help you in your guerrilla marketing efforts not only broadens your marketing reach, but it also creates goodwill. Numerous research studies show that recognition is directly tied to performance, so whether you're rewarding your team members or rewarding customers who help you guerrilla market, people who are recognized perform better.

Incentives for team members:

- Time off with pay
- Treat to lunch
- Celebration
- Cash or gift certificates

- A casual dress day
- Public recognition
- Entry into a drawing for large prize
- Special parking space

- Written thank you note
- Group outing
- Trophy or medal

- Fill up car with gas

Incentives for customers:

- Handwritten thank you card with discount coupon
- Special privileges
- Upgraded status
- "Customer of the month" bulletin board
- Special delivery or valet service
- iPod, cell phone, or digital camera
- Invitation to a special party

- Free services

- Gift certificates
- Recognition in newsletter
- Fruit basket

- Movie tickets

- Entry into a prize drawing

The Least You Need to Know

- What your message says is as important as how it looks or how it is delivered.
- No matter what guerrilla marketing method you use, you need an elevator speech.
- Less is more when it comes to writing.
- Make spreading your message easy and rewarding, and it's sure to reach more people.

Chapter 20

No Money, No Problem: Free (or Nearly Free) Guerrilla Marketing

In This Chapter

◆ Methods of customer appreciation

◆ Garnering press attention

◆ Partnerships and sponsorships

◆ Ways to accelerate guerrilla marketing

Guerrilla marketing is all about getting the biggest bang for your buck. But what if you have very few bucks? Don't despair. There's a world of opportunity out there that doesn't take a hefty marketing budget. All you need is a little creativity. Read on for some inexpensive methods you can try.

Customer Appreciation

Taking the time to show your customers how much you appreciate them is always a great idea. One way to shine the spotlight on your most faithful customers is a "Customer of the Month" program. You can implement this idea in whatever way works best for you—there are no rules. You can even make it a "Customer of the Day" or "Customer of the Week" program if that suits your purposes better. You could choose the 10th or 100th customer on a given day, week, or month and single them out for a reward; you could honor the customer who makes the largest purchase(s) in a predetermined time span or you could enter every customer into a random drawing. This method is also effective for giving kudos to customers who make referrals. Once you've outlined the criteria, anything goes for rewards. Here are a few ideas:

◆ Post customer's name and your message of thanks on a bulletin board, on a reader board, or in your newsletter

◆ Offer discounted or complimentary products or services

◆ Reserve a parking space for the honoree right in front of your business

That's thinking guerrilla. Low cost but high impact! And don't forget about the Internet. Your website is a great place to highlight your best customers. Keep a digital camera on hand to take the customer's picture while they are in your store; then feature the customer's photo and relevant details in a monthly or weekly column online. Customers might welcome this spotlight as an opportunity to showcase their own company offerings. One legal note: ask the customer to sign a release saying it's okay for you to use the picture!

Brainwaves

Bags, Inc., a retail packaging materials company based in Boulder, Colorado, has a fabulous Customer of the Month program in place. Bags, Inc., offers a variety of products that can be used in many different ways. Its ingenious customer of the month program is a win-win—it showcases the customer and the customer's business while simultaneously introducing different uses for Bags, Inc. products.

Each month Bags, Inc. selects a customer who has used its product in an innovative way to feature that customer on its website. Bags, Inc. devotes an entire web page to the Customer of the Month, explaining how the customer uses the Bags, Inc., product, as well as a company profile. Links to the Customer of the Month's website are displayed prominently at the top along with complete contact information. Very clever. Through this one program, Bags, Inc. is recognizing its customers and offering them something of value (free publicity), and it's shining the spotlight on its various product offerings and potential new uses.

Customer Appreciation Night

If keeping up with weekly or monthly prizes and recognition seems daunting, why not host a Customer Appreciation Night and use it to thank all your customers at one time? Offer discounts, refreshments, entertainment—whatever works for your audience. With a little legwork, you can probably find local entertainers who are willing to pitch in for the publicity and for the opportunity to hand out business cards or sell their CDs.

Alternately, you could have a Customer Appreciation Day during which you offer customers something extra special. You can repeat as often as possible. The "something special" could be as simple as offering Starbucks coffee along with a note of gratitude for your customers' business. At the time of press in our area, we could purchase a 96-ounce container of Starbucks coffee (with all the accoutrements including cups, sugar, creamer, stir sticks, and so on) for under $15. A 2.5-gallon container cost under $50. If you did this simple act once a week for your early morning customers, just think how much goodwill you'd create for less than $15 a week! (Along with the coffee, consider offering tea and bottled water for those who don't partake in the java.)

Here's the Buzz

Old-fashioned thank-you notes are an oldie but goodie. Each week, select ten random customers and handwrite them a thank-you note. Never underestimate the power of a genuine personal expression of gratitude.

And the Winner Is ...

Everyone loves a chance to hear those magical words: "You're a winner!" It doesn't even matter how valuable the prize is—people love the idea of getting something for free. Fortune 500 companies make regular use of contests to market products because contests can lead to big sales. (Think McDonald's Monopoly game and instant prizes under the lids of soda bottles.) Yes, big companies do it on a much larger scale, but so what? You can still get in this game. To pique people's interest and get them to enter, do one of two things:

◆ Offer lots of small prizes so the odds of winning are high or

◆ Offer one big prize so there's something really valuable for people to hope to win.

Either of these methods should drive people to enter, and having lots of entries is key because every entry provides valuable contact information for future mailings and promotions. Make sure your entry form has space for the entrant to provide their contact information.

Here's the Buzz

Pack some punch in your contest by designing it around your product or service. For example, if you own a local bakery, hold a contest to name a new or existing pastry. Ask people to write a short essay or draw a picture that relates to their experience with your product. Once all entries are submitted, hold a reception to announce the winner and unveil the new name. This is a great opportunity to get the media involved, especially if you're launching a new product.

Inexpensive Novelty Items

People love a free gift, especially if it's something fun or useful. Crazy, off-the-wall novelties certainly grab people's attention, but if at all possible choose something associated with your business, and more importantly, something of value. Logo-emblazoned junk will just end up in the hands of your customers' kids and will become yet another piece of "stuff" somebody has to clean up. Nobody wants a button or a 5 cent slinky with a company logo on it.

Determining what qualifies as "something of value" depends on your audience. If you own a second-hand computer store, you could give a free mouse pad with every purchase (or maybe just for stopping by your store). If you have a gas station, hand out free window cleaning wipes. Whatever you choose, don't forget to have your company name, contact information, or website and logo printed on the item. Buy these items in bulk and the cost per item will be minimal. Select an item that relates to your business and is highly appealing to your target audience. Here are some possible novelty items:

- Sticky note pads
- Water bottle lanyards
- Emergency flashlights
- Calendars or magnetic message boards
- Pens or pencils
- Travel alarm clocks
- Packets of flower seeds
- Stress balls

- ◆ Umbrellas
- ◆ Tote bags
- ◆ Piggy banks
- ◆ Pocket knives
- ◆ Pedometers

Of course, there are dozens of industry-specific novelty items. Golf tees, pet dishes, tennis balls, fishing lures—the list goes on and on. If your target audience is children or parents of young children, there are hundreds of inexpensive options that would hold their interest—stuffed animals, bath toys, puzzles, and other novelties can grab the younger audience's attention.

Be a Good Citizen

Being an active member of your community is guerrilla marketing at its finest. Best of all, it's a win-win. You contribute to a worthy cause and your neighbors get to know you better!

Sponsor a Local Sports Team or Event

If you aim to promote goodwill and get your name out in the community, sponsor a local sports team or a community event. Along with providing a sense of community pride, sponsorship of a team or event can provide some tangible benefits. For a modest sponsorship fee, teams will typically place your company name and logo on uniforms or T-shirts and may allow a banner prominently placed at the games or events. Many will also be willing to feature your logo on their plaques, certificates, and trophies, as well as put free ads in their programs or supporting materials.

> **Brainwaves**
>
> Sports and sporting events play a large role in many people's lives. By sponsoring a local team, you are granted access into an existing community comprised of people who probably prefer to do business with people they feel have an interest in their lives, as opposed to someone that they have no connection with.

Donate to Charity

Donate your services or products to charity fundraisers or charity events to build awareness of your company while providing a valuable service to the community. Best of all, there's more in it than the satisfaction of helping out, although that is definitely a big plus. Corporate philanthropy pays off in positive word of mouth, plus you give people an opportunity to experience your product or service (experiential marketing!).

Expertise Yourself

Being recognized as an expert in your field builds credibility. Credibility influences buying decisions. Here are a few ways to establish yourself as the go-to person in your industry.

Give Away Free Advice

How do you become a well-known expert in your community? Start by giving free lectures or workshops at local bookstores, libraries, community meetings, or churches. This requires a time commitment on your part, but it also lets you network with attendees in a non-sales-pitch setting. Just be sure you are well prepared to deliver helpful and insightful information on your subject and bring plenty of business cards.

Don't have the time for free lectures? Create a section on your website for expert tips. Post free, useful information and give customers a reason to tell others about you. This establishes you as a valuable resource. Winn-Dixie, one of the largest goods retailers in the nation, employs this method. Check out www.winn-dixie.com and you'll find all kinds of useful information. They offer recipes, food safety tips, healthy living guidelines, and hurricane preparation checklists, as well as other community resources.

Many newspapers and magazines also value contributions from experts who are willing to dole out advice for free. Contact a magazine that fits your demographic or get in touch with your local newspaper to determine submission guidelines.

Another way you can use your expertise to your advantage is by creating an informative handout that potential customers can take away with them. For example, if you own a landscaping company, consider creating a handout that includes plant care instructions, educational information, facts about your state tree, or coloring pages and puzzles about local flowers. As with all promotional materials, make sure you include your name, phone number, e-mail address, website address, and "elevator speech" so that it's easy for your new customers to contact you.

Blogging or Social Networking Sites

If your customer base includes people who are online (and almost everybody's customer base does), blogging or social networking is a great way to position yourself as an expert when your budget is slim. To be a successful blogger, you need writing skills (or a great editor) and a generous amount of time. (See Chapter 13 for in-depth info on blogging and social networking.)

Press Releases and Newspaper Coverage

Extra, extra read all about you! Are you the first of your type of business in your community? Are you launching an innovative new product or service? If you have a newsworthy angle, you might be able to get your story in the newspaper. Getting your story in the newspaper is extremely valuable because it provides instant credibility. Understandably, people trust a newspaper article more than paid advertising. But getting your story in print requires more than just sending press releases, according to Brent Manley, editor of the American Contract Bridge League's monthly magazine, *The Bridge Bulletin*. Brent has more than 20 years experience in the newspaper business; he worked as a reporter for several daily newspapers including the New Orleans daily paper, *The Times-Picayune*, and *The Memphis Press-Scimitar*. He also served as City Editor for *The Houston Post*.

"Before you approach a newspaper, read the publication for a few weeks," said Brent. "Pay attention to the type of stories they run, as well as the types they never run. This will give you an idea of what's likely to pique their interest." Brent advises that company representatives go by the newspaper and introduce themselves instead of simply e-mailing, faxing, or mailing stories over for the first time. "Drop by the news outlet and find out what the reporters are interested in and in what format they like to receive stories and tips," he suggested. "Most quality material that came to me didn't come by mail alone."

During his time at *The Houston Post*, Brent said that typically less than 10% of the material received via mail made it into the paper. "I received volumes of mail and there were people who would send 4, 5, even 10 press releases in a week. It got to the point that I'd recognize the envelope and wouldn't even open it. Bombarding a newspaper with puff press releases is not effective. It really turns people off. Newspapers have to answer for the material they run and they're not interested in printing a story that says nothing more than 'Here we are. We're in business.'"

"Newspapers look for stories that are of interest or value to their readers, which doesn't mean your story has to be monumental. If you have an employee who's worked for your company for 25 years and has never taken a sick day, that's interesting. Are you a local company that just got your foot in the door to doing business in China? That's interesting," said Brent. "It's better to wait until you have something with meat on it before you approach the newspaper. Give a reporter one or two bad leads and you'll probably find that he or she will get busy really fast when you come around."

In his current position, Brent receives requests from people who'd like publicity in *The Bridge Bulletin*, a highly specialized magazine that centers on duplicate bridge. "I get mass e-mails from many game producers and publishers of books and videos on bridge, but I don't respond to spam-looking e-mails" said Brent. What does get his attention? "If someone sends me a personal e-mail, I'll take a look and see if what they're promoting is something that would be useful for our members. If they've used my name, I know they've taken the time to read the publication and look up the editor. Those leads are more apt to turn into something of interest than the mass e-mails which often don't even apply to our organization. A personal e-mail is much more appealing than one that appears to have been sent to 600 other people."

Creating a Press Release

When creating a press release, include your company information, contact name, and info at the top of the press release followed by PRESS RELEASE in uppercase. Also include:

- ◆ Date for release
- ◆ Contact info for further information, including name, phone, e-mail, address, and fax number

The press release should begin with your city, state, and company name followed by a power sentence about what you're announcing. Remember, this is not a teaser: get straight to the point when writing a press release. What will happen, who's involved, and who or what is affected? Include answers to the five W's and one H: who, what, why, where, when, and how. If you have photos, facts, or quotes, include those. Typing -30- at the end of the release indicates the end.

Many people view newspaper stories as more credible than advertisements.

> **Brainwaves**
>
> Is your press release announcing an event that you hope the press will attend? Consider sending out a media advisory instead of a press release. Outline what's going to happen, when, and where.

Write an Article for an Online Publication

Write an article about your business for an online publication. Spotlight a new offering, announce a milestone achievement, or detail a unique service your company provides. You can find an online magazine, sometimes called ezines, to fit your needs by doing a search on your particular business. Like newspaper articles, online publications have more credibility than paid advertising. Keep in mind that the more detail you provide—photos, facts, and figures—the more likely you are to see your story in the ezine.

Create Joint Ventures

Two heads are better than one. Establish relationships with complementary businesses in your area and cross promote your products. It's the "you scratch my back, I'll scratch yours" principle. You could do this by offering your new partner's product as a free gift with the purchase of your product (and your new partner would do the same).

For example, if you are a florist, you might partner with a local candy or stationary store for a Valentine's Day promotion. When someone purchases a bouquet of flowers, he or she also receives a certificate for a discounted box of candy or a card.

You could also co-sponsor an event. If you own a hair salon, you could team up with a local massage therapist and a trendy boutique for an open house. The additional products and services your partners offer will make the event more interesting. They can also help shoulder the cost of hosting and promoting the event.

> **Brainwaves**
>
> Don't limit yourself to just one partnership; instead, create an entire network of complementary businesses. If you're a clothing store, you could cross promote with a dry cleaner, a personal shopper, and an upscale jeweler. You're an interior designer? Consider partnering with a general contractor, a painter, and a fabric store.

Testimonials

Every customer you've ever had is overjoyed at the product or service you provide. If only you had more of them! This is the perfect scenario for testimonials, and you may already have some on hand. Customers who are happy with your offerings may have already written in to express their adoration. If they haven't, why wait? Ask for feedback in the form of a testimonial.

To solicit testimonials, you'll need to do a little work beforehand. At the point of sale, ask your customers to provide basic information such as: name, address, phone number, and e-mail address. (Assure them you are not selling or otherwise abusing their information.) Use this information to follow up with your customers, ideally as soon as possible after their experience with you. You can create an online survey or you can send a follow-up letter including a postage-paid return envelope inside.

> **Brainwaves**
>
> Create easy-to-use and easy-to-tally surveys at www. surveymonkey.com. For a small fee, you can create your own survey to send out to whomever you choose via e-mail. (Be careful not to violate spam laws.) The results are compiled for you and are exportable in a wide variety of formats.

Here's a sample of the type of questions your customer satisfaction survey could include:

On a scale of 1 to 10 with 10 being extremely satisfied and 1 being extremely dissatisfied, please rate the following:

- Satisfaction with product or service offerings
- Satisfaction with the level of customer service provided
- Satisfaction with the overall experience

On a scale of 1 to 10 with 10 being extremely likely and 1 being extremely unlikely, please rate the following:

- If you are in need of this product or service again, will you do business with us again?
- If you have a friend in need of this product or service, would you recommend us to him or her?

Then have some free-form questions that allow users to write in their own answers. These questions could be:

- Is there anything you needed that we didn't offer?
- What could we have done differently to improve your experience?

Make sure the form clearly states that whatever customers write may be used in your promotional materials and provide a space for them to give their permission. As always, remember that offering quality products and services is the best way to ensure that those testimonials keep coming, so if opportunities for improvement are revealed in the survey results, use them to make adjustments.

Brainwaves

Testimonials have been used for marketing purposes for many years. Did you know that in the late 1800s, Pope Leo XIII provided a testimonial for Vin Mariani, a cocaine-containing wine? The tonic was created in 1863 by Angelo Mariani, a chemist, and was extremely popular even with royalty such as Queen Victoria. The Pope liked the wine so much that he awarded it a Vatican gold medal and appeared on a poster endorsing it. Now that's what we call a celebrity endorsement!

The Least You Need to Know

◆ There are a variety of affordable customer appreciation programs that can be used as guerrilla marketing tactics.

◆ Giving away expert advice is a benefit to others and can build your reputation and business.

◆ Partnering with other businesses can pump up a lean budget.

◆ Surveys are an effective way to identify areas that need improvement and they can also be a great source of testimonials.

21

Time vs. Money: When to Call in the Professionals

In This Chapter

- ◆ Calculating your marketing budget
- ◆ Ad agency, specialty boutique, or freelancer?
- ◆ Questions to ask before you hire
- ◆ Evaluating effectiveness

Many small- to medium-size business owners believe they have to conduct their own marketing for budgetary reasons. And many can, if they're willing to learn about the marketing process and invest the time it takes to effectively market their product. (Reading this book is a great first step!) But do-it-yourself is not the only option. Hiring a marketing or advertising firm isn't an extravagance reserved exclusively for big businesses.

Maybe budget isn't your only concern. Perhaps you feel that nobody can understand your business the way you do. But think about this: you don't expect your accountant to completely understand your line of work. You just expect him or her to be an expert in accounting. He or she is

100 percent focused on accounting day in and day out. Similarly, an ad agency or marketing firm knows advertising or marketing and how to apply it to your business.

When to Call the Pros

There are several reasons to consider bringing in external marketing or advertising support:

◆ Outside firms can offer an objective viewpoint about your products and services, as well as your current sales and marketing strategies. Many times business owners are too close to their business to be objective about advertising strategies that will generate maximum results.

◆ Outside firms are typically much faster at developing and deploying marketing concepts because that's their focus.

◆ Bringing in external support can help build momentum behind your marketing efforts—keeping things progressing, even when you have other operational or human resource issues to contend with. Unless you're in a full-time marketing role within your company, it's easy to back-burner marketing responsibilities in lieu of the crisis at hand. External marketing firms can help ensure you are deploying consistent marketing strategies year-round.

◆ When you think about the *opportunity cost* involved in devoting an entire day to focus on your marketing efforts (for example, the sales lost or the value of the business opportunities missed), it's often less expensive to hire a marketing firm.

◆ Certain types of marketing are best handled by experienced marketing teams. Full-scale ad campaigns, complex brochures, large direct-mail campaigns, and anything that may be picked up by the national media are a few examples of items you might want to farm out to the pros.

def•i•ni•tion

Opportunity cost is the value of the activity that you are forgoing so that you can participate in an alternative activity. If you dedicate an employee to a day of marketing in lieu of that employee's typical on-the-floor sales activities, the opportunity cost is the amount of sales that the employee would have likely generated had he or she been selling that day.

If you don't have the budget to hire a big-name marketing firm, consider hiring a new college graduate, an intern, or a freelancer. Besides being cost effective, these sources may provide a fresh spin on an old topic.

Calculating Your Marketing Budget

Before identifying the kind of support needed, you'll first want to calculate your marketing budget, because it obviously plays a large part in determining the type of firm that will best suit your needs.

Industry Average

There are several approaches to determining your marketing budget. One popular method is based on your industry's average ad spending trends. Reports of this kind will tell you what percentage of sales the top ad spending industries allocate toward marketing each year. These figures are compiled from publicly disclosed company financial reports and generally include both advertising and other marketing expenses. If you are a start-up company, wanting to gain share quickly, you may want to consider spending an extra percentage point or two beyond the industry average.

Where can you find the average that your industry spends on advertising and marketing? Visit www.advertisingage.com and enter "advertising to sales ratios" in the site's search field. For under $5, you can download the latest report, which is typically three to four years old. The report provides the annual percentage of growth in ad spending, so despite the age of the report, you are able to calculate a current-day figure. For example, let's say you run a restaurant, and the report provides this data:

2003 Advertising to Sales Ratios

Industry	SIC Code	Adv. as % of Sales	Adv. as % of Margin	Annual Growth %
Eating Places	5812	3.2%	14.5%	4.8%

According to this report, restaurants spent an average of 3.2 percent of net sales on marketing and advertising in 2003. In 2004, they would have spent an additional 4.8 percent of the 3.2 percent or $[(.032 \times .048) + .032] = .0336 \times 100 = 3.36$ percent. If you continue that process through the year 2007, restaurants were projected to spend an average of 3.88 percent of net sales on marketing and advertising.

Percentage of Prior Year

Another formula for calculating your marketing budget is to take last year's budget up or down a percentage or two based on your desired sales growth for the year. If you measured the effectiveness of your marketing efforts last year, meaning you are able to anticipate the incremental sales volume that a given budget range will generate, this should be a fairly decent indicator. Just be sure to also factor in any new competitive threats, economic indicators, and the like.

Brainwaves

This may seem like common sense but we think it bears repeating: the least expensive proposal is not always the worst option. Likewise, the most expensive one is not always the best. Cost is just one of the variables to consider when choosing a firm to market your product.

Value of a New Customer

Another way to project an appropriate marketing budget is to first determine what the annual dollars-and-cents value of a new customer is to your business. For example, if your average new customer spends $2,000 with your company in the first year working with you and your profit on that $2,000 is $1,000, then you can afford to spend up to $999 in marketing per year to generate that client and still generate a $1 profit. Naturally, you'd like to bring in that new client by spending as little as possible. By tracking your marketing efforts, in time, you'll be able to determine exactly what it costs to generate a new client. It might be $100 in the scenario just mentioned. If you want to generate 500 new clients in one year, then your marketing budget is $50,000.

Audience, Frequency, and Channel

One final way to determine your marketing budget is to start fresh, discarding your previous year's budget and dismissing industry averages. Instead, just ask yourself these questions:

- ◆ Exactly whom do I need to reach?
- ◆ What frequency of message is needed to get them to buy?
- ◆ What marketing channels are the most effective in reaching them?
- ◆ What is the cost for these channels at this frequency?

If the answer to this last question is reasonable from a financial standpoint, then you have your budget. If not, rethink number one, considering a more highly targeted market. If you're struggling with the answers to numbers one, two, or three above, that's where marketing or advertising firms can offer value. Determining target audience, message frequency, and appropriate channels is their bread and butter.

Deciding What Kind of Help You Need

Large or small company? Full-service or specialty boutique? Advertising agency or marketing firm? Finding the right group in which to partner can be challenging, but time invested in the search will pay off.

Big or Little

Once you've established your marketing budget, you'll have an idea of the size firm that will offer the right kind of support. Let's face it, ad agencies or marketing firms that work with clients with million-dollar budgets aren't going to be interested in your business if your budget is $5,000. Even if they do take your business, you will no doubt be quickly handed off to a less experienced, junior account executive. You don't want to be the smallest fish in a big pond. Of course you don't want to be the biggest fish in a small pond either, because it means your marketing firm or ad agency typically doesn't deal with clients of your size. Just like Goldilocks, you're looking for a firm that's "just right."

Full-Service or Specialty Boutique

In addition to the size of the firm, another consideration is the depth of service offering. Full-service ad agencies are best suited for companies with a variety of marketing needs (for example, mass media advertising, collateral, online advertising, PR). While full-service agencies generally have some of the highest hourly rates in the business, they may be your best bet if you're looking for a multi-channel, integrated plan, as efficiencies can be gained by having all of your marketing needs managed by one team. For those with media budgets that are fairly large (around $50,000 or more), full-service agencies have the advantage of "buying power" due to the volume of media they purchase each year, giving them the ability to negotiate better media rates (such as network TV, cable TV, newspaper, and magazine rates) for their clients.

Smaller, boutique firms often offer the same wide array of services, but they have lower overhead, typically resulting in lower costs. Why? Because they generally focus on their core area of expertise, hiring specialized freelance support to broaden their service offering when needed. The freelancers hired by boutique marketing firms may not be housed internally, generally don't receive benefits, and are not paid for down-time between projects, thereby reducing overhead. Generally, boutique firms are thought of having somewhere between 2 and 10 employees. In addition to the cost benefits, the principal players in boutique firms are typically more involved in day-to-day account service than with larger, full-service agencies. So you get more seasoned talent for your money. Good questions to ask any firm you are considering are:

♦ Who will be working on my account behind the scenes?

♦ Who will my day-to-day contact be?

♦ How many hours per week/month will you (the senior account exec. at the initial client meeting) be spending on my account?

Due to the desire to retain low overhead, boutique firms tend to focus less on full-scale, multimedia proposals designed to capture your business. They are often less apt than full-scale agencies to do spec work on the front-end.

Agencies provide spec work when they provide services for free in the hope of gaining a client's business. Most full-service and boutique agencies accept that some spec work is needed to land an account (for example, industry research, initial client discovery meetings, and proposal development). Boutique agencies are less likely than full-service agencies to provide a comprehensive marketing plan on spec. Why? Due to their size, they often don't have the resources to allocate to work that may not result in a paying client. Plus, they generally don't build enough overhead into their pricing models to allow for resources to be allocated for spec purposes. Keep in mind, too, that when a full-service agency agrees to spec work, you will likely pay for it in the end once they get the business.

Here's the Buzz

After determining which companies are best suited to handle your business, ask each firm to provide a presentation that includes samples of previous work and evaluations of other campaigns' effectiveness. Ask for references and check them out. Last but not least, listen to your gut. This is more than a business deal, it's a relationship, and you need to have chemistry with the agency players in order to be successful. Ask yourself if you feel comfortable sharing your thoughts with these people. Do they seem trustworthy and reliable? If not, keep shopping.

Both full-service and boutique firms play an important role in the marketing industry. When it comes to guerrilla marketing, which by definition is about identifying low-cost solutions, boutique firms are often a better fit.

Advertising Agency or Marketing Firm

You will often hear the terms "ad agency" and "marketing firm" used interchangeably. While they share some common traits, there are differences.

Ad agencies conceptualize and produce the ads that you see on TV, in magazines, in newspapers, and on billboards. Ad agencies help clients identify their target market and determine how best to appeal to that market. These agencies are often involved with brand development and promotion. Not only can a full-service agency develop ads, but it can also buy the print space and the TV or radio air time needed. Historically, ad agencies have been focused primarily on print and TV advertising, but for the last several years, they have been greatly enhancing their online/ digital media teams due to related market trends.

Before hiring an ad agency, it might help to become familiar with the various departments and roles that make up the typical agency.

Account management acts as the link between the ad agency and the client. It serves as the client's day-to-day contact—facilitating client meetings, sharing creative concepts developed by the agency's creative team, gaining ad approval from the client, and up-selling additional agency services. Account managers are the face of the agency.

The creative department develops concepts and creates ad designs. This creative team—made up of copywriters, print designers, web designers, and illustrators—produces both the words and images used in the ads. The creative director typically manages the entire creative department.

Production is responsible for making the finished product. Many agencies will produce print ads using in-house designers but outsource the production of TV and radio ads to outside production companies due to the cost of maintaining such an operation internally.

The media department is responsible for determining where ads should be placed based on market research it conducts, as well as purchasing the actual ad space. If the market it wants to target is business commuters, a billboard located along a well-trafficked highway or drive-time radio spots (7 A.M. to 9 A.M. and 4 P.M. to 6 P.M.) will likely be more effective than TV ads during the 5 P.M. news when most commuters are still on the road. If you are purchasing significant media, full-service agencies may be ideal for you because of the rates they're able to negotiate. Due to the volume of media purchased for all of the agencys' clients, they wield the power to bargain with media outlets for better rates.

Booby Traps

Ad agencies earn the greatest percentage of their revenue from media commissions. Magazines such as *People* or *Time,* or even your local newspapers, offer commissions to agencies for space purchased. The same applies to TV and radio. Because the lion's share of their revenue comes from media commissions, ad agencies are perhaps less apt to recommend marketing solutions beyond traditional advertising (for example, direct mail, guerrilla marketing strategies, point-of-sale materials).

Marketing firms are different from ad agencies. Large corporations typically have their own in-house marketing department, but small- to mid-size businesses often find it difficult to justify the cost of hiring a full-time marketing staff. That's where marketing firms come in.

Marketing firms offer sales development, market research, branding, and strategic planning support, in addition to traditional advertising. Most marketing firms generate the majority of their revenue through strategic consulting instead of media commissions, which often results in recommended solutions beyond just traditional advertising. Some marketing firms will pass along media commissions to clients in the form of media discounts. Other marketing firms opt to retain those media commissions, just like ad agencies. Regardless, the financial model for most marketing firms is not centered on media commissions.

The service offering provided by a marketing firm can be quite extensive. A marketing firm may help the sales force reassess how they target potential customers or may be involved in the development of a new product to ensure that consumer expectations are met.

Boutique Example: RedRover Company

RedRover Company, a boutique marketing firm based out of Memphis, Tennessee, is a relatively new player in the marketing consulting arena. Managed by two principals who spent years managing marketing teams in the corporate world, they know firsthand what clients want and don't want in a marketing firm. Managing partner, Lori Frazier, recalls her corporate days dealing with ad agencies and marketing firms:

"I found large ad agencies to generally offer tremendously creative, beautiful ads that might even be deemed works of art. Where some of these agencies fell short, though, was in truly understanding how our business operated and what drove consumer preferences. I also found that campaign measurement wasn't an area of focus for many of the larger ad agencies that we hired." When Lori and her business partner set out to open RedRover Company, LLC, they opted to offer a different model, one that is becoming more and more common.

"We really dig in and get to know a client's business," explained Lori. "We work to understand their operations, profit margins, customers, brand positioning, employees, and culture. A big-picture vantage point allows us to offer recommendations for growth that are much more likely to succeed. The best marketing campaign will fail without the right employee support and culture. A holistic approach is best."

Ad agencies, which have historically been less focused on sales development, product expansion, and employee culture than their marketing firm counterparts, are beginning to expand their service offerings to more closely match those of rival marketing firms due to market demand.

Freelance Support or Not

If you have one or two clearly defined marketing projects, hiring a freelance specialist could be a less expensive option than an ad agency or marketing firm. For the most part, freelancers have a single primary area of specialty (for example, print design, web design, or copywriting). While they may dabble in several areas, they are typically best known for their specialties. Because their service offering isn't soup to nuts and they have little overhead, they are an affordable choice. Use freelancers when you know exactly what you want and have the time to manage the project. Because freelancers are project focused, they usually don't know enough about your business to help you determine how the project you are tasking them with fits into your overall marketing strategy. They are looking for clear direction from you. Freelancers are most efficient when the scope of work is clearly defined.

Choosing the Right Group

Now that you've identified the type of firm that best suits your goals and budget, it's time to nail down the process by which you will select the ideal firm. To ensure that you have buy-in with your marketing efforts across your company, you may want to build a "review committee" responsible for hearing agency pitches and making a decision on the firm in which you'll partner.

Regardless of whether or not you create a review committee, it's always a good idea to develop a checklist of the most important factors driving your decision to ensure you don't make a decision based on a dynamic presentation alone. Here are a few items to consider for your checklist:

◆ The agency's average account is close to the size of your company both in terms of company size (revenue, number of employees) and marketing budget.

◆ You have met and are comfortable with the abilities of the team members who will be working on your account behind the scenes.

◆ You seem to connect or have chemistry with both the day-to-day contact and the agency as a whole.

◆ The agency has worked on clients within your industry and is willing to share related references.

◆ The agency is open to your contacting any of its current or past customers at your request versus just the ones it offers you.

◆ The agency has assured you that you will have availability to key personnel as needed.

◆ The agency is focused on delivering results versus just doing pretty creative work. It has presented proposed metrics for measuring the effectiveness of a campaign.

◆ You have the ability to get out of a contract with the selected agency if things are not going as planned.

Agency fee structures likely fall into one of these categories—retainer agreements, project rates, or by-the-hour rates. Some agencies use a combination of all of these based on client needs. Most agencies pass along all out-of-pocket expenses to clients—some adding in margin, others passing them along at cost.

Retainer Agreements

A retainer agreement is a fee charged in advance to reserve someone's time or services. There are typically two reasons that an agency would use retainer agreements. The first is for long-term clients. When an agency intends to work with a client over a long period of time (say a year or more), the agency wants to make certain that enough resource time is reserved to ensure it can be responsive to client needs. Sometimes, a retainer rate is less than the agency's typical hourly rate, because it's paid in advance. A marketing firm may also use retainers for new clients, particularly with small businesses, to ensure timely payment.

A retainer may just be for the number of hours of agency time deemed necessary to manage the account each month. It could also consist of the full advertising budget agreed upon, being used to pay agency fees as well as all production and media buying expenses. Either way, the client should insist on detailed and accurate invoices for expenses taken from the retainer.

Project Rates

If you have a well-defined project in which you are seeking support—one with a finite beginning and ending—then you or the agency may suggest project pricing. Contracts for projects are typically quite detailed, with the entire scope of the project mapped out. If the project varies from the plan, in terms of scope of work or timeline, additional fees may be incurred. Make sure that your project rate includes as many revisions to creative as you think may be necessary, as it's rare that clients approve creative with no changes. Two to three rounds of creative revisions is the industry standard.

By-the-Hour Rates

For ambiguous projects or when you just need a couple hours of an agency's time here and there, by-the-hour billing is generally used. By-the-hour is just as it sounds; you are billed an hourly fee for each hour of time that the agency spends on your account, broken down into 15- or 30-minute increments in most cases. With hourly pricing, you'll want to avoid long meetings where multiple agency employees are present, because you are paying an hourly rate for each person attending, which can quickly get expensive.

Brainwaves
Negotiate with agencies for a discounted rate for meetings attended by multiple agency representatives. For example, you may only be willing to pay for two people to attend. If they bring more, it's on their dime.
In addition, some agencies charge different hourly rates based on the level of experience of the person working on your account. So you may pay just $80 an hour for a designer and $150 an hour for your account executive. If there are junior agency reps working on your account, be sure you're not paying full rate for their time.

Out-of-Pocket Expenses

Ad agencies and marketing firms generally pass along the cost of all expenses they incur in relation to your account. It's important to find out upfront what they mark up (allowing agency margin) and what they don't. It's generally accepted that agencies make a commission on media purchased. But if an agency is hiring a photographer to shoot some custom photography for a brochure, are they marking up the photography expenses as well? This is good information to know ahead of time. Other out-of-pocket expenses might include:

- Outside contractor fees (for example, illustrators, event planners, video production teams)

- Travel fees (for example, mileage, hotel, airfare, meals)

- Shipping/courier charges

- Cost of copies and proofs

- Printing costs

- Postage expenses

- Media placement costs

What should you pay? Hourly rates for large, full-service agencies can range from $125 to $275 per hour. Smaller, boutique marketing firms often charge from $100 to $150 per hour. Freelancers' rates can vary greatly based on the specialty and demand in your market, as well as their level of experience and how in demand their services are.

The Least You Need to Know

- Sometimes opportunity cost makes hiring a marketing professional your best bet.

- Determine your marketing budget before you begin.

- Ask the right questions to be sure the professional you're hiring is a good fit for your company.

- Many options exist when it comes to hiring professionals. It's not advertising conglomerate or nothing.

Chapter 22

Are We There Yet?: Measuring Guerrilla Marketing

In This Chapter

- ◆ Benefits of measurement
- ◆ AIDA sales cycle
- ◆ Market research
- ◆ Connecting marketing measurement to bottom-line results
- ◆ Managing expectations

If you don't know where you're going, how do you know when you get there? Many small- to mid-size businesses, and even some very large corporations, do little in the way of marketing measurement. Many figure that if their overall numbers go up, why bother? This chapter will show you the benefits of measuring your efforts as well as a way of creating a method of tracking.

Benefits of Measurement

Measuring your marketing efforts is helpful for a variety of reasons:

Budget Ammo. The most important reason to measure is so you'll know how much money to set aside for your marketing efforts. Even if you aren't the business owner—perhaps you're simply in charge of marketing and you have to go through the dreaded budget request process each year—there's no better way to justify your requested budget than through solid measurement. If you can show that you deliver $10 in profit (or revenue—however you want to look at it) for every $1 in marketing spent, then you're providing the company a 10:1 ROI, impressive by almost any standard.

Continuous Improvement. If your marketing efforts aren't performing as you'd hoped, you may need to tweak your approach. But it's difficult to know what to improve upon if you're not tracking response rates and revenue generated from your various marketing strategies. If you distribute 10 different e-mail campaigns through the year and you track each of them, you're able to compare one campaign to another. You can see which creative treatments, offers, and target audiences generated the best ROI. This knowledge allows you to capitalize on what's working so you get increasingly higher ROIs with each campaign. Once you've measured and refined your marketing strategies for a year or more, a good rule of thumb is to:

◆ Spend 80 percent of your budget on channel, offer, and creative combinations that have proven to be successful over time and

◆ Spend the other 20 percent testing new combinations for potential implementation down the road. Don't ever rest on your laurels—campaign effectiveness diminishes over time without a fresh approach. It's similar to the economic *law of diminishing returns.*

def•i•ni•tion

The **law of diminishing returns** is a well-accepted economic concept stating that the more you invest in an area, overall return on that investment increases at a declining rate if everything else remains equal. A marketing example is a company that has saturated the marketing with billboard advertising but is considering adding a few additional billboards. Will these additional billboard ads provide the same rate of return as the others? According to the law of diminishing returns, probably not.

Efficient Spending. If you have a small "guerrilla-type" marketing budget, you need your limited dollars to stretch as far as possible. The best way to ensure that is to measure and calculate an ROI for each campaign, investing your limited budget in just those activities that are the most profitable. The mark of a truly successful marketer is doing more with less, not requiring a multi-million dollar budget to generate results.

Brainwaves

Unless you're a Fortune 1000 company, your marketing resources are probably stretched thin and you're lucky if you have a single person dedicated to marketing. More likely, whoever is in charge of marketing at your company may have other duties that take precedence over marketing. Under these circumstances, efficient guerrilla planning is key to not letting this important part of your business strategy slip through the cracks. And don't forget to plug in the cost of resources needed to execute the campaign, otherwise known as the opportunity cost, when determining ROI for marketing strategies deployed.

Job Security! One of the most popular reasons for marketing measurement is job security. If your primary role is that of marketer, it's important to continually justify your existence. The benefit of your measurement efforts to the company is a bonus!

Tracking Success: AIDA Sales Cycle

With some products, consumers make quick, impulse decisions, but with most they move through a fairly predictable sales cycle that can be explained with the acronym AIDA. AIDA stands for: awareness, interest, desire, and action. Your marketing measurement will be more meaningful and relevant if you track your success at each of these key milestones.

How do you track the various steps in the sales cycle? Let's take them one at a time.

Awareness

Awareness is created by simply bringing your product or service to the attention of your prospect. Depending upon the marketing vehicle used, awareness can be tracked in a number of ways. For example, imagine you sent out a direct mail piece that included a call to action encouraging prospects to visit your website. If you simply drove users to your homepage (mycompany.com), you'd have no way to differentiate direct mail responders from everyday web surfers. An increase in website traffic could be a coincidence or it could be genius marketing. You'll never know.

On the other hand, if you created a specific promotion URL (mycompany.com/promotion) you can track responses from the direct mail piece. Just be sure that the URL cannot be accessed from your homepage. The URL should be accessible only to those who type it in off your direct mail piece. You can then assume that you've generated awareness among all those visiting this web page.

Interest

Interest is generated when a customer allows you (or better yet, asks you) to demonstrate the features and benefits of your product or service. Taking the scenario just given, let's assume that the promotion web page (the one with the specific and different URL) has a link where prospects can request a free demo of your product. All those requesting a demo fall into the "interest" component of the sales cycle. Again, you need to be able to see that the requests came specifically from the promotion web page, so build in a differentiator of some sort to distinguish these "more info" requests from other "more info" requests that might come from your homepage.

Desire

You're closing in—you've reached the third stage in the sales cycle. It's called desire when your prospects believe that they need your product or service. Using the same example, if your prospect requests a quote after he's viewed the demo, he's moved into desire.

Action

Your prospects have reached the "action" stage of the sales cycle when they are actually ready to make a purchase (for example, complete an order, send in a signed contract, make a down payment). Because you've been tracking them from the beginning using your specific URL, you can now know exactly how many people were moved to action from the direct mail piece you distributed.

Here's the Buzz

Don't forget to monitor traffic to your website or brick and mortar location before you start your new campaign, you'll need a benchmark for comparison.

Response Tracking

The way you measure the effectiveness of your marketing campaign is dependent on two primary factors:

1. What stage in the sales cycle are you working to move your prospects into? It can be quite difficult to move customers straight from awareness to action. With most products or services, multiple *impressions* or contacts are needed to move a prospect to the action stage of the cycle.

2. What marketing channel(s) are you using to get your message out? Response tracking can be very different depending on the marketing vehicle used. So, let's review measurement strategies by marketing channel in some detail.

def•i•ni•tion

An **impression** is every contact point in which the prospect receives information about your product, service, and/or company. It's a single instance of your ad or message being displayed. In the online media arena, an impression is the number of times your ad is displayed for site visitors. For example, on any given day, if 1,000 people visit a website on which your banner ad is displayed, then you've generated 1,000 impressions that day. Impressions don't necessarily mean that you've created awareness. But you have created the possibility of awareness.

Print Advertising

Print advertising is priced and measured based on total circulation combined with reader demographics. Circulation is the number of copies of a newspaper or magazine sold. Larger, more established print publications will typically offer reader demographics. So, if the total circulation is 25,000 and 50 percent are in your target audience, the total number of impressions to your target audience is 12,500. The best way to know the effectiveness of the message you're putting in front of those 12,500 prospects is to include a call to action that can be tracked. It might be a unique toll-free number that you don't use anywhere else so you'll know that all calls coming in through this line can be attributed to your ad. Or it could be a page on your website (such as the specific URL mentioned in the previous section). If your call to action drives readers to that dedicated web page, you'll know they're responding to your marketing efforts. Alternatively, you could create a separate e-mail address just for tracking response to your ad. It doesn't matter what method you use, as long as you can separate responses to your ad from random inquiries.

Public Relations: Media Equivalencies

The effectiveness of public relations is most often measured in *media equivalencies*—the value of an ad the size or equivalency of the PR you received. So if your area TV station ran a three-minute segment dedicated to your business or product, the media equivalency would be equal to the cost of running three minutes' worth of advertising on that same station.

def•i•ni•tion

> **Media equivalency** is the cost of an ad the size or equivalency of the PR that you generated. If your city magazine ran a quarter page ad on your business and that ad costs $985, that's the equivalent value of your PR. Many PR specialists take this one step further by placing added value on third-party credibility—meaning, an article written by a third party is more valuable than an ad of the same size because editorial is generally found to be more credible than advertising. A common practice is to multiply the cost of the ad by three to allow for this added value. So in this scenario, the media equivalency for the quarter page article would be $985 × 3 = $2,955.

Online Advertising: Web Metrics

Online advertising is measured by the number of instances your ad is displayed for a site visitor (impressions) and the number of "click-throughs" that your ad generates. Online media outlets can tell you how many site visitors clicked on your specific ad, which is an indicator that you have both generated awareness and possibly interest. This click-through rate (CTR) is the number of click-throughs per hundred ad impressions shown as a percentage. CTRs measure the number of site visitors that clicked on your ad to arrive at the destination site. It does not include those that saw the ad, remembered your brand name, and visited your site directly on their own later on (without clicking through via your ad). These indirect clicks are difficult to measure, although it can be done via web cookies. CTR is seen as the immediate response to an ad and not the overall response.

Another more important measurement of web advertising effectiveness is called a conversion rate. The conversion rate is the percentage of those clicking through who actually took action (for example, bought your product). Some Internet media outlets can provide average conversion ratios by industry, but it's so dependent upon the ad and the product that these averages are often not helpful. There's nothing like testing your own ad with a limited number of impressions to determine its projected conversion rate.

Direct Mail Customized Calls to Action

Direct mail is perhaps one of the easiest marketing channels to track. With digital printing as affordable as it is, you can customize your call to action down to the individual direct mail piece if you like. Imagine you own a veterinary office and you want to promote your new boarding facility. In your company database, you have about 3,000 contacts. The direct mail piece offer is 50 percent off of boarding. You could actually track each direct mail piece by printing a different discount code on each direct mail piece. This would allow you to track response rates by customer. You could even use the contact's record number as their discount code for easy individual tracking. Imagine that!

Segmented tracking is far more common because it's easier to implement. Using the same veterinary office scenario as an example, you could break down the 3,000 people in the contact database into three segments:

> Group 1: Current customers
>
> Group 2: Customers who haven't visited the office for over one year
>
> Group 3: Prospects who have never used the facility

You could send the same basic direct mail piece to all three groups—the only variation would be in the discount code. Instead of having 3,000 individual discount codes to track by customer, you'd have three discount codes to track by segment. So in the group of mailers going to current customers, the call to action would read: "Mention code CC1000 when calling our office to receive 50 percent off your pet's first visit to our new boarding facility." The mailers to past customers might use a discount code of PC1000 and so on.

Direct Mail Tracking Against a Control Group

Another form of direct mail tracking is comparison against a control group. This method is especially effective when you are not providing a unique offer that is easy to track.

For example, hotels that cater to business guests often find that weekends are slower than they'd like. As a result, they offer special weekend rate packages as incentives for booking. They may promote these weekend rates in magazine ads, on their website, and via direct mail, making tracking by channel difficult. That's where a control group comes in. A control group is a portion of your target audience that does not receive your direct mail offer but whose purchase activity is nonetheless monitored.

In our hotel scenario, we might assume that the hotel desires to mail to guests who have stayed over the weekend at least twice over the past year. For simplicity's sake, assume that this amounts to 2,000 past guests. The hotel may then opt to mail to 1,000 randomly selected contacts from this group of 2,000, while tracking the purchase activity of the entire group over a set period of time, which could be the duration of the offer or perhaps 30 days from the date the mailer is received. If 100 customers out of the 1,000 receiving the direct mailer purchase a weekend package during the offer period and only 10 of those in the control group purchase this package (because they heard about it through another channel), you've had a successful campaign. Here's how you calculate your success:

10 percent response rate for those receiving the direct mailer – 2 percent response rate for the control group = 8 percent response rate attributable to the mailer alone.

 Booby Traps

When buying and measuring print advertising, take a hard look at the publication's total circulation number. It's usually made up of both paid subscribers and newsstand buyers. If a publication sells more newsstand copies than it has paid subscribers, be wary, as you may be paying for considerable waste. Readers who buy copies off a newsstand are typically less loyal than those who subscribe. Generally speaking, subscribers spend more time with a publication and read a larger percentage of the publication's content. The other downside to paying for advertising that goes primarily in newsstand copies is that accurate reader demographics are difficult to identify. That means you may not be advertising to your intended target market.

Sales Promotions: Direct and Indirect Sales

Sales promotions or any type of marketing for that matter can generate both direct and indirect sales. If you're promoting a specific product, like a new beverage at a local coffee shop, direct sales would be the sales revenue generated from the new product alone. Indirect sales would be the additional items purchased (for example, muffins, bagels) by those who responded to your marketing efforts to drive new beverage sales. In order to get a fairly accurate indirect sales estimate, you'll need to first determine what sales on these additional products would have been without the promotion. So if your projected muffin sales would have been $8,000 for the month without a sales promotion and your sales during the promotional period were $12,000, you generated $4,000 in incremental indirect bagel sales.

Cross-Channel Sales Trends

Oftentimes, marketing promotions are carried out via a number of channels and that makes tracking by channel time consuming. When measurement for a campaign as a whole is desired, it's often easiest to just measure new sales generated beyond projections.

So what do we mean by "sales generated beyond projections"? Say you are running a second quarter campaign using cable TV, print media, web media, point-of-purchase displays, and direct mail as your message delivery channels—perhaps too many channels to track individually. Your company sold $125,000 in the second quarter of last year with no marketing campaign during that time period and sales for the second quarter of this year are projected to be $150,000 with no marketing campaign. In this measurement model, all sales beyond $150,000 can be generally attributed to your marketing campaign.

As you can see, this is considered to be a fairly loose measurement but it is used quite often due to its simplicity.

Tracking Unusual Strategies

When it comes to measuring the effectiveness of unusual, guerrilla marketing strategies, the principles are essentially the same. Here are just a few examples of how to apply traditional measurement to nontraditional marketing.

- ◆ **Stunt marketing**—While the objectives of stunt marketing can vary, generally the goal is to generate awareness and foot traffic at your stunt or event. You could measure your effectiveness by simply placing employees with hand counters at all entrances to your event to measure foot traffic. If you're handing out fliers at the event, measurement can take the form of discount codes or unique URLs/phone numbers.

- ◆ **Blogging**—When starting a blog, it's important to establish your success criteria and measurement strategies before your blog is designed. You might include a link to a particular product page to which you'd like to drive web traffic. By using a web statistics program for your website, you can determine the number of click-throughs generated to that product page from your blog. If awareness is simply your goal, overall traffic to the blog may be the best way to measure your efforts.

◆ **Free seminars**—When offering free seminars, determine what you want to achieve as a result. For example, do you want to generate 10 new contacts per seminar who you can add to your sales prospecting database for future follow up? Your measurement is the total number of qualified prospects. Do you want to get 25 enrollments to your free eNewsletter for continued contact? Your measurement is your total number of enrollments. Do you want to generate publicity for your willingness to donate your time? Your measurement is the media equivalency of the PR generated.

Ask every new customer how they heard about you and record their answers. This is a guerrilla way to measure marketing campaigns that are hard to track.

Market Research

Market research is a method of marketing measurement often used to track the impact that your advertising is having. This type of research is typically conducted by firms engaging in significant local, regional, or national advertising where a market or target market is being fairly well saturated, resulting in fairly broad awareness for your product or company. There are two types of market research of this kind—aided awareness and unaided awareness. They can be measured via consumer focus groups, telephone surveys, or online/printed surveys.

Connecting Measurement to the Bottom Line

At the end of the day, the best form of marketing measurement is your impact on the company's bottom line. If you're able to show how your marketing efforts are impacting bottom-line profits, then you've found the Holy Grail. In order to do this, though, you must know:

1. The profit margin on the products/services you're promoting.

2. The sales volume you are generating as a direct or indirect result of your marketing efforts.

Sounds easy enough, right? Profit margins can be rather elusive in small- to mid-size businesses, but if identified, they offer powerful insight into what's impacting your bottom line most.

Managing Expectations

Companies with limited marketing budgets (and everyone else for that matter!) would understandably like every marketing dollar spent to generate a measurable return on investment. The reality is that for some products and services, particularly those that aren't conducive to impulse buying, this just isn't realistic. It's important to set expectations accordingly so that your efforts aren't seen as undeservingly ineffective.

Case in point: there is much banter in direct marketing about acceptable response rates. Many will tell you that one to two percent is good, three percent is average and anything higher is cause for celebration. As nice as it would be, you simply can't blanket all direct mail campaigns with this same benchmark. Many factors impact the effectiveness of your direct mail efforts or any advertising effort for that matter:

◆ The impact of your design.

◆ The type of packaging used (for example, window envelope, standard #10 envelope, oversized postcard).

◆ The sense of urgency you are able to create.

◆ The strength of your offer.

◆ The way you segment your audience.

◆ The time of year you send the mailing.

◆ The existing demand for your product.

The factors impacting your response rates are countless.

Another important aspect of marketing that many nonmarketers may not fully appreciate is the number of impressions it takes to get your audience to take action. It's different by industry, company, and product. You may find that you must get your message in front of your prospects a minimum of six times before they are ready to buy. The point is to stick with your marketing efforts long enough to see if they are truly effective. The "cut and run" approach results in a reactive, cobbled-together marketing strategy.

An acceptable response to your marketing efforts is also quite dependent upon the profits that can be generated from a single sale. Consider, for example, a country club. If the cost of membership is $100 per month, and the club has about $50 in monthly expense in that membership, then the annual value of a new member is $100 – $50 = $50 × 12 = $600. If this were your company, what would you be willing to spend in marketing in order to generate $600 in annual profit for a new customer? $100? $200? While in theory, you'd spend as much as $599 to generate $600 in revenue, you obviously are looking for the best return on your investment.

The Least You Need to Know

- Give some thought to measurement before creating and implementing any guerrilla marketing tactic.

- Before you decide how to measure, decide where in the sales cycle you're hoping to get people.

- Creating a method of tracking where sales leads come from is key in marketing measurement.

- Multi-channel marketing campaigns might need to be tracked using a broader analysis such as the year-over-year sales generated beyond projections method.

Chapter 23

What Not to Do: Bad Buzz

In This Chapter

- ◆ Stop bad buzz in the first place
- ◆ Prevent bad buzz even if something goes wrong
- ◆ Controlling bad buzz: preventing a feeding frenzy
- ◆ Handling bad buzz gone wild

Back in the olden days, just 30 years ago, in fact, news of achievements as well as evildoing didn't always become public knowledge; at least not five minutes after it happened, anyway. We elected politicians without knowing potentially damning information about their private habits, and we fought wars without knowing the details of troop movements as they happened.

You just can't keep anything a secret anymore. And it's not true that any attention, good or bad, is better than no attention at all. There are some things we'd all like to keep to ourselves.

When you're in the public eye, however, invariably along with the good comes the bad. And, given the public's penchant for dirt, bad press spreads just as fast (if not faster) than good press. Here's how to avoid creating an angry mob.

Playing It Safe

There are several ways to prevent negative buzz. The first and most important is to do things right, be ethical, and, when things go wrong, fix them right away.

Consider this classic case of a situation that could have completely destroyed a company.

In 1982, someone contaminated bottles of Tylenol with cyanide. It didn't happen on the company's watch; the bottles were tampered with after they were on retailers' shelves. But Johnson & Johnson did the responsible thing to keep the public safe. The company recalled 31 million bottles of the drug. The cost to the company was tremendous, not only in dollars lost recalling the product but also in loss of sales and consumer trust. Imagine watching your market share go from 37 percent to 7 percent almost overnight.

But within a year J & J had developed a solid caplet and a super tamper-proof bottle. The product went back on the shelves and regained its strong position.

This kind of response to negative publicity is flawless. The company acted responsibly and retained consumers' trust. In fact, people probably trust the company more as a result of its conscientious reaction than they would if the terrible situation had never occurred.

It's proof that you can deal with negative buzz even when the situation that caused it is dire.

Preventing Bad Buzz

What about when things are just status quo, with nothing in particular going wrong? That's the time when you most need to avoid bad buzz. Remember what we said about customer loyalty; that customers who are loyal will cut you some slack? The best way to keep your buzz positive is by keeping your customers happy. The best defense is a good offense, so prep your team to play a good, clean game.

Hire Friendly People and Put Them Out Front

There is absolutely no doubt that the best marketing is outstanding customer service. But how do you ensure that your customers get the best service possible?

It begins with hiring the right people.

Whoever interacts with your customers is the face of your company. Make sure the people you have interacting with the public are friendly, helpful, outgoing people. No exceptions. The people who represent your company, whether it be face-to-face or on the phone, need to be extraordinarily service-oriented and upbeat. You can teach someone to perform the tasks related to the job. It's much harder to teach someone to be friendly if it's not their nature. Take for example, Nordstrom's philosophy of "Hire the Smile. Train the Skill." This extremely profitable customer-centered company is a perfect example of this strategy. You can hardly attend a conference without hearing at least one speaker cite Nordstrom as a stellar example of how to take care of customers.

Naturally, we all think we're hiring service-oriented people when we sign them on. We certainly don't knowingly hire surly, bad-tempered employees. So where do we go wrong?

The interview process is the place to identify who has a great attitude and who doesn't. There are lots of books about behavioral interviewing that guide you in asking questions that reveal people's attitudes. One of the ways you can discover what people are really like is by asking them how they've handled difficult people in the past.

We recommend Dr. Paul Green's book, *More Than a Gut Feeling*, which tells you everything you need to know about how to hire the people you want.

Communicate the Big Picture

Do your employees know what your most important concern is? Do they know what you most want them to do?

A friend of ours named Carol worked as a front desk agent at a hotel when she was in college. Her manager was very vocal about the hotel's revenue goals and from what Carol could ascertain, ensuring that the books balanced at the end of her shift was her primary objective. One morning, when a guest disputed a long distance phone call charge at check-out, Carol refused to relent on the $1.35 charge. She was sure he was lying. Although she realized this was a very small amount to quibble over, Carol took pride in being a good employee. She wanted to do what her manager told her to do and to get every penny the hotel was due. What the manger *had not* discussed with Carol was the importance of customer service. He didn't explain that by insisting on collecting a measly $1.35 she could poison that customer to their brand forever. (Interestingly, they later discovered it was a housekeeping employee who had made the call from the guest's room. Oops.)

Often, it's little things like this that make the biggest impact on customers' perceptions. It's vitally important that your team members see and understand the big picture.

What You Measure Gets Done

Are you measuring the behaviors that most contribute to customer service? We've worked with a lot of companies that measure employees' performance. One of the things that always seems to come up when we're talking about telephone service reps is "average talk time." This refers to the time the person spends on the phone with each caller. Employees who spend too much time on calls with customers are penalized. Okay, so what message are your employees getting? They're being told very clearly, though indirectly, that you care more about them getting off the phone quickly than you do about whether the customer is satisfied.

Don't measure behaviors that are in conflict with good customer service. Measure things like effective problem resolution. That's what you're in business for.

Train Employees to Say "I'm Sorry"

Front line employees are under the gun when customers are unhappy. You owe it to your team members to support them in their efforts to satisfy customers when things go awry. Hardly any of us get training in conflict resolution when we're growing up. We just muddle along trying our best to soothe angry people who think we messed up their lives.

Provide training in conflict resolution for all of your employees. (It will come in handy not only with dissatisfied customers but also in situations with their co-workers.) Let your employees know that it's okay to say "I'm sorry," and that you back them 100 percent as long as they follow your guidelines for smoothing customers' ruffled feathers.

Create Service Recovery Tools

Unpleasant experiences are inevitable in every business. No matter how hard you try to avoid it, everyone has unhappy customers from time to time. Be sure you have service recovery tools already in place ready to transform that negative into a positive.

The best service recovery tool is a money-back guarantee. People know that you really want them to be happy when you are willing to refund their money.

Beyond that, you can demonstrate your remorse by using service recovery tools like a gift card to a nearby mall, movie ticket vouchers, a free service—any sort of gesture that communicates your intention to please and your desire to have another chance.

Be sure all your team members know that they have the power to use the service recovery tools. Unhappy customers will be pleasantly surprised when they find out that your employees don't have to get permission to solve their problems. The positive buzz you'll get will be so worth it.

Listen to Your Customers

When a customer gives you feedback, listen carefully and try to see things from their perspective. Don't interrupt and don't correct them, even if they have a misconception about the situation. If they take the time to fill out a comment card, pay close attention to what it says. Whenever possible, respond to their feedback and demonstrate that you care about their opinions and are making an effort to incorporate their suggestions. Think of it this way: if a person is upset enough to fill out a complaint card, they are definitely upset enough to tell their friends about their unpleasant experience with your product or company.

Monitor What People Are Saying

Take time to read comment cards, browse message boards, and read blogs. If you can identify a potentially sticky spot early on, you can act quickly to prevent it from becoming a bad buzz feeding frenzy.

Brainwaves

Monitor what's being said about you online by ordering Google Alerts (www.google.com/alerts) and Yahoo! Alerts (alerts.yahoo.com). Every time a mention of your name appears on Google News or Yahoo! News they'll send you an e-mail. This way, you can formulate a response *before* the local news gives you a call. Also, keep an eye on search engines like Technorati and any RSS feeds for blogs that apply to your industry or field.

A Few Caveats

Because guerrilla marketing is nontraditional, a lot of the traditional marketing rules don't apply; however, there are some basics that hold fast.

Under-Promise And Over-Deliver

Be realistic about what you can do. Customers can accept limitations if they're openly communicated on the front end. Even if they feel momentary disappointment, most will respect your honesty. If you don't live up to what you've promised after you've made the sale, it will seem like you tried to deceive them. On the other hand, if you deliver *more* than they're expecting, they'll be pleasantly surprised and remember that you exceeded their expectations.

Don't Tell the Customer They're Wrong

The customer is never wrong, because if you prove him or her wrong, they will no longer be your customer.

There's a story about Marshall Field, who founded the department store of the same name. Field was walking through his Chicago store one day and heard a clerk arguing with a customer. He asked the clerk what he was doing.

"I'm settling a customer complaint," said the clerk.

"No, you're not," said Field. "Give the lady what she wants."

> **Brainwaves**
>
> Always communicate a positive message. Tell people what you are *for* rather than what you are *against*. Instead of focusing on your competitor's faults, tout your benefits. There's enough negativity in the world already and people are hungry to feel encouraged and connected.

That became the title of a book about Marshall Field, and resonates as the ultimate reality of the phrase "the customer is always right."

Even if you have an explanation … even if the customer is claiming that monkeys are on Mars … even if you have to admit to a "mistake" that you know you or your team didn't make—you have to swallow your pride (and your sense of justice) and let customers think they're right. Telling customers they're wrong will do nothing but make them angry. We'll say it again. No matter how wrong the customer might be, remember: the customer is *always* right.

When Things Go Wrong: Buzz Control

Once bad buzz has started circulating, it's hard not to panic. But panic you must not. Stay calm and realize that most often, bad buzz is not personal. Still, you must take it seriously. Don't spend your time rehashing past events. What's done is done. Focus on damage control and on moving forward in a positive way. Here's what to do:

Step 1: Communicate Quickly. Issue a brief communication as quickly as possible. This shouldn't be an extensive statement because you need to consider all sides before saying too much; however, it's not prudent to wait too long to respond because bad publicity spreads so quickly. Responding immediately is often enough to defuse your customers' negative feelings and thus kill the fast-burning wildfire of negative buzz.

Step 2: Acknowledge the Mistake. Don't make excuses. And don't become defensive. Just apologize and take the blame for whatever went wrong. If there's an explanation that is important to communicate, make it brief. The majority of your reaction should be apologetic. People respect those willing to admit their faults.

Step 3: Remedy the Problem. Take steps to fix whatever caused the bad buzz. Even if you can't immediately rectify the situation, demonstrate movement in that direction.

Step 4: Follow up, Accentuating the Positive. When the chaos has subsided, emphasize some positive aspects of the company—community involvement, progressive workplace practices, or positive stories. This can help to improve your image in the long run and help people get over the negative publicity and focus on the positive.

Cautionary Tales

Thanks to the Internet, unhappy customers have numerous platforms on which to express their displeasure. There are even websites solely dedicated to logging consumer complaints. Check out www.complaints.com for an example.

The Orange Menace

A guy named Eddie has been engaged in a dispute with Cingular Wireless. Is it legitimate or not? We don't know. But he's telling his story to a lot of people who may not give big business the benefit of the doubt. Here's what Eddie says happened.

After dropping his cell phone service and starting it up again three weeks later, Eddie received an $8,677.29 phone bill. Apparently, when he reactivated his account the customer service representative did not give him the plan he had before—the one he'd used since 2003. Instead, he was signed up under a different rate plan. A much more expensive one. Eddie contacted Cingular to resolve the issue, but he was told somebody would get back to him. When someone finally did return his call, he spent "52 minutes on hold only to have my call dropped."

Eddie filed a complaint with the Better Business Bureau and the FCC, but the issue remained unresolved. Where was Eddie to turn? MySpace, that's where. Eddie created a MySpace page for his cell phone bill—myspace.com/theorangemenace. Eddie is now adding friends who support his cause. He's assembling his own angry mob.

Comcastic? Customers Don't Think So

The Internet is blanketed with complaint-oriented blogs and websites devoted to expressing users' loathing of Philadelphia-based Comcast, the nation's largest cable provider. And these aren't just mild complaints. The phrase "I hate Comcast," is so frequently used on the Internet, we can't even provide an accurate count. Experiences range from unhappiness over price hikes, lack of communication, product issues, incompetent and unfriendly installers and customer service agents, misrepresentation of prices and service … the list goes on and on. Finding a response from Comcast to the volumes of consumer complaints is a much harder thing to find.

Wendy's Chili Crisis

In 2005, fast-food giant Wendy's suffered from some seriously bad buzz. The source? Wendy's just couldn't put its finger on it. On May 22, 2005, the San Jose *Mercury News* reported that a 39-year-old female diner found a human finger in her bowl of chili at Wendy's. Naturally, the news spread like wildfire and before Wendy's could control the damage, the story was everywhere. Wendy's was the butt of countless jokes on late-night television. After about a month and an intense investigation into the company's practices and the chili supplier, it became clear that the "victim" had a history of scams and had *planted* the finger in her bowl of chili in order to extort money from Wendy's. So, in the end, Wendy's had nothing to apologize for. Even so, it lost millions of dollars in revenue, the employees at the restaurant lost wages as the branch shut down for several days after the incident, and the company suffered from a severe image problem as a result of the publicity it received.

When Guerrilla Marketing Backfires

General Motors recently launched a contest in association with *The Apprentice*, Donald Trump's reality TV show. The contest invited users to create and submit their own commercials for the Chevy Tahoe SUV. Unlike many similar contests, GM and *The Apprentice* provided video clips and soundtracks that entrants could use to create their commercials. Unfortunately, the attempt at viral video backfired. In just a few short days, thousands of negative videos were circulating on the Internet. Many of the user-generated ads charged GM with contributing to global warming. Others condemned the war in Iraq or simply slammed the product quality of the Tahoe. Of course whether this qualified the campaign as a failure or not is debatable. GM still considers it a success because most of the ads were favorable. With 2.4 million page views, more than 80 percent were positive. Still, the other 20 percent cannot be ignored, especially because so many people have access to the Internet these days.

The Right Way to Handle Bad Buzz

JetBlue was the recent recipient of a heaping handful of bad buzz after it had to cancel hundreds of flights due to extreme weather. Some passengers were trapped aboard planes, stuck on the runway for up to 11 hours. Countless more were stranded at the airport, their bags nowhere to be found. With customers in a rage and losses at roughly $30 million, it was a really bad time for JetBlue. Of course there was no way to undo the horrific situation, but how JetBlue handled the aftermath was brilliant and innovative.

In addition to taking out oversized ads in newspapers, JetBlue CEO Dave Neeleman used a variety of nontraditional media methods to get JetBlue's apology across. Neeleman sent an e-mail apology to JetBlue customers, he recorded a video apology and posted it on YouTube; JetBlue also posted the apology on its website. And it wasn't just talk. JetBlue also announced a new "Customer Bill of Rights" to prevent such things from happening in the future. Now that's how you do it.

The Least You Need to Know

- Solving customer problems on the spot is the best way to prevent bad buzz from getting started.

- When things go wrong, use service recovery tools to turn bad customer experiences into good ones.

- If negative publicity begins to spin out of control, communicate quickly.

- Monitor what's being said about you online so you can be prepared to respond.

Keeping Your Organic Buzz: Making Existing Customers Happy

In This Chapter

- Creating a culture of service
- Loyalty trumps satisfaction
- Training for results
- Recovery is more than rehab
- Measuring to stay on track

The best advertising is a good recommendation from a satisfied customer. If you attract gazillions of customers, how do you make sure they tell their friends how great your product or service is? Keep reading!

Your Best Spokesperson

When your customers are happy, what do they do? They come back. And they tell their friends. Their friends come to see you. They're happy. They tell their friends. And the circle of love just keeps on giving, contributing directly to your success.

When your customers are unhappy, what do they do? They get mad. They don't come back. They tell lots of their friends, who don't come to see you. Word travels, and pretty soon your bottom line is more like a bottomless pit.

According to research, it costs about five times as much to get a new customer as it does to keep an existing one. So is there a secret formula for hanging onto customers?

Customer Service and All That Jazz

It seems logical to say that if you're in business, you're there to serve your customer. And yet, how many times recently have you been in a customer role at a business and been treated as if you were inconveniencing the clerks, interrupting their time to chat with their friends, bothering them with questions, or causing them trouble by wanting something out of the ordinary? And then, if you have the audacity to suggest there's something wrong with what you've purchased, well, you've really pushed them over the edge.

Hardly a day goes by that we don't suffer some type of second-rate service. What's happened to the idea of "service with a smile"?

Consumers today are so jaded by the lack of service that they are actually surprised when they receive truly outstanding service. Most of the time, good old-fashioned service is a wonderful surprise! How do you create great service? Several factors contribute.

Here's the Buzz

With so many choices in today's world, often the only thing that sets one company apart from another is their commitment to customer service. Good customer service can have a meaningful impact on your bottom line, so let the world know that providing good customer service is a priority for your company. That's what RadioShack did. Their slogan, "You've got questions, we've got answers" highlights this philosophy brilliantly.

The People Factor

Business is made up of two things: a buyer and a seller. Typically, that means there are two people involved, one on each side. And in every single case, one of those people is always right: the customer. It doesn't matter if the customer is rude, lies, is stupid; no matter what the customer does, there is almost always a way to make him happy.

In order for one person to always be right under positively every circumstance, the other person has to be flexible, calm, cool-headed, patient, skilled at defusing anger, able to handle confrontation, well-trained in the goals of your business, and willing to be seen as wrong even if not. That's a tall order!

Can you possibly expect so much from your employees? Yes, you can, as long as you hire the right people, teach them what your expectations are, train them to handle all kinds of situations, and thank them profusely when they do so.

One thing's for certain: your business will succeed or fail on the quality of your people. Until we've completely automated every single purchasing activity, we've just got to get the people factor right.

You're Hired!

Believe it or not, good service starts with hiring. Recruiters talk about "Hire the attitude, train the skill." You can teach a friendly person to operate a cash register. You can't train an experienced cash register operator to smile and be friendly unless the person is already inclined that way.

One of the important ways to interview people is to ask what we call behavioral questions. In other words, give them a situation and ask them how they've handled it in the past. For instance, "Think about a time when you encountered a really unpleasant customer who was dissatisfied. How did you handle it?" You'll be amazed at the things you can find out by asking these kinds of questions. The person should, of course, tell you about how she turned the situation around and made the customer happy. If she doesn't, then just imagine that she would handle your customers the same way. Is that what you want?

> **Brainwaves**
>
> Is the potential new hire that's sitting in front of you smiling? If not, then you've learned all you need to know about this person. If he's not smiling at you—his potential new boss—then he sure as heck is not going to be smiling at your customers.

What Do You Expect?

New employees tend to be enthusiastic from the start as long as you give them something to feel excited about. Be sure you tell them how happy you are they've joined your team and let them know that you will be there for them to answer questions or offer guidance.

The most important thing you can do is to immediately set expectations so that the new employee knows exactly what you expect. The mistake some managers make is that they describe the job duties but they don't describe the outcome they want. Have you ever heard an orientation that sounds like this:

"Your job is to be here from 8:30 A.M. until 5:00 P.M. You get a half-hour lunch and two 15-minute breaks. When you arrive, unlock the register and sort the cash into the drawer. Then be ready to open the doors at 9 o'clock sharp …."

Nowhere in that did you ever hear the manager say, "Your job is to be friendly to everyone who comes in the door and to make sure that every customer leaves happy."

Here's the Buzz

One of the easiest ways to help new employees settle into their position is to assign them a mentor—someone who knows the ropes and is willing to share this knowledge with the new employee.

It seems silly that you have to come out and be that specific, but you do. Otherwise, your employees will see their job as a checklist of tasks, instead of whatever tasks contribute to customer satisfaction.

Give people examples of situations and tell them how you would expect them to act. What should they say to an irate customer? It's hard to draw on your own judgment when you're in the line of fire. If you've talked about real-life things to say, your team members will feel less threatened and more powerful and capable of handling tough situations correctly.

Power to the People

How far can your employees go to satisfy a customer? Do they know they can give refunds? Do they realize that they could even go out of their way to do something special to please a customer? At Embassy Suites hotels, team members know that they can do whatever it takes to satisfy a guest. As an example, they might buy a guest a birthday card, send a fruit basket to the room, or give the guest a free dinner to recognize a special occasion.

On the other hand, if your employees think that making money is your biggest priority, they'll try to make sure they never spend a dime that they don't have to. Many people are afraid of taking liberties on the job. You must tell your employees exactly what they're allowed to do, how much they can refund, and what they could spend to satisfy a customer.

Nordstrom department store history is filled with stories of how employees went out of their way for customers. One story tells of how a customer who was headed out of town left her airline ticket on the counter at a Nordstrom store. The employee called the airline to find out if it would print the woman a new ticket when she got to the airport. The answer, of course, was "no." The employee, who was a sales person paid on commission, got in her car and took the ticket to the airport for the customer. Can you imagine how relieved and delighted that customer was? Every Nordstrom employee knows that she can do anything necessary to meet her customers' needs, whether it relates to a purchase or not.

> **Brainwaves**
>
> Research indicates that most customers who've had a bad experience with you will continue to do business with you if you resolve their problem immediately. And that's why your employees must be empowered to resolve problems on the spot without waiting for the okay from upper management. Time is money.

Rewarding Good Performance

Why do team members leave? Not because of pay. Are you surprised? It's true that 70 percent of employees leave because their bosses don't give them enough attention, recognition, and/or guidance. They don't quit the job; they quit the boss.

Everyone likes to be thanked for a job well done. Some people like to be recognized in front of the team; others prefer a more private thank you. But everyone—absolutely everyone—needs to be told when they've done a great job.

Here are some ideas of ways you can reward individuals or your team.

◆ Keep a stash of small prizes to give out when you see someone go above and beyond. Movie tickets, restaurant coupons, ice cream coupons, or even a trip to the dollar store are things lots of people enjoy.

Here's the Buzz

An important part of recognition is to be sure you tell people exactly why you're so proud of them. Why? They need to know how to create a repeat performance in the future!

◆ Buy pizza for your team when they've worked through a difficult week or achieved something exceptional.

◆ Bring in the fixings for ice cream sundaes as a special treat.

◆ For an outstanding job, give someone the day off with pay.

Loyalty Goes Beyond Satisfaction

For many years researchers have used certain metrics to determine whether customers are satisfied. It was all based on the idea that if customers are satisfied, they'll keep coming back. But recently we've discovered something very important. Satisfaction doesn't necessarily lead to repeat business. All it does is indicate how a person felt at a certain time. It doesn't promise anything beyond that transaction.

The new definition is loyalty. What is loyalty? It's when a customer is:

◆ Willing to buy your product or service

◆ Will recommend it to friends

◆ Cuts you some slack when you mess up

◆ Gives you time to fix it

◆ Comes back again

When people are loyal, they're not so influenced by price. They'll buy your product even if it costs a little more.

You see, loyalty leads to action. That's why it has become so important to companies who want to keep their good customers.

Loyalty: More than Dogs and Boy Scouts

Loyalty involves creating an emotional connection with a customer. In fact, it implies a sort of love for the brand or the product. Can you think of a brand you're loyal to? My personal favorite is Coke. I will actually pass up having a cola drink if I can't have The Real Thing. In fact, Coke is kind of like a member of my family. Yes, it tastes good, but it also has some sentimental attachments for me. I remember the TV commercial in which all the children from different nations sang, "I'd like to teach the world to sing." It tugged at my heart strings. And it made me feel good about the company that created that message: the Coca-Cola people.

To move your customers beyond the day-to-day satisfaction of a product that meets their needs, you have to add a healthy dose of people power. Genuine connections, a friendly attitude, a smile, and making people feel like more than a number, these are all ways that you begin to forge a loyalty bond with your customers.

What Factors Create Loyalty?

People who have an overall great experience with your company are the ones who will become loyal. But what parts of their experience are the ones that make them feel really good about your product or service? In other words, what *touch points* influence them to be loyal?

Assume you operate a dry cleaner that delivers. There are a number of touch points. One is when the delivery person picks up your dirty laundry. How can you make it something more than a cut-and-dried pickup? Suppose the pickup is in the early morning and the delivery person brings the morning newspaper to the doorstep. Or maybe he greets the customer with a smile and a weather report. Or he pets the dog and tells the customer about his own pooch. Now you're making a connection.

> **def•i•ni•tion**
>
> **Touch points** are specific times during a transaction that you have a chance to either make a customer really happy or not.

At each of the touch points, there is an opportunity to exceed your customer's expectations and to turn a transaction into an experience.

Now, when you're considering those touch points, you'll want to get feedback from your customers so you'll know what's important to them at each of the touch points. Put your effort toward the touch points that the customer feels contributes to a great experience.

Touch Points from Afar

Sometimes you aren't face to face with your customer at the touch point times, such as over the phone or when you're e-mailing them. Can you still make the moment special? Of course. Here's a very simple trick to make a telephone touch point magical. Begin by smiling as you talk. Research shows that customers can actually "hear" your smile. Can you make a comment about the customer's nice voice, accent, or cheerful disposition? Try greeting people with a phrase like, "Good morning!" instead of the cold, "Joes' Body Shop."

If you're communicating via e-mail, always include a salutation or greeting such as "Hello Bob," or "Good Morning" instead of simply beginning with "Bob:" or launching directly into the message without even naming the recipient. And naturally you should always close with a note of appreciation or good wishes.

Any opportunity you have to make a personal connection is a chance to win friends.

The Tools

Aside from creating an emotional bond with your customers, there are several ways you can demonstrate how committed you are to their satisfaction. One of the most important is your approach to problem resolution. Studies show that if a customer has a problem and you resolve it in a way that exceeds that customer's expectations, he'll become more loyal than if he had never experienced a problem.

When your customer has a complaint, do you view it as a big fat pain in the neck or do you consider it a wonderful chance to regain his trust and restore his loyalty? When a customer tells you he has a problem, you should be grateful; some customers are dissatisfied but just go away mad without ever letting you know anything was wrong. Once you know about the issue, then you can take quick action to make things right.

Satisfaction Guarantees

When you've failed to deliver on the promise you make to customers, either through a product malfunction or a service slip up, you can instantly win their approval by giving them their money back. So many times customers report problems and expect to have to argue with management. If you immediately offer a refund, they'll be pleasantly surprised!

Want to make them even happier? Make it an unconditional guarantee, meaning that you don't ask any questions, you just do whatever it takes to make them happy.

L. L. Bean is famous for their You Have Our Word 100% satisfaction guarantee. You can return anything (without receipt) that you are unhappy with no matter how long it's been since you purchased it. Now that's putting your money where your mouth is.

Here's the Buzz _____

Get the most mileage out of your satisfaction guarantee by posting it in a highly visible place. This lets the customer know that you're willing to let everyone know the policy and there won't be any haggling over it. You're proud of your guarantee and actually want to give people their money back if they're not happy.

Bargaining for Happiness

If you want to really irritate the stew out of unhappy customers, start bargaining with them about how much of a refund they're entitled to. This shows that you only want to give them as little as possible to shut them up.

When you're trying to earn back people's respect, you certainly don't want them to think that you're looking for a cheap solution. You want them to know that you'll do more than they expect.

Ask and Ye Shall Receive

Certainly the easiest way to find out what your customers think is to ask them point blank when they shop with you. Try this: next time a customer is standing at your check-out stand or is on the phone with you, start a conversation like this:

"Mrs. Green, I appreciate your business and want to make sure that we're doing everything we can to earn it. Is there anything we can do better to make your shopping with us more satisfactory?"

Mrs. Green will probably be so shocked that you actually asked her opinion you will already have made a friend! If she indicates that she's satisfied, probe a little more by asking her if there are any products she needs that she can't find at your place of business. Whatever you can do to get a conversation started will enable you to hear tidbits about Mrs. Green and make her feel like you truly care about her opinion and well being.

Granted, you won't have time to have an in-depth conversation with every customer, but you can randomly choose people to ask when things are slow or when you have someone else to cover your station.

> **Here's the Buzz**
>
> Free shipping is an excellent and relatively inexpensive way for mail order and online companies to provide customers with the incentive to place future orders.

Filling Out Surveys Pays Off

There are more formal ways you can learn about your customers' desires, too. A simple written survey works as long as you keep it brief and make it easy for people to fill out and get it back to you. Don't make it more than four or five questions at the most; a majority of people won't take the time to answer more than that.

Also be sure to steer clear of creating a survey that allows the responder to mark the middle of five options—such as "strongly agree, agree, neither agree nor disagree, disagree, strongly disagree." This allows people to mark the neutral option, which doesn't give you useful information. It's better to give them only four choices so they have to lean more toward the positive or negative. It gives you a better idea of their true feelings.

Focus Groups Get You Focused

To get more in-depth information about what your customers want, how happy they are with your product or service, and investigate what additional ways you can serve them, conduct a small meeting. Invite no more than six customers to participate so that everyone has a chance to be heard.

Here's the Buzz

Offer an incentive to customers to give you feedback. They'll appreciate the fact that you recognize they're investing their time to help you and that you value their participation. It doesn't have to be anything huge; a small token of your appreciation will suffice.

You can take a kind of formal approach by doing it in a meeting room and offering coffee and soft drinks or you can invite people to dinner and make it a more relaxed setting. Let them know that you want to hear both good and bad news about how you're currently serving them. If you sincerely listen, you'll hear what you need to improve your business and will simultaneously create more loyal customers.

You can also hire a local firm to conduct a focus group for you. It will give you more objective information than if you conduct the research yourself. It also has a price tag.

Rewarding Your Best Customers

In the last 20 years, businesses have invented *frequency programs*, or reward programs, to show their most devoted customers appreciation for their business. The idea behind frequency programs is that the reward is sufficiently enticing to make a customer keep shopping there to earn the reward.

The best example of a frequency program is the airline industry, where frequent fliers earn points that they can use to get tickets, choose upgrades, or purchase gift items or hotel rooms. The airline lets fliers earn different levels of status such as silver, gold, or platinum that give them higher and higher levels of service or rewards.

def•i•ni•tion

Frequency programs are gimmicks that businesses use to encourage customers to shop with them repeatedly. The gist of a frequency program is that if you show up a certain number of times, spend a certain amount of money, or in some way demonstrate repeated business, the company gives you something for free. They can do this by awarding you points that you can redeem for your choice of rewards, such as airline tickets or by giving you a free item or dollars-off coupon after you've spent so much.

If you're thinking of creating a frequent buyer program, just be sure you don't create something that could backfire and generate ill will. Recently, the airlines have made some frequent fliers mad because they've made it too difficult to redeem points for tickets. By limiting the number of "reward" seats available on each flight, they've made it so inconvenient to travel that the rewards have turned into de-motivators.

What kind of frequency program could you develop for your customers? If you own a restaurant, give away a free meal after the purchase of 10 meals. What do you have to lose? When your customer redeems her free meal, she'll probably bring a paying friend. And that's your chance to create two loyal customers.

The Least You Need to Know

- ◆ Customer satisfaction is simply the cost of entry for businesses today.

- ◆ You can create customer loyalty by making each transaction a magical experience and building an emotional bond with your customers.

- ◆ Feedback is essential to keeping your product and service relevant to your customers.

- ◆ Besides providing a product or service, give your customers an incentive to keep coming back.

Glossary

aided awareness   Also called prompted awareness, is the percentage of respondents who indicate that they are familiar with an ad when provided some type of stimulus material.

amplified WOM   Engineered word of mouth.

astroturfing   An orchestrated public relations campaign that gives the impression of being grass roots oriented. It gets its name from Astroturf which is, of course, fake grass.

B2B marketing   Marketing of products or services from one business to another.

B2C marketing   Marketing directly to consumers.

behavioral questions   Questions formulated to elicit specific relevant examples from your past.

bluejacking   Unsolicited messages sent via Bluetooth to mobile devices.

Bluetooth technology   Technology that allows mobile devices to connect with each other wirelessly, using a small radio transmitter and receiver.

blog   Abbreviation for weblog. Online journal that anyone can read.

blogosphere   All weblogs or blogs that exist on the Internet.

blogrolls   Lists of other blogs that are linked to any blog entry.

borrowed equity   A celebrity endorsement transfers some of the celebrity's "equity" to the product, giving the product qualities it might not have had otherwise.

brand promise   What you tell customers they can expect from your brand.

buzz marketing   Techniques intended to get people talking about your company, service, or product.

call to action   The part of the sales pitch where you ask someone to do something, to take some action that will lead them closer to doing business with you.

COGS   Cost of goods sold.

consumer-generated media (CGM)   Word of mouth on the Internet. It comes in a variety of forms including blogs, message board posts, commentary in forums, and so on.

conversion rate   Percentage of those clicking through your website who actually bought your product.

customer service   Customer-oriented philosophy that integrates and manages all the elements of the customer interface within a predetermined cost-service mix, according to the American Marketing Association.

demographic   Selected population characteristics including age, gender, location, language, lifestyle, socioeconomic status, and so on.

e-mail client   Another word for e-mail programs such as Entourage and Microsoft Outlook.

elevator speech   A short description of what you do—one that could be recited in the length of time it takes to complete a typical elevator ride.

Ethernet   The most widely used local area network (LAN) technology.

experiential marketing   Marketing experiences designed to immerse the potential customer in the brand. Ideally, experiential marketing engages as many of the five senses as possible.

ezine   An online magazine devoted to a particular subject matter.

Facebook   A largely college-centered online network founded in 2004.

Federal Trade Commission (FTC)   An independent U.S. government agency responsible for regulating methods of competition and advertising in America.

folksonomy   A user-generated taxonomy for categorizing web content.

frequency   Defines how often your message will be seen.

frequency programs   Gimmicks that businesses use to encourage customers to shop with them repeatedly.

friend of a friend (FOAF)   Term used in social networking.

Gen X   People born between 1966 and 1982. Also called the Me Generation or MTV Generation.

Generation Y   People born between 1983 and 2000. Also called the Internet Generation or "Millenials."

grassroots marketing   Spontaneous marketing that occurs when consumers love your product so much that they can't stop talking about it.

green marketing   Marketing which takes into account the product's effect on the environment.

guerrilla marketing   Unconventional marketing techniques intended to get maximum results from minimum resources invested. The term was coined by Jay Conrad Levinson in his book, *Guerrilla Marketing*.

hit   Measurement of unique users visiting your website.

HTML   Hypertext markup language. The primary language used to create web pages.

impression   Every contact point in which the prospect receives information about your product, service, and/or company.

influencers   People whose opinion is highly valued by others.

IP address (Internet protocol address)   Used to identify an item on a computer network. Computers, routers, Internet fax machines, and even some telephones have IP addresses.

law of diminishing returns   Well-accepted economic concept stating that the more you invest in an area, overall return on that investment increases at a declining rate if everything else remains equal.

leaners   People hired to promote products undercover and in person.

linkback   Method that allows blog authors to receive notification when somebody links to one of their documents. Also called trackback, pingback, or refback.

market segment   Groups of people driven by similar motives and similar needs.

mass e-mail Marketing campaign conducted via e-mail. Also called bulk e-mail.

media equivalency Cost of an ad the size or equivalency of the PR that you generated.

message diffusion Process of gaining market acceptance for your product or service.

Metcalfe's Law Term formulated by Robert Metcalfe which states that the value of a telecommunications network is the square of the number of users of the system.

netiquette Basic etiquette as it applies to digital communications.

online community Group of people that interacts via the Internet. Also referred to as a virtual community and web community.

Open Directory Project Search system that feeds Google, AOL, AskJeeves, Netscape, EarthLink, Lycos, and hundreds of other sites.

open source software Type of software that is available for others to use and/or change or improve.

opportunity cost Value of the activity that you are forgoing so that you can participate in an alternative activity. The value of the next-best alternative that must be sacrificed.

opt-in e-mail marketing Strategy that allows your potential consumers to request to receive your product messages via e-mail, instead of receiving them automatically (like spam).

organic WOM Word of mouth that occurs naturally when people like your product.

out-of-house advertising Advertising that reaches your customer when they are out of the house.

pay-per-click advertising *See* PPC advertising.

performance incentives Financial motivation to complete specific activities.

permalinks URLs that allow blog entries to be viewed even after the source has been archived.

ping Alert sent out to inform readers that a blog has been updated.

podcast Media file distributed via the Internet for playback on mobile devices and personal computers.

positioning statement   Concise statement conveying the benefits of your product/ service offering.

PPC advertising   In pay-per-click advertising, companies bid on keywords they think their customers and potential customers will type in to search for their type of services. Whoever wins the bid gets to appear in the area of the search return results that is called "sponsored ads." These are typically featured at the top and to the right of the ads that are naturally optimized. Advertisers who engage in PPC advertising only pay when someone clicks on their ad.

product advocate   Someone who is willing to talk about your products to other people. Also known as buzz marketers, product evangelists, or word of mouth marketers.

product placement   Advertising method whereby a company pays for their product or logo to be used in a movie, TV show, video game, or other form of media.

product seeding   Providing your products, free of charge, to people you think are a natural match for your product, and who also are likely to become brand loyalists.

profit margin   A company's measure of profitability. Calculated by dividing net income by revenue.

proximity marketing   Geo-targeted advertising and marketing using Bluetooth technology.

reach   Term that refers to just how broad the extent of the medium's impact will be.

reciprocal linking   Practice of exchanging links with an associated business to mutually boost your website ranking.

return on investment (ROI)   Performance measure used to evaluate the efficiency of an investment or compare the efficiency of a number of different investments.

roach bait marketing   Process of putting people paid to promote your product in a situation where they can promote it, while giving the impression that they are not being paid to do so.

RSS (Really Simple Syndication) feed   Data format used to publish digital content such as blogs, news feeds, or podcasts that are updated frequently.

search engine optimization (SEO)   Process of improving the traffic flow to a website by making it easy to find with search engines.

shotgun marketing   Sending messages to a broad audience that includes a large percentage of people who are not potential customers.

SMS (short message service)   A technology which allows users to send a text message via their mobile telephone or PDA.

sneezing   Telling someone about an interesting website. (It's a continuation of the "viral" marketing terminology.)

social networking   Practice of connecting with people with similar interests via online communities.

spec work   Work that agencies provide for free in the hope of gaining a client's business.

splog   Abbreviation for spam blog. Blog accounts created to promote affiliate websites by artificially boosting search ratings.

stealth marketing   Undercover or deceptive marketing efforts intended to appear as though they happened naturally.

stunt marketing   Unusual marketing techniques (often performed by actors) intended to draw attention to your product.

subliminal messages   Messages designed to influence behavior by appealing to the subconscious mind.

swapping   Informal type of bartering within Internet communities where items are traded with a virtual handshake.

tag cloud   Display of the most frequently used tags.

tagline   Descriptive or emotional phrase that follows or precedes a business name.

targeting   Selecting a market segment and creating marketing messages that will speak to that distinct demographic.

target audience   Primary group you are marketing your product to.

target demographic   Common characteristics of prospective customers in which you are focusing your marketing efforts.

taxonomy   Hierarchical classification system.

testimonial   A written statement from someone who's used your product or services, endorsing your company.

third-party credibility   Occurs when someone not formally associated with your company endorses your product.

third-party endorsement   When someone not associated with your company says good things about your product or service or about your company's way of doing business.

thread   Software-aided, usually chronological, grouping of messages that are related to a particular message board post.

touch points   Specific times during a transaction that you have a chance to either make a customer really happy or not.

trial usage   Offering discounts, coupons, or samples of your product in the hopes that after trying it, consumers will like it and continue to choose it.

unaided awareness   Also called spontaneous awareness, is the percentage of respondents who indicate familiarity with a product when provided with no stimulus material.

user-generated ad campaigns   Campaigns where the company encourages viewers to submit ads they've created.

value proposition   How you differentiate your company from your competitors.

viral marketing   Refers to a strategy that inspires people to pass along your marketing message like a virus. Technological equivalent of word of mouth marketing.

Web 2.0   Term used to represent the second generation of web-based services that emphasize collaboration and sharing among users.

WiFi   Wireless fidelity. Technology that allows computers to connect to each other or a network wirelessly.

wikis   Websites that allow visitors to edit or change content.

wireframe   A basic visual guide, similar to a flow chart, that illustrates how users will navigate around a website.

word of mouth marketing   Passing of information from person to person, often called buzz marketing.

YouTube   Online video community.

undercover marketing   *See* stealth marketing.

Resources

Books

Drake, Susan, M. *Light Their Fire: Using Internal Marketing to Ignite Employee Performance and WOW Your Customers*. Dearborn Trade Publishing, 2005.

Gladwell, Malcolm. *The Tipping Point: How Little Things Can Make a Big Difference*. Back Bay Books, 2002.

O'Conner, Patricia, T. *Woe is I*. A Grosse/Putnam Book, 1996.

Documentary

Green, Dr. Paul. *More than a Gut Feeling*. American Media Corporation, 1984.

Agencies and Organizations

American Association of Advertising Agencies, www.aaaa.org
American Marketing Association, www.marketingpower.com
Direct Marketing Association, www.the-dma.org
Federal Trade Commission, www.ftc.gov
Interactive Advertising Bureau (IAB), www.iab.net

International Reciprocal Trade Association (IRTA), www.irta.com

Mobile Marketing Association (MMA), www.mmaglobal.com

Utility Consumers' Action Network (UCAN), www.ucan.org

Word of Mouth Marketing Association, www.womma.org

Websites

Adopt-A-Highway, www.adoptahighway.com

Advertising Age, www.advertisingage.com

Agencyfinder.com, www.agencyfinder.com

BzzAgent, www.bzzagent.com

Encompass Media Group, www.encompassmediagroup.com

Facebook, www.facebook.com

Famous Quotes, www.famousquotes.com

Game Show Placements, www.gameshowplacements.com

Google Alerts, www.google.com/alerts

Guinness Book of World Records, www.guinnessworldrecords.com

International Data Corporation, www.idc.com

Mascots & Costumes, www.mascotsandcostumes.com

Monster Media, www.monstermedia.net

Myspace, www.myspace.com

Name Extractor, www.nameextractor.com

Quoteland, www.quoteland.com

RedRover Company, www.redrovercompany.com

Signature Marketing Solutions, www.signatureadvertising.com

Sugar's Mascot Costumes, www.sugarcostumes.com

surveymonkey.com, www.surveymonkey.com

Technorati, www.technorati.com

The Complete Idiot's Guides, www.idiotsguides.com

Think Exist, www.thinkexist.com

ThinkMap, www.thinkmap.com/visualthesaurus.jsp

TSNN.com, www.tsnn.com

Yahoo! Alerts, www.yahoo.com/alerts

YouTube, www.youtube.com

Wetpaint, www.wetpaint.com

Popular Search Engines

Ask.com, formerly AskJeeves, www.ask.com

Google, www.google.com

Yahoo!, www.yahoo.com

Mamma, www.mamma.com

AOL Search, search.aol.com

Windows Live Search, www.live.com

LookSmart, search.looksmart.com

Lycos.com, www.lycos.com

Netscape, search.netscape.com

Free or Nearly Free Message Boards

Aceboard.net

ActiveBoard.com

Bestfreeforums.com

BoardHost.com

BoardServer.com

Bravenet.com

Conforums.com

ezboard.com

Forumhoster.com

FreeForums.org

GetFreeBB.com

GoGetForum.com

GreatBoard.com

HWForums.org

Hyperboards.com

InvisionFree.com

Jconserv.net

LiveBoards.com

MinuteBoard.com

MyProBB.com

Network54.com

Onvix.com

ProBoards.com

RunBoard.com

SuddenLaunch.com

WebsiteToolbox.com

WebringAmerica.com

Yabbers.com

Message Board Services

BuildACommunity.com

Communityservers.com

ChatSpace.com

ForumExperts.com

Invisionboard.com

Lithium.com

Multicity.com

Netvillage.com

Peoplelink.com

Webcrossing.com

Xsorbit.com (also offers free and low-cost options)

Popular Business-Focused Social Networking Sites

LinkedIn, www.linkedin.com

Ryze, www.ryze.com

Soflow, www.soflow.com

Business Entrepreneur Networks, www.bizpreneur.com

Tribe, www.tribe.net

XING, www.xing.com

Ecademy, www.ecademy.com

Blogging Hosting Services

Blogger, www2.blogger.com

LiveJournal, www.livejournal.com

Wordpress, http://wordpress.com

TypePad, www.typepad.com

Moveable Type, http://moveabletype.com

Xanga, www.xanga.com

Places to Create a Blog

Windows Live Spaces (formerly known as MSN Spaces), http://spaces.live.com

Livejournal.com, www.livejournal.com

Blogger.com, https://www2.blogger.com/start

Xanga.com, www.xanga.com

Vox.com, www.vox.com

Tagging Systems

Flickr, http://flickr.com

Del.icio.us, http://del.icio.us

Youtube, www.youtube.com

Technorati, www.technorati.com

IceRocket, www.icerocket.com

Highlights from Our Guerrilla Marketing Plan

We're currently developing a guerrilla marketing plan for *Light Their Fire*, an internal marketing book by Susan Drake and Sara Roberts. Although the plan is still in development, we thought we'd share a few highlights with you so you could see how you might begin to put the pieces together.

Overview: *Light Their Fire* shows you how to engage your team members and solidify customer relations using internal marketing. (By the way, it's a must-read for any manager!) The book has been well received and even been printed in Russian! But good is never enough for us. We want everyone who's anyone to read our book and use it as their manual for success! Of course it would be great to hire a high-end agency out of New York or Los Angeles to promote it, but right now that's not possible. Sound familiar? It looks like we need a little guerrilla marketing of our own!

Our goal in conducting guerrilla marketing for *Light Their Fire* is to use the book to generate interest in our internal marketing consulting services.

Our audience: CEOs, company executives, business owners, human resource professionals, and department managers.

Our competition: In the field of internal marketing, it's actually sparse. And the few competitors there are, well, we don't want to give them publicity here!

Guerrilla Marketing Methods to Consider

Here are the different techniques we think will help us put *Light Their Fire* on the bookshelf of every CEO in the country!

Influencer Marketing

The people who will benefit most from *Light Their Fire* are managers. Managers at every level can probably find something of value in the book, but they won't have the opportunity to realize this benefit if they don't read the book. So we've got to make sure that they read the book. But how? Who do managers listen to? Other managers, of course. But not just any other managers—the big guys: the senior vice presidents, CEOs, and business leaders of their communities. Even better are the business leaders who speak to groups or write articles that people consider must-reads. Here's how we might get the book into the hands of the people we think would be influencers.

◆ Give It Away. It's not hard to find out who the business leaders are in different communities. So we figured why not do a little research and create a list of influencers in cities we want to touch? All we have to do is stick a copy of the book in the mail with a personalized note to the recipients. They may or may not read it, but chances are, they won't throw it away. They'll certainly put it in their bookshelves in their offices or pass it along to others—both of which are good for us!

◆ Leave It Behind. Where might business people be when they're not at work? Fancy restaurants, high-end car dealerships, airplanes, and airports … the list is endless. And when they're waiting, they generally need something to read, right? Why not leave a copy of the book in a first class seat pocket on a weekday flight from New York to Atlanta? Chances are that it could appeal to whoever picks it up. And right on the book flap there's information about how that person can reach us. Our website delineates our services.

◆ Use Our Friends. Of course we don't mean we're going to "use" our friends, but we're likeable people, and we have a lot of friends. And our friends have a lot of friends. With all those friends of friends of friends, we have access to some really influential people, who will doubtless be a lot more receptive to receiving the "gift" of this book from someone they know. Word of mouth has more credibility than any other form of marketing because people trust other people's opinions more than paid advertising.

Expertise Ourselves

Having written *Light Their Fire* and worked in internal marketing for longer than we care to admit, we feel confident that we're pretty darn good at it! In fact, in the words of the Charlie Daniels Band, we just may be "the best there ever was"! But what's the use of being an expert, if you can't capitalize on it? Throughout the book we've covered various online tools. We're going to put a couple to use for ourselves, including:

◆ Write a Blog. Blogs are everywhere. We plan to set up a blog devoted to using internal marketing and communication to motivate teams and customers. To be prepared, we'll be sure to read other marketing blogs and stay on the look out for great blog topics to keep our blog up to date and interesting.

◆ Contribute to a Wiki. If you've ever researched anything online, you've probably come across Wikipedia, an online encyclopedia covering every subject under the sun. Anyone can contribute to entries either by editing existing entries or creating whole new ones. We're considering adding our internal marketing expertise to this great online resource!

◆ Be an About.com Guide. This is a website on which subject matter experts weigh in on a wide range of topics. Right now there isn't a subject topic available that relates to internal marketing, but we will continue to check back to see if there's a spot for us to become a new contributing expert.

Our Websites

Our spellbindersinc.com and lighttheirfire.com websites are currently being revamped. We're adding more content and we're optimizing the sites to rank higher among search engines.

We'll add more testimonials and even set it up so we can sell books from our site.

E-Mail Marketing

Obviously writing is a strong suit for us, so an eNewsletter is a natural fit for promoting our book and our internal marketing services. We're currently considering content for our own eNewsletter. We could give readers hints about internal marketing implementation; we could share case studies, or we could write about new trends in internal marketing and employee engagement.

Offline

While we can use lots of online tools to promote ourselves, we also know how valuable face-to-face marketing can be. We'll be staying in front of people in several key ways.

◆ Speaking events. It's pretty easy to get tapped as a speaker at conferences. We'll approach groups that are related to our industry or management groups that regularly host business conferences. These events give us credibility and also enable us to speak to qualified leads one on one.

◆ Develop related workshops. We have expertise in a number of areas that are related to internal marketing, such as coaching, presentation skills, writing, and project management. We can develop workshops that we deliver online as webinars and that we can sell to corporations as one-off segments.

◆ Writing articles. Many business publications are thrilled to have contributing writers for their monthly or quarterly publications. By submitting carefully crafted e-mail queries about a subject, we are pretty likely to be offered a spot in a publication. There's no money in it, but the exposure helps us become known as experts in our field.

Partnerships

For more than 20 years, our company, Spellbinders, Inc., has thrived almost exclusively through word of mouth. While this is a great testimony to how many happy customers we have, it can prove to be a challenge when we decide we'd like to grow our business in different directions. We just don't have any team members who are available to focus on sales! Lucky for us, one of the companies we often partner with, Signature Marketing Solutions, does have dedicated sales team members. We're currently exploring all the ways we can partner with Signature because their services are complementary to ours.

Measurement

We've chosen a wide variety of guerrilla marketing tactics, and we'll employ a variety of measurement tools to gauge our success in each of these areas.

Index

C

H

I